ECHOES OF VALHALLA

ECHOES OF VALHALLA

THE AFTERLIFE OF THE EDDAS AND SAGAS

Jón Karl Helgason

Translated by
Jane Victoria Appleton

REAKTION BOOKS

To my mentors
Gary Aho and Andrew Wawn

Published by Reaktion Books Ltd
Unit 32, Waterside
44–48 Wharf Road
London N1 7UX, UK

www.reaktionbooks.co.uk

First published 2017

Printed and bound in Great Britain by TJ International, Padstow, Cornwall

A catalogue record for this book is available from the British Library

ISBN 978 1 78023 715 2

Contents

A NOTE ON THE SPELLING OF NAMES

Names of characters and places from the eddas and sagas are given in the most common English translated form. Spellings of names in quoted translations are left intact. Titles of medieval Icelandic texts and manuscripts are provided in Icelandic, and titles of published works are given in their original language, all with English translations in brackets the first time they appear.

Prologue

You know Gandalf, don't you?

Well, it may depend which Gandalf I'm talking about. If we are to believe palaeontologist Ross Geller, of the American sitcom *Friends*, Gandalf is 'like, the funniest guy in the world'.[1] Gandalf's real name is Mike Ganderson, but the nickname suits, since he 'is like the party wizard', as Ross explains to Joey Tribbiani in the fourth season of the long-running television series. Joey clearly misses the point:

> Joey: Why do you call him 'Gandalf'?
> Ross: Gandalf the Wizard. Hallo! Didn't you read *The Lord of the Rings* in high school?
> Joey: No, I had sex in high school.[2]

Sadly, this Gandalf cancels his proposed get-together with Ross and Chandler Bing, and is never seen in this or any other episode of *Friends*.

If instead we are to believe philologist J.R.R. Tolkien, author of the fantasy novel *The Hobbit* (1937) and its sequel *The Lord of the Rings* (1954–5), Gandalf is one of the most powerful wizards of Middle-earth. In the first chapter of *The Hobbit* he sets the narrative in motion by tricking Bilbo Baggins into accommodating a party for Thorin Oakenshield and his twelve dwarf companions: Dwalin, Bifur, Bofur, Bombur, Nori, Oin, Fili, Kili, Gloin, Dori, Ori and Balin. On this occasion, Gandalf the Grey is characterized as

> an old man with a staff. He had a tall pointed blue hat, a long grey cloak, a silver scarf over which his long white beard hung down below his waist, and immense black boots.
>
> 'Good Morning!' said Bilbo, and he meant it. The sun was shining, and the grass was very green. But Gandalf looked at him from under long bushy eyebrows that stuck out further than the brim of his shady hat.
>
> 'What do you mean?' he said.[3]

Even if you too were busy with something other than reading fantasy in high school, it is highly probable that you have come across a version of this imposing party-wizard by other means. You might know him from Arthur Rankin Jr and Jules Bass's animated television movie *The Hobbit* (1977), Ralph Bakshi's animated film *The Lord of the Rings* (1978) or more recently, as portrayed by Ian McKellen, from Peter Jackson's two blockbuster trilogies, *The Lord of the Rings* (2001–3) and *The Hobbit* (2012–14).

Last, but not least, if we are to believe the testimony of *Snorra Edda* (also known as the *Younger Edda* or *Prose Edda*), a thirteenth-century manual of poetics attributed to the Icelandic chieftain and poet Snorri Sturluson, Gandalf belongs to a group of midgets within the ecosphere of pagan Nordic mythology. Originally, after the gods Odin, Vili and Ve had created the Earth from the corpse of the giant Ymir, a fraternity of dwarfs quickened in Ymir's flesh as maggots. Later 'they became conscious with intelligence and had the shape of men though they live in the earth and in rocks'.[4] Verifying this clarification, the author of *Snorra Edda* quotes a few stanzas from *Völuspá* (The Prophecy of the Seeress), one of a series of early eddic poems (generally known as the *Elder Edda* or *Poetic Edda*) embodying Nordic pagan myths and Germanic heroic legends. The stanzas in question include an apparently banal list of dwarf names:

> Nyi, Nidi, Nordri, Sudri, Austri, Vestri, Althiolf, *Dvalin*, Nar, Nain, Niping, Dain, *Bifur, Bafur, Bombor, Nori, Ori*, Onar,

> *Oin*, Modvitnir, Vig and *Gandalf*, Vindalf, *Thorin*, *Fili*, *Kili*, Fundin, Vali, Thror, Throin, Thekk, Lit, Vitr, Nyr, Nyrad, Rekk, Radsvinn . . . Draupnir, Dolgthvari, Hor, Hugstari, Hlediolf, *Gloin*, *Dori*, *Ori*, Duf, Andvari, Heptifili, Har, Siar.[5]

As it happens, *Völuspá* was a part of the native literary canon that I was made to read during my Reykjavik high-school years in the early 1980s, and it was also a part of the vast medieval corpus that Tolkien focused on as an academic and was inspired by as a novelist. 'Virtually every day of his working life as a Professor of Anglo-Saxon, or of English Language and Literature, he found himself reading, teaching, or referring to works like *Beowulf*, the *Elder Edda*, or Snorri Sturluson's *Prose Edda*', explains Tom Shippey, a leading authority on Tolkien's fictional universe and his medieval literary sources.[6] And as every *Lord of the Rings* buff will tell you, these unremarkable stanzas from *Völuspá* not only lie behind the name of Gandalf the Grey – and thus, by extension, the nickname of Mike 'Gandalf' Ganderson – but the names (italicized above) of twelve of the thirteen dwarfs who pop up in Bilbo Baggins's hobbit-hole in the early pages of *The Hobbit*. Lately, manufacturers of toys and games have reproduced this group for younger generations. One of the most recent creations of this industry is LEGO *The Hobbit* (2014), an action-adventure video game featuring the cast of Tolkien's novel as Lego characters, who themselves are also available in a range of Middle-earth Lego sets.

This animated existence of the dwarfs from *Völuspá* is symbolic of the contemporary afterlife of the medieval eddas and sagas, which is the principal concern of this book. In our modern age the adaptation of these texts is not limited to the northern European philologists, translators, writers and artists who were most active in cultivating the Nordic literary heritage in the late eighteenth and early nineteenth centuries. Over the past century, adaptations of the eddas and sagas have appeared in a variety of formats and platforms: from radio, cinema and television, to LPs, CDs and DVDs, to travel books, comics and digital media. Leading entertainment companies in Europe, North America and Southeast Asia have eagerly engaged with this exotic old northern literature, distributing their multimedia products to the four corners of the world.

The links between these variations and one or more 'original' works from the corpus of the eddas and sagas – the 'real' stories, as we can call them for now – are naturally quite diverse. Modern adaptations of older literature do not represent 'our historical past so much as they represent our ideas or cultural stereotypes about that past', according to Fredric Jameson's analysis of postmodernism and consumer society.[7] However, that does not make these works any less interesting or important:

> Cultural production has been driven back inside the mind, within the monadic subject: it can no longer look directly out of its eyes at the real world for the referent but must, as in Plato's cave, trace its mental images of the world on its confining walls. If there is any realism left here, it is a 'realism' which springs from the shock of grasping that confinement and of realizing that, for whatever peculiar reasons, we seem condemned to seek the historical past through our own pop images and stereotypes about that past, which itself remains forever out of reach.[8]

In other words, a contemporary reader of *Völuspá* or *Snorra Edda*, who is familiar with the most influential adaptations of Tolkien's Middle-earth, is likely to connect the name Gandalf in the line 'Vig and Gandalf, Vindalf, Thorin' with either the bearded face of Ian McKellen or the fierce-looking plastic mini-figure designed by Lego. A third (and least likely) option is that the reader will recall the psychedelic LP cover of *Gandalf* (1968), the debut album of an obscure but somewhat legendary American rock band of the same name.

The primary objective of this book is to consider this connection between the eddas and sagas and their modern legacy. In particular, I am fascinated by the way in which texts that were originally written many centuries ago in the isolated rural areas of my native Iceland have become a part of our (almost) universal cultural memory. At the same time, I hope to offer insights into some of the diverse intentions and constraints that have shaped individual adaptations and framed the afterlife of the eddas and sagas as a whole. As Linda Hutcheon has pointed out, 'the urge to consume and erase the memory of the adapted text or to call it into question is as likely as the desire to pay tribute by copying.'[9]

Just like the works on which it focuses, my research is a part of a well-established tradition. The post-medieval reception of the eddas and sagas as an area of study has flourished within academia over the past twenty years or so, as can be seen by the number of conferences and essay collections devoted to the topic. Impressive individual monographs by Jöran Mjöberg, Mats Malm, Klaus von See, Klaus Böldl, Margaret Clunies Ross and Andrew Wawn have focused on the afterlife of Iceland's medieval literature and its ideological footprint in seventeenth-, eighteenth- and nineteenth-century Scandinavia, Germany and Britain. Specific studies have also concentrated on translations and rewritings of one or more sagas into particular languages, or of individual sagas into a variety of languages. However, relatively few of these earlier studies are cross-culturally comparative and, apart from the attention given to the reception of the eddas and sagas in early twentieth-century Germany, modern adaptations have been somewhat under-represented. Two recent books by British medievalists, Heather O'Donoghue's *From Asgard to Valhalla* (2007) and Martin Arnold's *Thor: Myth to Marvel* (2011), as well as a series of interesting studies published by German scholars during the past few years, indicate that the focus is changing fast and the present book will hopefully contribute to that development.

In the following chapters, I draw particular attention to those genres that combine a rewritten text with other modes of expression, either visual or aural. The primary focus is on comic books, plays, pilgrimage, music and films. In each case, I will deal with characters that, just like Gandalf, have enjoyed international exposure. These include the Nordic gods Thor and Odin, the saga characters Hallgerd Long-legs, Gunnar of Hlidarendi and Leif the Lucky, as well as the medieval writer Snorri Sturluson. The majority of those I discuss who have adapted the ancient texts are Scandinavian, British and American, but I also examine German, Italian and Japanese artists. The group comprises cartoonists Jack Kirby and Peter Madsen, playwrights Henrik Ibsen and Gordon Bottomley, travellers Frederick Metcalfe and Poul Vad, composers Richard Wagner and Edward Elgar, rock musicians Jimmy Page and Robert Plant, novelists Ottilie A. Liljencrantz and Dorothy James Roberts, film directors Roy William Neill and Richard Fleischer, and many more.

In addition, I hope to demonstrate how misleading it can be to judge adaptations primarily on the basis of their fidelity to the 'original' texts, or the 'pre-texts', as I prefer to call them. I agree with Linda Hutcheon's claim that 'Adaptation is repetition, but repetition without replication.'[10] The fact is, firstly, that for most of the adaptations we will encounter, the artists in question are working from a range of pre-texts. Secondly, these pre-texts are themselves adaptations of one kind or another. Due to their origin within an oral society, it is difficult to pinpoint precisely when specific medieval works belonging to this corpus were truly created. At the same time, their innumerable contemporary reformulations suggest that the creative potential of this literature is far from exhausted. Hence, I approach the eddas and sagas as a flourishing cultural tradition: an accumulation of texts, images, sounds and ideas that reverberate through the fabric of various cultures at various times.

The story of Odin and the mead of poetry – as related in *Snorra Edda* – can be regarded as an allegory of this perpetual creative process:

essentially this is a narrative describing amalgamation, metamorphosis, brewing, devouring, digesting and spewing. The story is communicated through a frame narrative; a conversation between characters named Bragi and Ægir. Bragi explains at the beginning that the groups of pagan Nordic deities, the Æsir and the Vanir, had a serious dispute,

> and they appointed a peace-conference and made a truce by this procedure, that both sides went up to a vat and spat their spittle into it. But when they dispersed, the gods kept this symbol of truce and decided not to let it be wasted, and out of it made a man. His name was Kvasir.[11]

Kvasir turned out to be a wise person but was killed by two dwarfs who made mead out of his blood by mixing it with honey. According to Bragi, anyone who drinks the mead becomes a poet or scholar. A giant called Suttung acquired the mead from the dwarfs after saving them from a submerged skerry. He took the liquid home, 'setting his daughter Gunnlod in charge of it'.[12] The mead is kept there in three vessels, named Odrerir, Bodn and Son.

At this point in the narration, Ægir asks Bragi by what means the gods in Asgard came to possess the mead. Bragi replies by relating how Baugi, Suttung's brother, hires Odin (under the pseudonym Bolverk), as a summer worker. When Bolverk says he wants a sip of Suttung's mead as payment, Baugi claims he has no say in its disposal and that Suttung wants it all for himself. Subsequently, Bolverk gets Baugi to help him drill a hole into Suttung's abode and sneaks into the room where Gunnlod safeguards the magic potion. After spending three nights with the guest, the giant's daughter allows Bolverk to drink just a mouthful from Odrerir, Bodn and Son. He, however, consumes the entire contents of all three vessels, before changing himself into an eagle and flying away:

> And when Suttung saw the eagle's flight he got his own eagle shape and flew after him. And when the Æsir saw Odin flying they put their containers out in the courtyard, and when Odin came in over Asgard he spat out the mead into the containers, but it was such a close thing for him that Suttung might have caught him that he sent some of the mead out backwards, and this was disregarded. Anyone took it that wanted it, and it is what we call the rhymester's share.[13]

This passage underlines the metafictional aspects of the story about the mead of poetry and of *Snorra Edda* in general; we are reading fiction about the origin of fiction, and its constant ingestion.

Snorra Edda was composed partly to help thirteenth-century Icelandic poets understand the complex system of *kennings* (fixed metaphors) that had been characteristic of skaldic poetry for centuries (*skáld* or skald means a poet; this Icelandic term is generally used in English for medieval Scandinavian court poets). Accordingly, Bragi explains to Ægir how poets can refer to the narrative about the poetic mead when they want to discuss poetry in their works:

> That is why we call poetry Kvasir's blood or dwarfs' drink or the contents or some term for liquid of Odrerir or Bodn or Son, or dwarfs' transportation, because the mead brought them deliverance from the skerry, or Suttung's mead.[14]

There are many similar comments in *Snorra Edda* that highlight how pagan and Christian poets reprocessed the ancient myths in the tenth, eleventh and twelfth centuries. However, it is unclear to what extent the story about the mead of poetry can be regarded as an authentic pagan myth. Instead, it may well be a radical adaptation of various older pre-texts.

Roberta Frank has systematically analysed the fixed metaphors for poetry that are discussed in *Snorra Edda*, along with examples from older skaldic poems where these images are used. In her view, the story of the mead of poetry is probably based on Snorri Sturluson's misunderstanding of some of these metaphors. Snorri, she claims, seems to have mistaken a set of regular nouns in these poems for proper nouns (names of characters and places). One such skaldic poem quoted in *Snorra Edda* is by the court poet Einar 'Skalaglamm' Helgason: 'Land's magnanimous guardian I bid hear – hear, earl, Kvasir's blood – fiord-bone's [stone's] men's [dwarfs'] yeast-surf [mead].'[15]

Etymologically the word *kvasir* is generally traced to words that mean an alcoholic beverage made from 'quashed' fruits.[16] In view of this, Frank suggests that Kvasir's blood can simply mean the blood of the quashed fruit and refer to an alcohol of some sort, just like when William Shakespeare refers in *Timon of Athens* to 'the subtle blood o' th' grape' (IV.3).[17] Frank highlights that according to the pagan worldview, there was a definite connection between alcohol, intoxication and poetic abilities but she doubts that a giant by the name of Kvasir was at any point a part of the mythological world of pagan Scandinavia. In the same way, she doubts that the vessels Odrerir, Bodn and Son existed before *Snorra Edda* was written.

In my opinion, it is not likely that the author of *Snorra Edda* misinterpreted these and other similar metaphors and then, on the basis of that misunderstanding, tried to construct a narrative merely in order to make some sense of them. It seems more probable that he was following the example of pagan storytellers who, according to the 'Prologue' of *Snorra Edda*, produced myths about the creation of the Earth 'to be better able to give an account of this and fix it in memory.'[18] The story about the myth of poetry can similarly be a mnemonic device for young poets. My primary point here, however, is that the text of *Snorra Edda* is an inventive 'digestion' of various earlier pre-texts, both written and oral, in verse and prose. The same applies, more or less, to the comics about the god of thunder, Thor, that we are about to explore.

Well, you know Thor, don't you?

'Thor's wedding band' illustration, from Peter Madsen's *Thors brudefærd* (1980).

ONE

Thor: From Superhero to 'Kitchin'-maid

'She is yoo-ung, she is beautiful and . . .', sings the dog at the piano, smiling out at the guests in a cave-like hall.[1] He is part of a quintet entertaining at the wedding of the goddess Freyja and the giant Thrym in *Thors brudefærd* (Thor's Wedding, 1980) by Peter Madsen, from the Danish comic book series *Valhalla*. The storyline is based on the eddic poem *Þrymskviða* (The Lay of Thrym) but the wedding band is borrowed from Jim Henson's television series *The Muppet Show*. In addition to Rowlf the Dog, the musical group includes members of the Muppet rock house band Dr Teeth and the Electric Mayhem, with the drummer Animal, saxophonist Zoot, bass player Floyd Pepper and keyboardist Dr Teeth. But several elements are at odds with the Muppet pre-text. Instead of his usual red cavalry jacket, borrowed from George Harrison on the cover of the Beatles' album *Sgt Pepper's Lonely Hearts Club Band*, Pepper wears a hessian tunic and plays a lyre. Zoot also plays an old-fashioned instrument that seems to be a cross between a clarinet and the Bronze Age 'Brudevælte lurs'. He is almost bald, and the way his pointy ears stick up suggests a common ancestry with Tolkien's hobbits, or the Vulcans from the television series *Star Trek*. Dr Teeth, who usually sports a floppy purple top hat, instead wears Gandalf's blue, pointed wizard's hat, and there is a black gap in his upper gum where his gold tooth normally shines. With reference to the words that Zoot directed towards Charlie Parker in one episode of *The Muppet Show*, it is easy to imagine Madsen whispering as he finished this frame: 'Forgive me, Jim Henson, wherever you are.'[2]

The *Valhalla* series is one of a great many examples of how the eddas have enjoyed a colourful afterlife within the genre of comics. The best-known adaptation of this kind is an American comic series devoted to the Mighty Thor. He first appeared during the 1960s in magazines issued by the American publishing company Marvel Comics. Since then he has resurfaced in various television series, films and computer games. Writing on the influence of Icelandic medieval literature on Japanese manga, Halldór Stefánsson has suggested that the artists at Marvel have 'been instrumental in determining many people's conceptions of ancient Nordic mythology in the English-speaking world'.[3] Both in Marvel's production and the Danish *Valhalla* series, the myths themselves are, however, still just one of numerous pre-texts that the artists in question have been working from. In some cases, the medieval influences seem to be operating at second or even third hand.

'The most exciting superhero of all time'

The idea of turning Thor into a superhero is generally attributed to Stanley Martin Lieber, better known as Stan Lee, who worked as an editor at Marvel Comics in New York. Martin Goodman founded the company in 1939 as Timely Publications and it quickly became a big player on the American comic book scene. Among the popular material published by Goodman in the early years were stories about Captain America, a patriotic superhero created by Jack Kirby and Joe Simon in 1941. Stan Lee was involved in the making of some of the Captain America stories but in the 1940s he also took part in creating characters such as the Destroyer and Jack Frost. The conception of the Mighty Thor is usually traced back to 1960 when DC Comics began publishing a new series called the *Justice League of America* in which all the principal superheroes of that company – including Superman, Batman and Wonder Woman – play a part. Goodman asked Lee to create a parallel super team for Marvel and soon he and his colleagues had shaped a diverse group of new characters, many of whom would live on for decades. These include Spider-Man, the Hulk, Iron Man and Thor, all of whom were introduced in comic magazines between 1962 and 1963.

At around the same time, Marvel began publishing stories under the title *The Avengers* in which three of the above-mentioned figures joined Captain America and other superheroes in their struggle against darkness and evil. Involved with Lee in this project were, among others, his younger brother and scriptwriter Larry Lieber, and Jack Kirby, who illustrated the first comics devoted to the Hulk and Iron Man.[4] Reportedly, Lieber (script) and Kirby (pencils), along with some other artists, worked with Lee on the first story about Thor, which appeared in the comic magazine *Journey into Mystery #83* in August 1962. The cover shows a muscular, blond warrior in a winged helmet, standing on the edge of a high-rise in a modern city, swinging his hammer around. A spaceship hovers above his head, out of which jump armed, green stone men, one of whom has already been struck down by the hammer. 'Introducing the Mighty Thor!' is written in large letters to the left of the spaceship, and to the right: 'The most exciting super hero of all time!!'

The feature story was published in the magazine in three different parts: 'Thor the Mighty and the Stone Men from Saturn!', 'The Power of Thor' and 'Thor the Mighty Strikes Back!' (the first title will be used here to represent all of them). The storyline, in brief, is that an American doctor, Donald Blake, is travelling through a mountainous region of Norway when the stone men land their space fleet there. Their mission is to breathe in oxygen, which gives them superhuman powers and would, in the course of time, enable them to conquer the Earth. Blake escapes into a cave where he finds an old wooden cudgel. When he hits it against a stone, the cudgel turns into a hammer and transforms the doctor into Thor, the Nordic god of thunder. After practising how to wield the hammer (to split a giant tree trunk, for example) he attacks the enemy forces, drives them away and saves the day. The story ends with their spaceships flying off, to the great surprise of American NATO soldiers who have taken up position in the area.

'Thor the Mighty and the Stone Men from Saturn!' could be interpreted as a modern adaptation of the myths describing Thor's struggle against the giants of Jotunheim. In *Snorra Edda* we learn that Thor is 'strongest of all the gods and men' and that among his possessions is the hammer Mjolnir, 'well known to frost-giants and mountain-giants when it is raised aloft, and that is not to be wondered at, it has smashed many a skull of their fathers and kinsmen'.[5] In *Þrymskviða*, which describes the consequences of Thor's hammer being stolen by the giant Thrym, the trickster Loki explains that the

Covers of *The Mighty Thor* #229 (1974) and *Justice League of America* #36 (1965).

fate of the pagan gods very much depends on this instrument: 'The giants will be settling in Asgard, / unless you get your hammer back', he explains to Thor.[6] In 'Thor the Mighty and the Stone Men from Saturn!' these circumstances are transposed from the fantasy world of Nordic mythology into the solar system (Asgard becomes Norway, on Earth; Jotunheim becomes Saturn) and linked to American military activity in northern Europe during the Cold War.

Thor adopts the split personality of an archetypal superhero who, half the time, also leads an ordinary life far removed from his role as saviour of mankind. In the Marvel comic, Dr Blake walks with a cane and before he finds the cudgel in the cavern, his monologue reveals that he is neither brave nor resourceful: 'The cave is so dark – so gloomy – and airless! It seems no human has set foot in here for ages!! (sigh) I might as well wait for the Stone Men to find me – I-I'm trapped!'[7] It is only with the aid of the hammer that he changes from a middle-class wimp into a masculine hero. The episode can be associated with *Þrymskviða,* where the loss of the hammer leads to Thor's transformation into a woman. In the eddic poem Thrym says he is willing to return the hammer to the gods if he gets to marry the goddess Freyja. When she proves unwilling to do this, the gods dress Thor in a bridal gown and send him to the wedding in Freyja's place. The plot ends with Mjolnir being laid in the lap of the bride, who then recovers her (or his) virile qualities:

> Thor's heart laughed in his breast,
> when he, stern in courage, recognized the hammer;
> first he struck Thrym, lord of ogres,
> and battered all the race of giants.[8]

The comparison drawn here does not necessarily mean that Lee, Lieber and Kirby pored over English translations of the eddas before they began creating the first Mighty Thor comics. In looking for the pre-texts these three consulted, it makes more sense to study earlier

American comics in which Thor plays a significant role. Kirby was involved in several such projects for DC Comics in the 1940s and '50s and it is customary to consider these as a part of the creative process that would later bear fruit in his collaboration with the Lieber brothers.[9] The oldest story, 'The Villain from Valhalla', appeared in the magazine *Adventure Comics #75* in the summer of 1942 and was, just like the first Captain America stories, designed by Kirby in collaboration with Joe Simon. Here, superheroes Sandman and Sandy fight a group of Vikings who visit modern-day New York. On the splash page, the bearded leader of the group can be seen standing on the banks of the East River with the Brooklyn Bridge and the Empire State Building in the background. The commanding warrior has pulled Sandy up by the hair and swings his hammer threateningly over Sandman's head. The iconography is the same as on the cover of *Journey into Mystery #83* twenty years later, except that instead of stone men equipped with guns and a spaceship we have Vikings armed with swords and a longship with a dragon prow. At the bottom of the page, the situation is elucidated:

> From the misty caverns of the past rises Thor, ancient god of war . . . no kindness pulses in his body: instead only hate and savage ruthlessness guide him as he invades a modern world . . . wielding his magic hammer . . . he beats a mad tattoo upon the forces of society![10]

Even if Thor here plays the role of the rogue, the story is identical to that told in 'Thor the Mighty and the Stone Men from Saturn!' and, indeed, in thousands of other American comics. Society struggles against the invasion of an evil force but before all is lost the protagonist manages to restore law and order. At the end of the narrative we learn that the rascals were not real Vikings from the past, but merely a group of contemporary criminals in disguise. The group's leader is a university professor called 'Fairy Tales' Fenton who has combined his knowledge of mythology and technology to design a bulletproof suit and an electric hammer that can smash police cars and blast bank vaults. Chris Sims has pointed out that Kirby's decision to present the villain as a Germanic god of battle was decidedly meaningful in the context of growing American participation in the Second World War in 1942:

> Thor, the *blitzkrieging* Norse god that was being held up by the Nazis as the ideal of the Master Race is revealed to be just another common crook who gets the living crap kicked out of him and ends the story in traction, with the Sandman and Sandy showing up to mock him in the hospital. Is it any surprise that this is the same artist who introduced Captain America by having him punch Hitler right in the mouth?[11]

Another wartime comic featuring Thor that has been attributed to Kirby and Simon is 'The Shadow of Valhalla' published in the magazine *Boy Commandos #7* in the summer of 1944. By that time, both artists had been drafted so it is uncertain to what degree the storyline, reportedly ghostwritten by Don Cameron and ghost-drawn by Louis Cazeneuve, is a part of Kirby and Simon's oeuvre.[12] The heroes of the *Boy Commandos* series, which had kicked off in 1942, are four orphan boys from France, England, the Netherlands and the USA who, under the leadership of Rip Carter, fight the Axis Powers on different military fronts. In 'The Shadow of Valhalla' the action takes place in German-occupied Norway, or more specifically in an old building where the commandos are supposed to search for artillery. It turns out that this is the castle of Valhalla, Odin's residence, occupied by a Nazi troop. The two parties engage in a battle, causing part of the bastion to explode. At that point, the Nordic gods Thor, Freyr, Bragi and Heimdall – they all have yellow beards and are wearing Viking clothing and horned helmets as uniforms – intervene and bring the intruders to the seat of Odin. The Nazi lieutenant claims that he represents the gods' 'chosen leader, Hitler!' and adds that Carter and his commandos 'must be destroyed! Our fuehrer has ordered it! We shall be masters of the world.'[13] But Odin is not impressed: 'Who is this upstart Hitler?' he asks. 'I never chose him for a leader!'[14] At that point Carter explains that 'Hitler has appointed himself master of the world – and now we are fighting his armies in order to be free! We refuse to be slaves!'[15] Odin decides to settle the matter between the commandos and the Germans by one-on-one combat. Luckily, Carter wins, granting him and the boys safe passage to 'the world of life', while Thor uses his hammer to dispatch the Nazis 'to the world of darkness'.[16] At the end of the story it is suggested that the whole episode is a dream of the American commando – his name was Brooklyn and he 'sounded and acted a lot like Kirby' – but that does not alter the blunt message of the story as defined by Odin: 'Valhalla is the Norse heaven . . . not German!'[17] By aligning the pagan gods on the side of the Allies, 'The Shadow of Valhalla' contradicts 'The Villain from Valhalla' and can be seen as anticipating Thor's future recruitment in Marvel's league of superheroes.

Kirby's third comic about Thor, 'The Magic Hammer', published in *Tales of the Unexpected #16* in 1957, can be read as a simple fable in which greed is condemned. It is the story of a Native American who accompanies a Caucasian gold-digger, Gerald Bard, into the Wild West and finds a hammer lying out in the open. The two men discover that if the hammer is struck, it produces thunder and lightning. Consequently, Bard strikes a deal with the regional authorities whereby he will produce rain on demand (probably a reference to remarkable rainmaking operations in the USA during the 1950s).[18] Bard is successful in selling this service but when he realizes that the hammer also has the power to split trees in half, he decides to change professions: 'Why, with that magic hammer, I can blast my way through bank walls', he thinks to himself, much like Fenton in 'The Villain from Valhalla'.[19] But before Bard gets a chance to act on this idea, a bearded Viking appears at his side, introduces himself as Thor and says he wants his weapon back:

> 'I come from a land you know not – and there I rule as master of thunder and lightning . . . Centuries ago, while at the great banquet hall, mischievous little Loki stole my hammer . . . Racing over the clouds, I pursued Loki – but he hurled the hammer into the hills below . . . As punishment for letting Loki do this, I was reduced to the size of you mortals – and made to roam the earth in search of my hammer.'[20]

The story ends with the gold-digger losing his mind when Thor has reclaimed his hammer and returned to his godly stature. The god's final words suggest he will seek revenge on the thief: 'Ho, ho, ho, ho hí! Loki! . . . I have my hammer back!'[21]

'The Magic Hammer' clearly draws on the heritage of the eddas. Kirby (or some other artist who contributed to the story) was undoubtedly familiar with Thor's role as the god of thunder and also with the lore describing Loki's repeated attempts to get the inhabitants of Asgard into trouble. A well-known example is a narrative in *Snorra Edda* describing how Loki lures the goddess Idunn out of Asgard and enables one of the giants to abduct her to Jotunheim.[22] There are no sources suggesting that Loki kidnapped Mjolnir in the same way, but given that *Þrymskviða* begins *in medias res* – Thor wakes in the morning, doesn't find his hammer and turns first to Loki who is somewhere nearby – it is conceivable that the trickster is somehow responsible.[23] A more conclusive connection between *Þrymskviða* and 'The Magic Hammer' is that Thor's joyful reaction when he gets the hammer in the comic story echoes the poem's description of the god in the same situation ('Thor's mind laughed in his breast').

In the three early Thor comics that can be partially attributed to Jack Kirby we find various elements that reappear in 'Thor the Mighty and the Stone Men from Saturn!' Still, there are at least two stages missing in the progress from the malevolent Fenton/Thor in 'The Villain from Valhalla' to the Marvel superhero Blake/Thor. These can be found in two additional comic stories featuring the Nordic god of thunder, one from 1940 and the other from 1959.

Weird Comics was the title of a short-lived comic magazine which Fox Feature Syndicate, a company founded by Victor S. Fox and Robert Farrell in 1939, began issuing the following year. The volumes in question contained a truly pioneering comic series opening with the story 'Thor God of Thunder'. The stories were attributed to Wright Lincoln (possibly a pen name used by several writers) but the drawings have been ascribed to Pierce Rice, a young artist who was to work with Stan Lee in the 1950s.[24] In the first story the reader meets 'the ancient god, Thor, son of Odin, supreme ruler of Valhalla', who looks down on Earth from Asgard and surmises that mankind has use for his powers.[25] Emphasis is placed on the god's hammer and how he can wield it to cause thunderstorms and discharge lightning. For some reason Thor decides to give a timid American, Grant Farrel, the ability to transform himself into a thunder god when needed. On those occasions, Farrel ducks out and then reappears shortly afterwards in the guise of Thor. His suit and tie is replaced by a costume of sash, boots, cape and winged helmet that not only enables him to fly but makes him more reminiscent of Peter Pan or Superman than Kirby's archetypal Vikings.[26]

The stories devoted to Thor in *Weird Comics* describe, on the one hand, Farrel's hopeless attempts to attract the attention of the modern girl Glenda and, on the other hand, Thor's successful efforts to save her and the Earth from villains, who more often than not are agents of the Axis powers. In the story 'Thor Goes to War' Farrel is, for example, terribly concerned when he hears that Glenda is planning to sail from America to Europe where war is raging. He decides to go along, using his flying ability and hammer to clear mines from their ship's path. Later, he applies the same method to fight Nazi bombers attacking Paris. After blowing several of them to pieces he ties up the German air fleet with a large chain and throws them down onto the Brandenburg Gate in Berlin.[27] Appropriately, Glenda does not realize that Farrel and Thor are the same person and her admiration of the latter makes Farrel jealous. It is a classic paradox of superhero stories that had surfaced, for instance, in the relationship between Clark Kent/Superman and Lois Lane, and would reappear in the relationship of Dr Donald Blake/Thor with the nurse Jane Foster (who was originally named Jane Nelson).

Another comic that Stan Lee and his colleagues were evidently familiar with is 'The Hammer of Thor', published in the magazine *Out of This World #11* in 1959. The author was Steve Ditko, who had started his career as an apprentice to Kirby and Simon in the 1950s and later worked with Lee at Marvel on the first Spider-Man comics.[28] The story is set in medieval Scandinavia and serves to explain the origins of the myths about the thunder god. Thor is a delicate boy with little interest in the Viking games of his peers, who bully him. His parents disagree about how to handle the situation. The father wants to toughen the boy up; the mother prefers a different tactic. When Thor subsequently flees into the forest, he finds a strangely lit underground cave and, inside, an amulet shaped like a hammer. The brightness fills the boy with powers he has never felt before; he becomes muscular and discovers by accident, much like the gold-digger in 'The Magic Hammer', that the tool can be used to split trees. 'Though I may never have to fight anyone, this will make a great weapon', says Thor to himself.[29] Later, after his parents have died an untimely death, a group of Huns go rampaging around Scandinavia and the hammer comes in handy. Thor uses the weapon first against two East-Asian-looking warriors with the result that they disappear off the face of the Earth. In the next frame he is seen from behind, having employed the power of the hammer, but instead of the enemy army he is encircled by a red glow and two yellow bolts of lightning. The caption reads: 'The Huns were driven back, discouraged by the strange terrible weapon, and peace came to Scandinavia again but Thor stayed in his happy forest.'[30]

Here, several comparisons can be made with 'Thor the Mighty and the Stone Men from Saturn!' In both stories, a fragile man finds the thunder god's hammer in an underground cave and uses it to fight off an army of vicious enemies. It is possible that the appearance of the Huns in Ditko's story referred to the Korean War, in which Americans became involved in the early 1950s, but the description of 'the strange terrible weapon' that drives the Huns back rather suggests that it is a *sub rosa* glorification of the effect of the nuclear attacks on Hiroshima and Nagasaki in 1945 in bringing the Second World War to an end and maintaining the armed peace of the Cold War.

It seems credible that most or even all of the five comic book stories from the 1940s and '50s that we have been discussing were part of the texts which Lee, Kirby and Lieber built on when they created the earliest story about the Mighty Thor. It is more problematic to demonstrate the relationship of the oldest Marvel stories to the Icelandic medieval sources. As in the frame that features Dr Teeth and the Electric Mayhem in *Thors brudefærd*, there are several references in 'Thor the Mighty and the Stone Men from Saturn!' that simultaneously point in widely different directions. The stone men from Saturn that Blake/Thor encounters in Norway are an illuminating example. Medieval scholars might assume that these characters are related to the mountain giants described in *Snorra Edda*. But for readers who know Jack Kirby's body of work, it is evident that these are based on the extraterrestrials that he drew in four comic stories in the period 1959 to 1961, inspired by the moai stone sculptures of Easter Island in the southeastern Pacific Ocean. In some of these stories the leader of these stone sentinels is named 'Thorr', but Richard Kolkman has proposed that the explanation for this is that Kirby had been reading *Aku-Aku: The Secret of Easter Island* (1958) by the Norwegian explorer Thor Heyerdahl:

> Is it reasonable to believe that not only was Jack inspired by this book, but that he also later paid homage to its author

> named 'Thor' by combining such diverse concepts as the Easter Island statues with the Norse god of thunder?[31]

In the wartime stories about Thor that we have explored, the villains were variously linked to the Axis powers. Similarly, it seems logical to link the stone men invading Norway in *Journey into Mystery #83* with the impending threat from Moscow. In the 1960s, only two NATO members in Europe shared a border with the Soviet Union: Turkey and Norway. Such political references became an important part of Thor's calling at Marvel. In the following issues of the magazine, Thor was to struggle both with communists who were dictating a small country in South America, and one of his future arch-enemies, Zarrko, The Tomorrow Man, who was planning to take over the world. Martin Arnold has emphasized how the whole series about the Mighty Thor became a mouthpiece of American ideology and conservatism as it developed from one decade to another:

> In due course, Thor would go on to be depicted as the one-time enemy of Hitler and the subsequent bane of all far-right organizations, a bulwark against the Soviet Union and as a combatant in Vietnam (against another superbeing). Thor also shares Middle America's social anxieties and is, in the late 1960s, for example, a critic of slothful hippies.[32]

Another of Thor's arch-enemies, who was introduced in 1962, was the trickster Loki. He plays the role of the villain in 'Trapped by Loki, The God of Mischief', published in *Journey into Mystery #85*. The first part takes place in Asgard, where Odin has imprisoned Loki inside a tree, cursing him never to escape unless someone sheds a tear for him. Using the power of his mind, Loki manages to make a leaf fall from the tree and injure Heimdall's eye, causing him to shed a tear. Thus Loki is freed and heads for Earth, where he intends to obtain Thor's hammer. He uses deception to succeed, causing the thunder god to

Thor waxwork from Madame Tussauds' Marvel's *Avengers* exhibit, New York, 2012.

change back into Dr Blake for a while, but before the day is over Thor turns the tables back on Loki.[33] In the first part of this story, we hear a faint echo from the *Snorra Edda* account of the gods' attempt to free Odin's son Baldur, who had been killed by his brother Hod, from the underworld of Helheim. Hel, who rules in Helheim (literally meaning 'the world of Hel'), promises to allow him to return to Asgard 'if all things in the world, alive and dead, weep for him'.[34] Everything appears to go to plan when Loki, disguised as the giantess Thokk, says she cries dry tears for Baldur. Furthermore, Thor and Loki's fight over control of Mjolnir in the latter part of 'Trapped by Loki, The God of Mischief' can possibly be linked to Thor and Thrym's fight over the hammer in *Þrymskviða*. Still, it probably makes more sense to see the comic here as a reworking of Kirby's 'The Magic Hammer' from 1957, in which Loki unquestionably steals the thunder instrument.

In the half-century or so that has passed since the publication of these early stories, Marvel has published hundreds of comics about Thor and his adventures. More than a dozen narratives were adapted for television in the cartoon series *The Marvel Super Heroes* (1966), produced by Marvel and Grantray-Lawrence Animation. The most recent adaptations of this kind are the fantasy action movies *Thor* (2011), directed by Kenneth Branagh, and its sequel *Thor: The Dark World* (2013), directed by Alan Taylor. Both of these films, featuring the Australian actor Chris Hemsworth as Thor, developed marketing tie-ins such as video games and plenty of merchandise, ranging from T-shirts, Legos, hoodies, jewellery, cufflinks, key chains, patches, alarm clocks, salt and pepper shakers, glasses, magnets and business card holders to wallets, wristbands and dog tags. Thor's role in the comic series *The Avengers* has contributed to his colossal international fame. Offshoots of this material, including Joss Whedon's films *The Avengers* (2012) and *Avengers: Age of Ultron* (2015), have also made their way into cinemas, televisions, computers and video game consoles.

Most of these adaptations are variations on the fundamental themes that emerged in the earliest stories of the Mighty Thor and their American prototypes. In several cases, the artists seem to have consulted the eddas or their nineteenth- and twentieth-century adaptations, including Richard Wagner's operas.[35] More importantly, however, an independent mythological sphere has developed around these Marvel characters – a world which has become at least as multifaceted as the one we read about in *Þrymskviða* and *Snorra Edda*. According to the medieval pre-texts, for example, it is never quite clear why Loki lives among the gods in Asgard. In Marvel Universe 'mythology', on the other hand, we learn that Odin adopted Loki from an early age after killing his father, the giant Laufey (who in the eddas is Loki's mother). Furthermore, the stories produced by the illustrators at Marvel have influenced a range of other artists. One curious example, which rejuvenates Kirby and Simon's interpretation of Thor in 'The Villain from Valhalla', is David Brin's *Thor Meets Captain America* (1986). This novella of alternative history, which later inspired Brin and Scott Hampton's acclaimed graphic novel *The Life Eaters* (2003), describes how the Nordic god of thunder teams up with German Nazis and ensures them victory in the Second World War.

'Then they dressed Thor in a bride's head-dress'

'The hallmark of all comics aimed at younger readers is violence made entertaining.'[36] Although this statement of Heather O'Donoghue's applies to most of the comic stories that we have already discussed, other comics about the Nordic gods can be found in which the material is treated differently. One early example is a manga series that the prolific and respected Japanese comic artist Shōtarō Ishinomori began working on in 1964 under the title *Saibōgu Zero-Zero-Nain* (Cyborg 009, issued from 1964 to 1981). Possibly stimulated by Ian Fleming's early novels about the espionage adventures of James Bond, alias 007, or more straightforwardly by Terence Young's 1962 film adaptation of Fleming's *Dr No* (1958), this material was serialized in various Japanese comic magazines, before later being published in book form.

Shōtarō Ishinomori, 'Joe Shimamura Saves Françoise Arnoul', from the manga *Saibōgu Zero-Zero-Nain Edda-hen* (1976).

Saibōgu Zero-Zero-Nain focuses on a multinational group of characters: eight men and one woman. They are captured by the evil Black Ghost organization and changed into half-robots with different superpower abilities. The Black Ghost aims to produce weapons of mass destruction and bring about a devastating world war. The cyborgs, led by the Japanese-American Joe Shimamura, do not succumb to the control of their captor and manage to foil his plans. They then continue working together in the battle against various villains and monsters, including mythological characters from the past. In some respects the team can be compared to the Boy Commandos and the

Avengers, but in other respects their stories are, as Halldór Stefánsson has demonstrated, suited to 'Japanese idiom, sensibilities and tastes'.[37]

In 1976 Ishinomori created *Saibōgu Zero-Zero-Nain: Edda,* a three-part story that describes the group's visit to Iceland. The nine cyborgs arrive by passenger jet and then journey into the harsh interior of the country, where they encounter the mythological world of the pagan gods, with the world tree Yggdrasil towering over a settlement of small timber houses. The foreign guests make themselves at home, but soon have to deal with ruthless beasts and gigantic creatures that are familiar to anyone who knows the eddas: among them the wolf Fenrir, the eight-legged horse Sleipnir, the World Serpent and the thunder god Thor. The most curious opponent, however, is a vicious incubus that makes several attempts to strangle the female member of the group as she lies asleep in her bed in one of the houses. The scene, which clearly pays homage to Henry Fuseli's painting *The Nightmare* (1781), ends with Joe Shimamura storming into the room and shooting the uninvited guest. Much like in 'The Villain from Valhalla', it turns out that behind the enemy army stands a crazy scientist who has planted an atom bomb within the world tree and who succeeds in blowing it up. There is certainly an echo here of the description of the apocalyptic Ragnarok from the eddas but it probably makes more sense to connect the end of the story with the critical view of weapons and warfare that has been a recurring theme in public Japanese ideology in the post-war period and is prominent in Ishinomori's *Saibōgu Zero-Zero-Nain* stories.

The most ambitious European attempt to transpose Nordic mythology onto the medium of comic books is no doubt the Danish *Valhalla* series mentioned at the onset of this chapter. A total of fifteen volumes came out, most of which were based not only on characters from Nordic mythology but more directly on the narratives found in the eddic poems, *Snorra Edda* and several other sources. The first six volumes were issued by the comic book publisher Interpresse and the rest by Carlsen Comics. Although the series is usually attributed

Cover of Peter Madsen and Hans Rancke-Madsen's *Ulven er løs* (1979).

to comic artist Peter Madsen alone, an impressive group of writers and artists was involved. Henning Kure, editor at Interpresse, initiated the project and took an active part in developing the concept from the beginning. From the seventh volume on, Kure was included alongside Hans Rancke-Madsen and Per Vadmand as one of the official writers of the *Valhalla* series.[38]

One of the primary sources of the earliest comic, *Ulven er løs* (Cry Wolf, 1979), written by Hans Rancke-Madsen and drawn by Peter Madsen, is *Snorra Edda*'s account of Thor's journey to Utgarda-Loki. According to the medieval source, Thor and Loki seek lodging at a farm on the way to Jotunheim and it is noted that the farmer had two children, Thjalfi and Roskva – a boy and girl respectively. In the evening, Thor slaughters the two billy goats that drag his carriage, cooks them, invites the farmer and his family to eat with him and orders them to throw the bones onto the goat skins at the end of the meal. The next morning, Thor consecrates the remains of the meal with his hammer, bringing the billy goats back to life; only one of them is now limping. It turns out that Thjalfi, not satisfied with gnawing the thighbone in question, broke it to get to the marrow. This infuriates Thor, but he calms down when the head of the household offers to compensate him for the loss. It is decided that the children will become 'Thor's bondservants and they have attended him ever since.'[39]

The first part of *Ulven er løs* closely follows this part of the narrative from *Snorra Edda,* with a few additions. For instance, at the beginning of the comic story it is made clear that Roskva is much more courageous than Thjalfi, even though she is younger. (When Thor and Loki first arrive at the farm, the girl is out walking an enormous dog of which her brother is obviously afraid.) Another addition is that in the comic book it is Loki who quietly encourages Thjalfi to break the goat's thighbone and suck the marrow from it, explaining that 'one bone does not play much of a part – there are so many of them.'[40] This accords well with how the trickster Loki is responsible for various misdeeds in other myths. Understandably, it is also up to him to calm the angry Thor in *Ulven er løs.* Loki proposes that Thjalfi should enter their service in order to make up for his transgression. Roskva is not a part of the arrangement in the comic version but she is unhappy about being left behind and so sneaks onto Thor's carriage to be with her brother ever after. Introducing the siblings at the beginning of the story in this way is quite clever as their main role in the series then becomes that of representing the perspective of young readers in this unfamiliar setting. Unlike the account in *Snorra Edda,* Thor and Loki do not head to find Utgarda-Loki following this episode – Madsen and his colleagues did not have that journey take place until the fifth volume of the *Valhalla* series. Instead, they travel to Asgard, where the children are little by little introduced to all the main gods and their places of residence, especially to the palaces of Bilskirnir, where Thor lives with his wife Sif, and Valhalla, where Odin reigns alongside his wife Frigg.

The other imperative pre-text of *Ulven er løs* is the account in *Snorra Edda* of the gods' attempts to tie up the giant wolf Fenrir. According to the medieval account, the gods fostered the wolf in Asgard and Tyr saw to feeding him. As the creature grew larger, the gods attempted to tie it up using the strong fetter 'Leyding', and then an even stronger one, 'Dromi', but Fenrir easily broke free both times. It wasn't until a couple of dwarfs – at the request of Skirnir – made the refined fetter 'Gleipnir' that the gods finally succeeded in restraining the wolf. Tyr held his own hand in the beast's mouth as security, with the unfortunate result that it was subsequently bitten off. 'Then they all laughed except for Tyr', according to *Snorra Edda*.[41] In *Ulven er løs* Frigg tells Thjalfi and Roskva a simplified version of this story on their first night in Valhalla. The children have already discovered that there is a crisis in Asgard because the wolf is roaming free. Obviously, the fetter proved less reliable than the gods had wanted. In the last part of *Ulven er løs*, the gods fail to restrain the wolf again, but the story ends with Roskva succeeding without much trouble, thanks to her previous experience back home of keeping a fierce canine beast under control. The girl simply loves animals and has her heart in the right place, and for those reasons has greater success than the rash gods.

Although individual threads in the story are taken from different places, *Ulven er løs* is certainly an independent creation and above all else an emblematic adventure story that serves to boost the confidence of young readers, especially girls. In this way, the moral of the Danish comic is far removed from that of most Marvel comics about the Mighty Thor, where might is normally right. Furthermore, *Ulven er løs* also reflects contemporary issues, which in the Denmark of the late 1970s included significant reforms towards gender equality – a concern Madsen and his co-workers continued to be preoccupied with.

Cover of Peter Madsen's *Thors brudefærd* (1980).

Thors brudefærd, drawn and chiefly written by Peter Madsen, was the second book in the *Valhalla* series. Unlike the first book, its entire subject-matter was drawn from one primary pre-text. The storyline of *Þrymskviða* is mostly unchanged in the comic story, but Madsen weaves various elements into the plot and interprets it in a fairly modern way. It is unclear from the eddic poem how Thrym comes to possess Mjolnir, but on the first page of *Thors brudefærd* this question is answered definitively. Shadowy giants are shown approaching Bilskirnir in the dead of night and taking something from one of the tower rooms while the gods are busy singing and drinking elsewhere in Thor's palace. Other additions include Thor and Loki, disguised as women, staying one night at the hall of Utgarda-Loki on their way to Thrym's quarters. A new scene is added at the end of the comic too, illustrating Thor triumphantly returning home with the hammer in his luggage. Sif, who is pregnant at the start of the narrative, welcomes her husband with twins in her arms, thereby revealing a new side of the thunder god as a proud father.

Scholars' understanding of *Þrymskviða* partially depends on the way in which they interpret the symbolic meaning of Mjolnir. There is a long tradition of seeing the hammer as a thunder instrument and interpreting the poem as an allegory of natural phenomena. In that case, Thrym and the other giants of Jotunheim represent the forces of winter, attempting to delay the coming of spring – the prolific rain – by capturing Mjolnir or, even better, Freyja, the goddess of fertility.[42] But it is also possible to regard the hammer as a symbol of social power. Freyja's reluctance to accept Thrym's proposal suggests that the gods of Asgard have little respect for the giants and regard them as socially inferior. She explains to Thor: 'You'll know me to be the most sex-crazed of women / if I drive with you to the land of the giants.'[43] The third alternative is to interpret Mjolnir as a symbol of masculinity and even literally as Thor's phallus, as the medievalist Margaret Clunies Ross has pointed out: 'on a symbolic level the god has had the emblem of his masculinity removed while in the passive state of sleep. It is as if he had been castrated.'[44] In the absence of the hammer the thunder god is turned into a transvestite or a transwoman.

Peter Madsen does not work with the first interpretive option, except that he draws a clear distinction between the fertile landscape of Asgard and the cold and barren environment in Jotunheim. Greater emphasis is placed on the class distinction between the gods and the giants. While Thor lives in a grand palace with many towers, Thrym lives underground in a warren of big caverns and dark tunnels. It is indicative of the low cultural status of the giants that all of the written instructions that are visible in Thrym's abode are misspelled; a sign above the door into the kitchen, for instance, reads 'Kitchin'.[45] While the gods in Asgard look like regular people and are nicely dressed in *Thors brudefærd*, Thrym's court mostly consists of trolls and monsters, many of whom resemble, to modern audiences, ugly characters from *The Muppet Show* or the early *Star Wars* films. Thrym is the most anthropomorphic of them all, but his small red skullcap, which looks a bit like a Muslim taqiyah, may suggest an Islamic background. In this context, it is worth noting that there was a growing influx of immigrants from Turkey, Pakistan and Yugoslavia into Denmark in the 1970s. Conversely, Madsen gives Thrym big lips that make him suspiciously similar to Dirch Passer, one of the most celebrated Danish comedians of the period.[46]

In *Þrymskviða*, the giant is not only wealthy, but materialistic. When Loki meets him for the first time in the poem we are told:

> Thrym sat on a grave-mound, the lord of the ogres,
> plaiting golden collars for his bitches,
> he was trimming the horses' manes.[47]

Later, Thrym boasts of his belongings:

> Gold-horned cows walk here in the yard
> jet-black oxen to the giant's delight;
> many treasures I possess, many necklaces I possess,
> Freyia was all I seemed to be missing.[48]

Although Madsen does not recycle these stanzas in his comic version (except for having Thrym sit on a mound rather than a throne), he is highly receptive to the giant's materialism. During the preparation for the wedding, Loki enters a large cavern where Thrym stores all of his gold and even swims in it. The scene alludes to Scrooge McDuck's money swim in Walt Disney's Donald Duck universe; later it is revealed that Thrym, just like Scrooge, cherishes his very own 'Number One Dime'.[49]

Thrym's claim in *Þrymskviða* that Freyja is the only thing missing in his portfolio clearly suggests that women are considered to be items of property in Jotunheim. The status of women does not seem to be much better in Asgard, but the eddic poem can nonetheless be read as a radical criticism of a patriarchal, medieval society with its fixed gender and social roles.[50] These same issues are also at the forefront in *Thors brudefærd*. Right from the first pages of the comic, Thor is characterized as a chauvinistic husband who orders his pregnant wife to prepare breakfast, and pretends to be worried when he sees that she is carrying heavy loads but never offers to give her a hand. Similar sexism can be detected in Thrym's dealings with his sister and in the common view of the giants of Utgarda-Loki's farm that the only language women can understand is the language of violence. But these ideas are also undermined in the comic book, such as when some of the gods and goddesses try to convince Freyja that she should indeed marry Thrym. She ferociously retorts by asking Idunn: 'What should you say to being traded away for a stupid old hammer, like a commodity?'[51] It is not until her father shows up and scolds her that Freyja hesitates, but right at the same moment Loki has the bright idea of dressing up Thor as a woman so that he can retrieve the hammer.

In the eddic poem, Thor's makeover is described in detail:

> Then they dressed Thor in a bride's head-dress
> and in the great necklace of the Brisings,
> they let keys jingle about him
> and women's clothing fall down to his knees,
> but on his breast they displayed [big stones],
> and arranged a head-dress suitably on his head.[52]

Peter Madsen obviously had these lines in mind when he sketched the scene in question. He left out the keys and added a burka that hides Thor's beard, but what is particularly interesting is the way in which he turns the poem's stones, most often interpreted as jewels, into artificial breasts. In spite of his feminine figure, Thor finds it difficult to play his female role in *Thors brudefærd*, in particular when the chauvinists among Utgarda-Loki's men start to harass him and he is forced to wash the dishes along with the 'other' females in Thrym's household. He loses his temper when he discovers that the male supervisor working in the 'kitchin' is on a higher salary than the women who work there: 'Why on earth is he better paid than I am? I did much more!!?!', Thor frantically asks, but the only reply he gets is that the supervisor is a man, 'so his work is worth more than yours'.[53] Thrym's sister, who has been wary of the bride all along, witnesses this conversation and becomes convinced that her future sister-in-law cannot possibly be a woman. These examples show how responsive Madsen is to the gender issues in *Þrymskviða* and to the ways in which they can be used to reflect on contemporary society. In that context, it is worth recalling that the equal pay act was not passed in Denmark until 1976, merely four years prior to the publication of *Thors brudefærd*.

It is indeed remarkable to witness the most masculine character of the Nordic mythological world – the prototype for Marvel's the Mighty Thor – becoming a victim of sexual harassment, jingoism and the gender pay gap. This leitmotif ripens when Thrym turns a deaf ear to his sister's warning regarding the phony bride and scolds her: 'What are you doing here, you lazy slag!! Get out of here and find something useful to do.'[54] One of the lessons of the comic book is that men should listen to what women have to say. But another lesson is that it is hard to teach an old dog new tricks. When Thor returns to Asgard at the end of *Thors brudefærd* he says that he is shocked by the ways in which women are treated by the giants, but at the same time he wryly declines Sif's request for him to give her a hand around the house. As a result, the gods and goddesses open a debate about the inequality of the sexes. While Sif reproaches everyone present for trying to let Freyja marry the ugly brute Thrym, and sneers at Tyr when he claims that men should rule and women obey, Thor is busy taking care of his newborn twins. Briefly, hope is raised that the roles of the sexes within the family might be turned around, but as soon as the baby girl starts to urinate, the father hands her over to the mother saying: 'She's wet.'[55]

In comparison to the first volume of the *Valhalla* series, Thjalfi and Roskva do not play big roles in *Thors brudefærd*. Still, they accompany Thor and Loki to the wedding and the girl is once again more of a star than her brother. She shows, for instance, great courage when she sneaks down into the 'secrit treesure-chamber', guarded by armed giants and a green dragon.[56] There she finds Thor's hammer but unfortunately is not strong enough to carry it away with her. The page devoted to this adventure is a good example of how Madsen develops interesting subplots in his adaptation of *Þrymskviða*. Some of these subplots are revealed in the background of individual illustrations, for instance a comic description of a young giant-boy who sits on the tie beam of Utgarda-Loki's hall and fishes for food from the hands of the grown-ups below.[57] In the hall of Thrym, attentive readers will also notice another rowdy giant-boy named Quark who attempts to steal a sausage from a girl in the kitchen and sets fire to the hair of one of the wedding guests.[58] Details of this sort, including the allusion to *The Muppet Show* mentioned at the opening of this chapter, are designed to make the reading and rereading of the story more pleasurable and encourage the reader to study each drawing in detail. Personally, I had read through *Thors brudefærd* several times before realizing that a group of five rather ordinary-looking wedding guests looked suspiciously similar to the five creators of the comic: Madsen, Kure, Rancke-Madsen, Per Vadmand and Søren Håkansson.[59]

The third volume in the *Valhalla* series, *Odins væddemål* (Odin's Wager, 1982) was based on several medieval sources. Furthermore, the *Valhalla* artists started preparing the production of an animated film based on the characters they had been developing, giving the giant-boy Quark a leading role. An original plot was created around his character, though in the second half of the film the plot from *Snorra Edda* describing Thor's trip to Utgarda-Loki was recycled to some degree. The film premiered in 1986 and also inspired the next two comic books in the series: *Historien om Quark* (The Story of Quark, 1988) and *Rejsen til Udgårdsloke* (The Journey to Utgarda-Loki, 1989). As time went by, the first five volumes were translated into all the Nordic languages, as well as Dutch, German and Indonesian, with three of them also translated into French. Though the remaining ten books of the series have not enjoyed as wide a circulation, all of them are available in Danish, Norwegian and Swedish. The last book in the series was *Vølvens syner* (The Sibyl's Visions, 2009), which was inspired by the eddic poem *Völuspá*.

During the thirty-year period in which the creators of the *Valhalla* series were active there was a substantial growth in the publication of Japanese and South Korean manga series that were influenced by the eddas and sagas, but possibly, and also more generally, by the international success of Marvel's series *The Mighty Thor* and the exemplary Japanese manga *Saibōgu Zero-Zero-Nain*.[60] These include *Suishō no Dragon* (Crystal Dragon, started 1981, ongoing) by Yuho Ashibe, *Akai Tsurugi* (The Scarlet Sword, 1986–93) by Ryō Azumi, *Ragnarok* (started 1995, now on hiatus) by Lee Myung-jin and *Matantei Loki* (The Mythical Detective Loki, 1999–2004) by Sakura Kinoshita. Some of these have been adapted into animated television series and computer games; *Ragnarok*, for instance, has been turned into a successful, massive multiplayer online role-playing game titled *Ragnarok Online: The Final Destiny of the Gods* (2002). More recent releases in this field include the American graphic novel *Gods of Asgard* (2007) by Erik E. Evensen, the Japanese computer game *Viking: Battle for Asgard* (2008) and the Icelandic 3D animated comedy feature film *Hetjur Valhallar: Þór* (Thor: Legend of the Magical Hammer, 2011), directed by Óskar Jónasson, Toby Genkel and Gunnar Karlsson.

In view of the sexual politics that we identified in *Þrymskviða* and the Danish *Valhalla* series, it is only fair to note that in the autumn of 2014 Marvel started to publish a new comic book series, simply titled *Thor*, which features a thunder goddess with 'big stones' and the qualities of a superhero. In the early issues of the series, written by Jason Aaron and illustrated by Russell Dauterman, the identity of the young, adorable woman employing Mjolnir to fight evil was irritatingly not revealed. Readers had to wait eight months before learning that the winged helmet mask of the superheroine concealed the face of none other than 'Dr Jane Foster, a former girlfriend of the hero who has been battling breast cancer', as explained by George Gene Gustines in the preface to an interview with Jason Aaron published in the *New York Times*:

> 'Jane Foster has been part of the Thor comics and the Thor mythology from almost the very beginning', Mr Aaron said. 'The very act of picking up this hammer, of becoming Thor, is killing her. Where we go from here is the real story.'[61]

The same can be said about the present book, as we now turn our attention to some of the pre-texts that we have been discussing so far; the 'real' stories habitually attributed to Snorri Sturluson.

Gustav Vigeland's statue of Snorri Sturluson, unveiled at Reykholt in western Iceland in 1947.

TWO

Snorri: The 'Real' Stories

'Mrs Moucheboume, do you enjoy Scandinavian literature?'[1] This question sets in motion one of the most tragicomic scenes in the French film *Le Petit Nicolas* (Little Nicolas, 2009), directed by Laurent Tirard. Nicolas' father has invited his boss, Mr Moucheboume, and wife to dinner, in the hope of improving his chances of a promotion. Nicolas' mother is beside herself about the evening. She feels her household is not refined enough and is afraid that she will make a fool of herself in conversation with these supremely intelligent guests. Trying to conceal her lack of education, she has memorized all kinds of information about geography, culture and art. Earlier in the film, we see her practising; reeling off convoluted definitions of the aesthetic qualities of the complex skaldic court poetry that, she believes, Snorri Sturluson once developed, she repeatedly runs into trouble when it comes to pronouncing the name of this medieval Icelander and the term 'periphrasing'. Inevitably, this is exactly where she stumbles on the fateful evening. 'I've a soft spot for thirteenth-century skaldic poetry', says the housewife when Mrs Moucheboume does not respond to her question about Scandinavian literature:

> The manner it has of using 'polyphrases' and metaphors instead of literal meaning. It's really very interesting . . . I simply adore Snorsi Struffl . . . Snorki Snuffn . . . Storki Stleft . . . Smurski Stroflt . . . Speaking of which, did you know that the word 'baroque' comes from Portuguese?[2]

The film about little Nicolas is based on a series of short comical novellas that René Goscinny produced for French newspapers and magazines in the 1950s. They later appeared in book form and enjoyed great popularity in France and have since been translated into numerous languages. The dinner party scene is based on the story 'À la bonne franquette' ('Pot Luck') from *Le Petit Nicolas a des ennuis* (Nicolas in Trouble, 1964), but the discussion about Snorri Sturluson appears to be the invention of the film's scriptwriters. It seems quite remarkable that they saw fit to include knowledge of skaldic poetry among the topics that a French housewife thinks well-to-do people might chat about over aperitifs. The point, of course, is that Nicolas' mother has completely overestimated her guests' intellectual capacities, but the humour would miss its mark if the audience of the film had no idea at all about the subject-matter. The difficulty she faces in pronouncing the name of Snorri Sturluson is amusing to some extent because generations of French school children have themselves struggled with this tongue twister with varying levels of success. Indeed, over the years several variations of the name have been developed. At Place du Panthéon in Paris, for example, we can find lists of more than 800 famous thinkers and writers carved in stone on a building at the renowned Sorbonne University; the Icelandic name dutifully chiselled onto this roll of honour is Snorro-Sturleson.

Snorri's (or Snorro's) fame in France and further afield derives from his being credited with writing at least two canonical works: *Heimskringla* (The Circle of the World), containing histories of Norwegian kings, and our already much quoted *Snorra Edda*. Snorri is also recognized as the author of skaldic poetry, including a lengthy praise poem about King Hakon Hakonarson and Earl Skuli Bardarson, who ruled Norway jointly for the last two decades of Earl Skuli's life. The poem, which is generally published with annotations as the fourth and final part of *Snorra Edda*, relates to significant episodes in Snorri's eventful career as chieftain and politician, during which

The plaque at the Sorbonne, Paris, bearing Snorro Sturleson's (Snorri Sturluson) name.

he spent two periods in Norway and had a good relationship with Earl Skuli, but seems never to have won King Hakon's confidence. Furthermore, it has been suggested that Snorri might be the author of *Egils saga*. Some even entertain the possibility that he composed the skaldic poetry attributed to that saga's colourful hero, Egil Skallagrimsson. In light of this, Nicolas' mother's belief that Snorri is the instigator of the skaldic tradition is not as far-fetched as it may seem.

But is it possible that Snorri's contribution to the world of letters is greatly overrated? Does he truly deserve the honoured position that he, or his misnomer, commands on the stone tablet at the Sorbonne? In this chapter, I want to cast some doubt on the nature and extent of Snorri's role. To begin with, the evidence confirming his authorship of any of the aforementioned works is scanty, quite apart from the fact that medieval prose texts were seldom attributed or attributable to individual writers. Scholars exploring these issues in recent times have emphasized that the distinction between the oral transmission of stories and written literary traditions is by no means as clear as was once thought. It seems less misleading to use concepts such as distributed authorship or rewriting to describe the process by which *Heimskringla* and *Snorra Edda* came into being.[3] From my perspective, there is no significant difference between the writer(s) of these works and those artists producing comics about Thor which we encountered in the previous chapter. Snorri Sturluson, in other words, represents just one link – clearly a very important one – in a long line of individuals who jointly deserve the respect of Nicolas' mother.

'Gudrid spoke the chant so well'

Looking back to the Middle Ages, we can identify two kinds of sources for most of the works attributed to Snorri and his contemporaries. First, there are the pagan oral traditions of poetry and narrative of those from Norway and the British Isles who settled in Iceland in the ninth and tenth centuries. Second, the arrival of Christianity in Iceland around the year 1000 paved the way for a learned Latin literary culture in the country. In the eleventh century, monasteries and other educational institutions were established, but it is widely held that Iceland's age of writing did not begin in earnest before the twelfth century. Not surprisingly, Iceland's settlement, its people's conversion to Christianity and the settlers' relationship with their ancestral homelands emerged as important themes in Icelandic literature during the following centuries.

Some of the sagas recorded on vellum manuscripts during that time tell of the conflicts that arose between pagan belief and Christianity. Descriptions in some sagas also give an indication of how pagan poetic tradition was passed from one generation to the next. *Eiríks saga rauða* (Erik the Red's Saga) is a case in point. It describes the settlement of its eponymous hero in Greenland and the voyages to North America made by his son, Leif Eriksson, and other explorers, at the beginning of the new millennium. Early in the saga, Leif's future sister-in-law, Gudrid Thorbjarnardottir, recites a pagan poem called *Varðlokur* (Ward Songs). She has just moved from Iceland to Greenland and is visiting a farmstead, which is in the grip of a famine. The recitation of the poem will help Thorbjorg the 'little seeress', a soothsayer engaged by the people at the farm, to predict when the famine will end. Gudrid is the only woman present who knows the poem, having learnt it from her foster mother:

> The women formed a warding ring around the platform raised for sorcery, with Thorbjorg perched atop it. Gudrid spoke the chant so well and so beautifully that people there said they had never heard anyone recite in a fairer voice.[4]

This scene outlines a poetic and musical tradition maintained by women. Interestingly, the main emphasis is placed on the individual who is reciting. Neither Gudrid nor her foster mother are said to have composed the verse; instead it seems to exist independently as part of the traditional pagan ceremony associated with soothsaying.

It is generally thought that the eddic poems, which describe both pagan gods, such as Odin and Thor, and legendary Germanic heroes, such as Sigurd the Dragon Slayer, Gunnar Gjukason, Gudrun Gjukadottir and Brynhild Budladottir, were preserved in a similar way, transmitted from person to person until they were first written down in Iceland during the twelfth or thirteenth century. Opinions vary as to the form and manner of their transmission, but the repeated phrases, stanzas and narrative patterns found in the poems strongly suggest that these texts developed as part of an oral tradition.

Other branches of medieval Icelandic literature, such as the Sagas of Icelanders, Kings' Sagas and Contemporary Sagas, are also based, to some extent at least, on witness accounts of historical events and extended oral traditions. In the first part of *Ólafs saga helga* (St Olaf's Saga) in *Heimskringla*, for example, several chapters seem to be based on skaldic poems by identifiable poets serving King Olaf Haraldsson. One chapter of the saga begins:

> Then King Óláf sailed south to Frísia and hove to before the coast of Kinnlimi in heavy weather. Then the king disembarked with his men, but the people of the land came riding against them and fought them. So says Skald Sig[h]vat.[5]

The prose is followed by a skaldic poem by Sighvat Thordarson that reveals that the king's ship had withstood a confrontation 'off Kinnlimi's shoreline, / when gallant foemen galloped / grimly 'gainst the ruler's / vessels'.[6] In this case Sighvat may reasonably be regarded as the genuine 'author' of the scene. The rest of the text in this chapter of *Heimskringla* is basically a prose translation of the verse.

Another stage in the evolution of the sagas took the form of recitation by practised storytellers in front of a large audience. One of the most renowned descriptions of such an event in medieval Icelandic literature is the account of a wedding at Reykjaholar in western Iceland in the year 1119. It is preserved in *Þorgils saga og Hafliða* (The Saga of Thorgils and Haflidi), one of many sagas collected in *Sturlunga saga*, dating from about 1300. The wedding took place during a week-long Mass of St Olaf. The saga mentions many kinds of entertainment: 'dancing, wrestling, and storytelling'.[7] The tellers of tales, present at the wedding, include the local priest Ingimund and the farmer Hrolf. Earlier in the saga, Ingimund has been depicted as an accomplished poet, 'a very well-read man and a good story-teller; he entertained people with poems and composed verses; he himself wrote good poems and was famous thereby in other lands.' Similarly

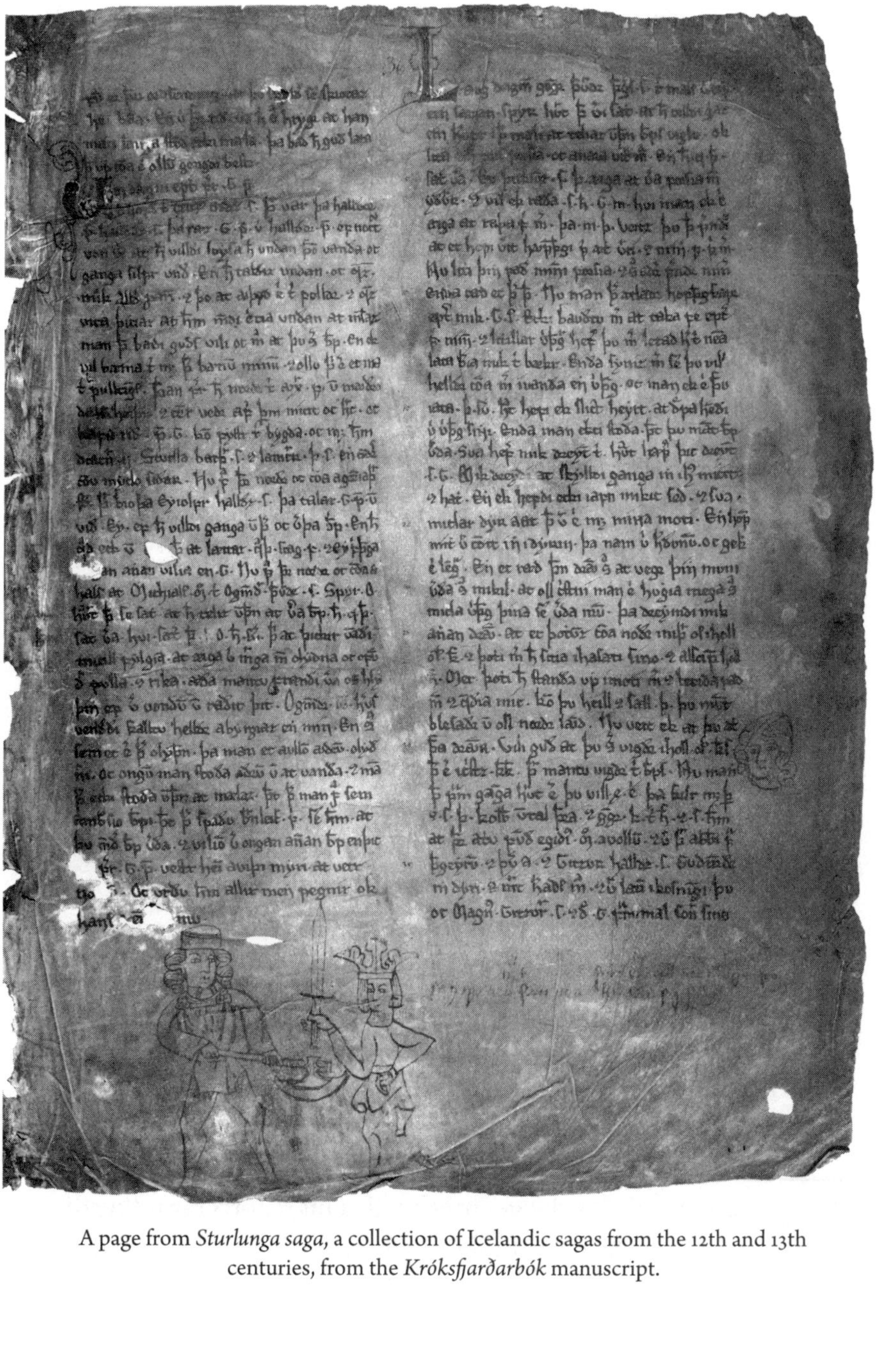

A page from *Sturlunga saga*, a collection of Icelandic sagas from the 12th and 13th centuries, from the *Króksfjarðarbók* manuscript.

we have learned that Hrolf was 'a historian and wrote fine poetry'.[8] In other words, these are professionals in their field, even though they appear to differ in their attitudes to storytelling:

> Hrólf from Skálmarnes told a saga about Hröngvið the viking and about Óláf, the Liðsmen's King, about the barrow-robber, Þráin the berserk, and about Hrómund Grípsson – with many strophes too. These sagas delighted King Sverri[r] who said such lying stories were very enjoyable. Men could even trace their lineage back to Hrómund Grípsson. Hrólf himself had put this saga together. Ingimund the priest told the Saga of Orm the Skáld of Barra, with many verses.[9]

While Hrolf tells a tall story that he has invented, Ingimund's tale appears to be a true – or at least plausible – account of actual events.

The third stage in the creative process occurs when stories of this kind are written down. Here we can again turn to *Þorgils saga og Hafliða,* which was probably recorded on vellum sometime during the thirteenth century. Following the description of the Mass of St Olaf, but before the passage devoted to Hrolf and Ingimund's recital, we read:

> About such occasions it is sometimes reported, though it is not in itself very important, who told stories and about whom stories were told. This is contained in an account which many now deny and pretend not to have known; for many men reject the truth, think that what is invented is true, and that what is true is a lie.[10]

The saga writer acknowledges in effect that his reports regarding the saga recital at Reykjaholar are disputed among those who claim to be knowledgeable about this event. Still, he downplays this uncertainty, and it is more as though he is answering anticipated criticism about the credibility of his narrative.

Another well-known description of a story recital can be found in the so-called *Sturluþáttur* (Sturla's Tale) in *Sturlunga saga*, focusing on the poet and historian Sturla Thordarson. In the year 1262 Sturla was reportedly sailing south along the coast of Norway, with King Magnus the Law-mender and Queen Ingeborg. One evening he was asked to entertain the crew before bedtime: 'Then he told them the saga of Huld better and more knowledgeably than any of them had ever heard it.'[11] The queen heard about this well-received performance and sent for Sturla the next day:

> asking him to come to her and bring with him the saga about the trollwife. . . . The queen then bade him tell the same story which he had told in the evening. He did so, and spoke for a great part of the day. When he had told the story the queen and many others thanked him and thought him a knowledgeable and a wise man.[12]

Apparently, Sturla is not the author of *Huldar saga* (The Saga of Huld). Members of the crew have, at least, heard the tale before the Icelander tells it. On the other hand, the queen asks Sturla to 'bring with him the saga', which may suggest he is travelling with a saga manuscript or at least some notes. Perhaps what we glimpse here is an intermediate phase between the oral and the written traditions.

It is worth noting that the tales allegedly told by Ingimund, Hrolf and Sturla have not been preserved in manuscripts. This serves as a reminder that the picture we can paint of medieval Icelandic literature from the meagre pallet of surviving vellum manuscripts is far from perfect. Hence chance has played its part in determining that *Snorra Edda* and *Heimskringla* are generally regarded as among the most important works of the period.

'Compiled by Snorri Sturluson'

Though the oldest manuscripts of *Snorra Edda* are from around the year 1300 or shortly thereafter, Snorri died a whole generation earlier, when his enemies attacked and killed him at his home at Reykholt (also named Reykjaholt) in western Iceland in 1241. Only one of these manuscripts, *Uppsalabók,* names Snorri as the producer of the whole work, stating in the foreword: 'This book is called Edda. Snorri Sturluson has compiled it.'[13] Snorri is also identified as the author of 'Háttatal' ('Enumeration of Verse Forms'), the last section of *Snorra Edda,* in *Uppsalabók* and various other sources. But there is no author named in the other two oldest full-length manuscripts of *Snorra Edda*. In fact, it is not until the second half of the sixteenth century that Snorri is decidedly characterized as the producer of the whole work, when a description of his death in a chronicle is followed by the claim that 'he compiled the Edda, and many other scholarly texts[,] Icelandic sagas'.[14]

Snorri's connection with *Heimskringla* is even more tenuous. Nowhere in the extant manuscripts is it suggested that he wrote that work. There are passages in one of the fourteenth-century Kings' Sagas, *Ólafs saga Tryggvasonar hin mesta* (The Greatest Saga of Olaf Tryggvason), that refers to Snorri as the source of certain of its episodes. One such reference reads: 'Snorri said so that King Svein set his ship against the Long Serpent, but Olaf the Swede set his ship's stern against Olaf Tryggvason's outermost ship.'[15] However, there is no specific reference to *Heimskringla* here or to any other written account. Again, it is not until 1551, in a Danish translation of several Kings' Sagas, that the idea of Snorri's authorship is suggested. Scholars generally believe that the idea derived from a manuscript of *Heimskringla* that was lost sometime after its use by the translator.[16] Still, this is only an assumption.[17] In a history of Icelandic literature, philologist Sverrir Tómasson discusses these fragmentary references and notes: 'It may be that some consider the sources describing

Snorri's writings to be rather thin on the ground, but there is no other known evidence, and these testimonies have not been challenged to date.'[18] This turn of phrase might well prompt the thought that such a challenge is long overdue.[19] However, at this point my interest is more in the nature than the extent of Snorri's authorship. Accordingly, I will focus my discussion here on the creative process that lies behind the various works attributed to Snorri.

The clearest contemporary evidence of Snorri's involvement in saga writing can be found in *Íslendinga saga* (The Saga of the Icelanders), written by Sturla Thordarson in the second half of the thirteenth century and preserved in the *Sturlunga saga* collection. Sturla notes that one of Snorri's relatives 'spent some considerable time at Reykjaholt and gave much thought to having copies made of the saga books which Snorri was [compiling]'.[20] It is interesting that both here and in *Uppsalabók* the same phrase is used to describe Snorri's literary activities. The reference to his *compiling* (the Icelandic term is '*setja saman*' which literally means 'place together') also applies sufficiently well to both *Heimskringla* and *Snorra Edda* that it may be more appropriate to refer to Snorri (or whoever else it was) as the compiler rather than the author of these works.

Heimskringla is usually divided into sixteen linked narratives, most of which detail the life of a particular Norwegian king. When

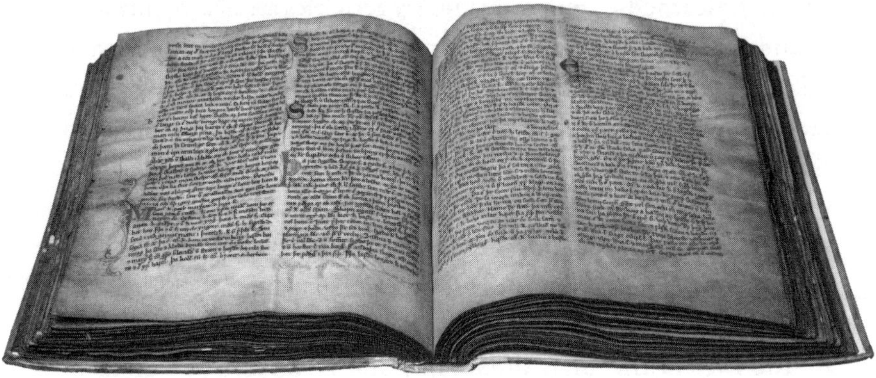

An early 13th-century manuscript of *Heimskringla*, in the *Codex Frisianus*.

these texts are set in a literary-historical perspective it becomes clear that their compiler assembled a wide variety of material from older manuscripts, made major and minor changes to his sources and added other fragmentary material, and ended up with a continuous history of the Norwegian monarchy from the ninth to the end of the twelfth century. Nowadays, such compositional methods might lead to accusations of plagiarism and even to litigation.

However, the line modern readers draw between original works and copies or other kinds of adaptations was much less clear in the Middle Ages, insofar as it existed at all. Thus, the pre-texts for *Heimskringla* included several works, still preserved, that were written in Norway during the twelfth or early thirteenth century. One of these is *Noregs konunga tal* (Catalogue of the Kings of Norway). They also involved an uncertain number of other works that are no longer available to us. Two of these lost texts might have been written more than a century earlier than *Heimskringla* by the pioneering Icelandic historians Sæmund Sigfusson the Learned and Ari Thorgilsson the Wise, both born in the latter half of the eleventh century. In a twelfth-century poem which Snorri's stepfather, Jon Loftsson, wrote about his relationship to the Norwegian royal family (King Magnus Barefoot was Jon's grandfather), he claims to have counted ten descendants of King Harald Fairhair, 'as Sæmund / said, the learned'.[21] Sæmund's literary activities are also mentioned in an Icelandic translation of *Ólafs saga Tryggvasonar* (The Saga of Olaf Tryggvason), which was originally written in Latin around 1200 by the Icelandic monk Odd Snorrason. In that text we read that King Olaf had '"given people good law and good custom." So wrote Sæmund about King Olaf in his book.'[22] More decisively, the writer of the prologue to *Heimskringla* pays a special tribute to Ari the Wise, who, he claims, has written on ancient and modern science, on the settlement of Iceland and also on other topics relating to 'the lives of the kings of Norway and Denmark, as well as of England'.[23]

While it may seem futile to compare the texts from *Heimskringla* with any of their lost pre-texts, the case of *Haraldssona saga* (The Saga of the Sons of Harald) merits particular attention. The narrative includes a description of the twelfth-century conflict between the sons of King Harald Gilli, on the one hand, and King Magnus the Blind and Sigurd Gadabout-Deacon on the other. At one point, the compiler of *Heimskringla* interrupts his narrative in order to offer an account of his sources:

> Hall, the son of Thorgeir Steinsson, the physician, was one of King Ingi's bodyguards and was present at these happenings. He related them to Eirík Oddsson who wrote down this account. Eirík wrote the book which is called *Hryggjarstykki*. In that book we are told about Harald Gilli and his two sons; also of Magnús the Blind and of Sigurth Gadabout-Deacon, down to their death. Eirík was a man of good understanding and had at that time been long in Norway. Some of his account he wrote according to what he was told by Hákon Maw, a landed-man under the two sons of Harald. Hákon and his sons took part in all these fights and counsels. Eirík mentions still other men who told him about these events, men who were both of good understanding and reliable. They were close by, so that they heard or saw what was happening. But some things he wrote according to what he himself heard or saw.[24]

From this we can see that many men have contributed to Eirík Oddsson's narrative in *Hryggjarstykki*, a manuscript no longer extant. Eirík seems in some parts of his narrative to have functioned as a typist or reporter, in modern occupational terms, while elsewhere his role is that of eyewitness or historian. The words quoted above – 'Eirík Oddsson who wrote down this account' – suggest that the compiler of *Heimskringla* merely copied his pre-text without making significant changes. A comparison between *Haraldssona saga* and parallel texts from the other medieval manuscripts based on *Hryggjarstykki* seems to support this view.[25] The compiler's contribution may well have been significantly greater in other parts of *Heimskringla* than in *Haraldssona saga*, but it is hard to verify this, given that he may have used several additional sources that were subsequently lost. There is no doubt that he is an active and creative participant in a written literary tradition that is in several ways analogous to the oral traditions that preceded it. That said, the work he produces is multi-layered; the text assembles the voices of many individuals who have each added, changed or omitted elements from their inherited narratives.

To help us appreciate more fully the multi-layered nature of this narrative tradition, we can examine briefly a single scene as treated in three different Kings' Sagas: *Noregs konunga tal*, *Ólafs saga Tryggvasonar* by Odd Snorrason and, lastly, *Ólafs saga Tryggvasonar* in *Heimskringla*. The scene features King Olaf, who is busy converting Norway to Christianity in the late tenth century. When he visits Gulen on Norway's western coast the locals make it a condition of their conversion that the king marry off his young sister Astrid to Erling, a young local chieftain. In *Noregs konunga tal* this development is described in a very concise manner:

> King Olaf had those leading chieftains who were likely to oppose Christianity killed, some he granted much holding to further his cause. Erling Skjalgsson married Astrid, Olaf's sister, and he became the King's envoy in the entire eastern part of the country.[26]

In Odd Snorrason's *Ólafs saga Tryggvasonar* the episode is described in greater detail, with conversations between the king and the local people dramatized:

> The King spoke: 'What is it that you ask?'
>
> They asked him to espouse his sister to Erling, who had never lacked high birth.
>
> 'We have heard that he is the most eligible of men, and if here be so much to gain, that then your will to the tenderness of God's mercy turn, if there be so much benefit, then this is my will.'
>
> And then he converted many hundred men and all the districts to Christianity, and Erling married Astrid and acquired with her great wealth.[27]

Things don't go quite so smoothly in *Heimskringla*. Astrid initially protests against the marriage but then succumbs after the king sends her symbolic threats:

> The king said, 'What would you have me do so that we come to a fair agreement between us?'
>
> Then Olmóth said, 'First this, that you marry your sister Ástríth [Astrid] to Erling Skjálgsson, our kinsman, whom we consider the most promising of all young men in Norway.' King Óláf replied that to him that match would seem a good one, adding that Erling was of high birth and seemed indeed most eligible, but that Ástríth herself would have to give her consent. Then the king discussed this with his sister.
>
> 'Little do I benefit', said she, 'from being a king's daughter and a king's sister if you wish me to marry a commoner. I would rather wait some years for another match.' And with that they ended their discussion.
>
> ...
>
> King Óláf had one of Ástríth's hawks taken and its feathers plucked, whereupon he sent it back to her. Then Ástríth said, 'Angry is my brother now.' Then she arose and went to the king. He made her welcome. Then Ástríth said that

> it was her wish that the king was to act in her behalf as he thought best.
>
> 'I had thought', said the king, 'that I would obtain the power to raise to high estate in this land whom I will.' The king then had Olmóth, Erling, and all their kinsmen called to him to discuss the matter of this marriage; and in the end Ástríth was betrothed to Erling. Thereupon the king had the assembly meet and bade the farmers accept Christianity. And then Olmóth and Erling were the leaders in speaking for this matter, important to the king, as well as all of their kinsmen. No one dared to oppose him. Then all the people there were baptized and converted.[28]

We can understand from this passage why Snorri has been praised for his clear character descriptions, vibrant dialogue and memorable scenes. A comparison of passages such as those discussed here is generally used to justify such praise. The problem, however, is that we cannot be sure whether the passage by Odd Snorrason was the only pre-text to which the *Heimskringla* compiler had access when finalizing his own version of the scene. There may well have been intermediate sources, oral or written, that have not been preserved. Gunnlaug Leifsson, a fellow monk of Odd's at the monastery at Thingeyri in northern Iceland, is known to have written another saga about Olaf Tryggvason in Latin around the year 1200. Though that work is no longer extant, chapters from it are thought to have been preserved in several later works, including *Ólafs saga Tryggvasonar hin mesta*. Based on these fragments, scholars suggest that Gunnlaug used Odd's text as a source but elaborated on it significantly. For instance, the description in *Ólafs saga Tryggvasonar hin mesta* of events leading up to Erling and Astrid's wedding closely resembles the one in *Heimskringla*, but it is difficult to know which of these is the pre-text of the other, or indeed, if both texts are based on the extant *Ólafs saga Tryggvasonar* by Gunnlaug Leifsson. This example serves to confirm just how complicated it can be to chart the relationship between different medieval texts and manuscripts.

As I have sought to demonstrate, it is somewhat misleading to credit Snorri with the authorship of *Heimskringla*, at least in the modern sense of the term. Not only are the connections between his name and this remarkable collection of Kings' Sagas somewhat vague, but we are dealing with a text that generations of witnesses, storytellers, historians, writers, editors and scribes have helped to shape. While I have no wish to downplay the remarkable achievement represented by the *Heimskringla* compilation, it may be fair to say that the compiler's contribution to the text is probably every bit as diverse as Eirík Oddsson's contribution to *Hryggjarstykki*. As would later be the case with the creation of *The Mighty Thor* comics, the creation of *Heimskringla* involved weaving together material from different sources. Undoubtedly, the compiler has reshaped and supplemented chapters of the work with certain aesthetic and ideological principles in mind, but because some of his sources are lost, it is difficult to identify his own contributions with any precision.

'People must not believe in the truth of this account'

Before we adopt the same sort of comparative approach for *Snorra Edda* that we have just used for *Heimskringla*, let us briefly reconsider the reference in *Uppsalabók* which credits Snorri with having compiled the work. The relevant sentence refers to three of the work's four parts, 'Gylfaginning' ('The Tricking of Gylfi'), 'Skáldskaparmál' ('Poetic Language') and 'Háttatal', but there is no mention of the short introductory section, known as the 'Prologus' ('Prologue'). The full *Uppsalabók* reference is as follows:

> This book is called Edda. Snorri Sturluson has compiled it in the manner in which it is arranged here. There is first told about the Æsir and Ymir, then Skáldskaparmál . . . and

> (poetical) names of many things, finally Háttatal . . . which Snorri has composed about King Hákon and Earl Skúli.[29]

It is somewhat remarkable that this description does not correspond to the sequence of material in *Uppsalabók*, where we find lists of skalds and law-speakers inserted at two places in 'Skáldskaparmál', and a grammatical essay included between 'Skáldskaparmál' and 'Háttatal'. In another thirteenth-century manuscript of *Snorra Edda*, 'Háttatal' is similarly separated from 'Gylfaginning' and 'Skáldskaparmál'. Accordingly, Anthony Faulkes, an expert in the manuscript tradition of *Snorra Edda*, believes it likely that originally the four parts had an independent existence, and that none of the four oldest manuscripts preserve the text as Snorri compiled it.[30]

'Háttatal' is an annotated version of the lengthy praise poem about King Hakon of Norway and Earl Skuli attributed to Snorri. There is thus little doubt that he composed this final part of *Snorra Edda*, but that is not to say that he is in that same sense the author of the other three parts of the work. If the words from *Uppsalabók* are interpreted literally, we may infer that Snorri's primary contribution consisted of assembling the available material in a particular order. Be that as it may, it is clear that both 'Gylfaginning' and, to some degree, 'Skáldskaparmál' are cases of rewriting. In both sections the author is working from pre-existing poetry and myths.

Before examining the relationship between *Snorra Edda* and its pre-texts, I would like to consider briefly the distinction Tzvetan Todorov draws in his *Poétique de la prose* (The Poetics of Prose, 1971) between two branches of literary studies; namely *criticism* and *poetics*. While literary criticism sets out first and foremost to evaluate or interpret meaning within specific literary works, poetics aims primarily to understand literature as a form of expression, shedding light on those forms and traditions upon which all literary creation rests. Todorov claims that the danger of pure poetics is that the conclusions become too general. He similarly cautions against the type

'The Deluding of Gylfi', an illustration from Thomas Bartholin's *Antiquitatum danicarum* (1689). The image is based on a drawing from a 13th-century manuscript of *Snorra Edda*.

of criticism that does nothing more than replicate or reorganize texts or the meaning of particular literary works; such an interpretation can too easily be confused with its subject-matter. Ideally, he suggests, these two approaches should be reconciled, with the particular shedding light on the general, and vice versa.[31]

At first glance, 'Gylfaginning' looks like an example of criticism based on reorganizing and rephrasing the texts of particular literary works. Its subject-matter is the world of the Nordic pagan gods that finds expression in the eddic mythological poems; the author draws together in prose many themes from individual poems and also cites some seventy stanzas from them. To show how this material is reworked in 'Gylfaginning', we can consider the discussion in *Snorra*

Edda about Ragnarok – the end of the world – which proves to be little more than an interpretation of the final stanzas of *Völuspá*. Here is a revealing example:

> Then brothers will kill each other out of greed and no one will show mercy to father or son in killing or breaking the taboos of kinship. Thus it says in Voluspa:
>
> > Brothers will fight and kill each other, cousins will break the bonds of their relationship. It will be harsh for heroes, much depravity, age of axes, age of swords, shields cloven, age of winds, age of wolves, until the world is ruined.
>
> Then something will happen that will be thought a most significant event, the wolf will swallow the sun, and people will think this a great disaster. Then the other wolf will catch the moon, and he also will cause much mischief. The stars will disappear from the sky. Then there will take place another event, the whole earth and mountains will shake so much that trees will become uprooted from the earth and the mountains will fall, and all fetters and bonds will snap and break. Then Fenriswolf will get free.[32]

The first paragraph is merely a summary of the stanza from *Völuspá* quoted below it, while the latter paragraph is a loose prose translation of six other stanzas from the poem.

However, it complicates matters considerably that the author of 'Gylfaginning' creates a narrative frame around his rendering of the eddic poems. Everything in the chapter is presented to the reader in the form of a conversation between the Swedish King Gylfi and his neighbour Odin, where Gylfi introduces himself as Gangleri and Odin disguises himself in the form of three kings named High One, Just-as-High and Third. This narrative frame is marked by a pattern discernible in many of the poems that describe how the pagan gods or their representatives travel from Asgard to Jotunheim, either to reclaim something they have lost to the giants or simply secure something they desire. The pattern emerges for instance in *Vafþrúðnismál* (Sayings of Vafthrudnir), where Odin, using the alias Gagnrad, meets with the giant Vafthrudnir in search of wisdom. The god and the giant duly take part in a quiz about the origins and development of the world of the pagan gods. Much of the subsequent poem consists of Odin's questions and Vafthrudnir's answers. In the 'Gylfaginning' these roles are reversed, so that it is Odin (alias High One, Just-as-High and Third) who answers Gylfi's (alias Gangleri) questions about the ancient fables.

The foundations of the framing narrative of 'Gylfaginning' are laid down in the 'Prologus' to *Snorra Edda*, where the author traces the genealogical roots of Odin and his kin to Asia Minor, noting that King Menon and Troan, the daughter of Priam of Troy, had a son 'Tror; we call him Thor.'[33] The descendants of these individuals, under the leadership of Voden (another of Odin's names), went to Sweden and settled there. The world of the framing narrative in 'Gylfaginning' is therefore not the divided pagan universe of Asgard and Jotunheim depicted in the eddic poems, but the historical Europe of an earlier time, notably a particular area of Sweden. When King Gylfi goes to meet Odin in disguise, his host also greets him with a series of illusions. The castle, the three kings and all the other sights and sounds to which Gylfi is exposed are fictitious, unlike the 'real' world described in the 'Prologus'. This is restated at the end of 'Gylfaginning' when High One indicates that there have been enough questions:

> Next Gangleri heard great noises in every direction from him, and he looked out to one side. And when he looked around further he found he was standing out on open ground, could see no hall and no castle. Then he went off on his way and came back to his kingdom and told of the events he had seen

> and heard about. And from his account these stories passed from one person to another.[34]

In other words, the narrative of the 'Prologus' about the Trojans, Gylfi (King of the Swedes) and Voden aims to create two levels of reality, one that accords with the geographical knowledge of contemporary Scandinavians and another that is clearly imaginary.

By framing the mythological information in this way, the Christian writer of 'Gylfaginning' makes it clear that everything which the pagan people had believed to be true should be regarded as deception. Gylfi heads for Asgard in *Snorra Edda* with the same purpose as Odin when he visits Vafthrudnir – he goes in search of wisdom. Both return home with similar information. The difference is that while Odin achieves his aim in *Vafþrúðnismál,* Gylfi ends up with pure fiction; he is Voden's gullible fool. And yet this deception continues to have consequences, even after the virtual reality of Valhalla vanishes. The most notable sentence in the text describes how the fiction that Gylfi swallows, hook, line and sinker, spreads around society: 'And from his account these stories passed from one person to another.'[35]

Unlike 'Gylfaginning', which is built on testimony from the eddic poems, 'Skáldskaparmál' is predominantly a collection of examples of skaldic poetry that show how various poets have used certain stories of the pagan gods and the Germanic heroes to create their complex skaldic paraphrases. There are also retellings of several such stories. As mentioned previously, 'Skáldskaparmál' begins with a framing narrative similar to that of 'Gylfaginning'. It tells of Ægir, who makes his journey to Asgard but when the god 'became aware of his movements, he was given a great welcome, though many things had deceptive appearances'.[36] In the evening there is a great feast, during which Bragi explains to Ægir various things he wants to know. Ægir asks, for example: 'How did this craft that you call poetry originate?'[37] The story about the poetic mead is Bragi's answer to that question. But at the end of this narrative, somewhat surprisingly, it is as though the author of 'Skáldskaparmál' steps into the limelight and addresses his readers directly:

> But these things have now to be told to young poets who desire to learn the language of poetry and to furnish themselves with a wide vocabulary using traditional terms; or else they desire to be able to understand what is expressed obscurely. Then let such a one take this book as scholarly inquiry and entertainment. But these stories are not to be consigned to oblivion or demonstrated to be false, so as to deprive poetry of ancient kennings which major poets have been happy to use. Yet Christian people must not believe in heathen gods, nor in the truth of this account in any other way than that in which it is presented at the beginning of this book, where it is told what happened when mankind went astray from the true faith, and after that about the Turks, how the people of Asia, known as Æsir, distorted the accounts of the events that took place in Troy so that the people of the country would believe that they were gods.[38]

Although the writer later refers again to the fact that Bragi is telling Ægir ancient stories, little attention is paid to the narrative frame for the rest of 'Skáldskaparmál'. This makes it likely that the text of this part of *Snorra Edda* is a draft that has only been partially revised.

Thus far, we have seen how the four different parts of *Snorra Edda* most likely existed independently before and even after Snorri Sturluson arranged them in the way described in *Uppsalabók*. Few scholars suggest that these chapters were composed in the same order in which they appear, but most seem to agree that they were all written by Snorri. Of these chapters, 'Prologus' and 'Gylfaginning' are the most closely linked in regards to subject-matter and form a convincing whole. By comparison, 'Skáldskaparmál' is merely a draft which the writer has yet to complete, especially the narrative frame that he seems to have decided to create around the material. The final chapter, 'Háttatal', containing the praise poem about King Hakon and Earl Skuli, is almost certainly composed by Snorri and is also the part that has been least influential in post-medieval times. To a considerable extent, 'Gylfaginning' and 'Skáldskaparmál' treat the same myths of the pagan gods and heroes as the eddic poems do. Yet, just as in *Heimskringla,* we can also find in these two sections material that few, if any, other sources have preserved. Again, it is difficult to judge how big a part the writer (or writers) of these two different parts of *Snorra Edda* played in the creation of the material. As scholars have pointed out, some of the interpretations of the subject-matter of particular eddic and skaldic poems that are to be found in these sections present a misleading picture of the world of the pagan gods. Nevertheless, Asgard, with all of its characters, narratives and sub-worlds, is clearly not an independent creation by Snorri or others who produced *Snorra Edda* in thirteenth-century Iceland. His (or their) contribution clearly consists of gathering information on the chosen topic, adapting it into a new form and, last but not least, presenting it as an important source of background information for the otherwise incomprehensible 'polyphrases' of skaldic poetry.

The collected works of Snorri

Many scholars believe that Snorri Sturluson, as well as 'compiling' *Heimskringla* and *Snorra Edda,* also created *Egils saga,* which relates the life of one of Iceland's most famous medieval poets, Egil Skallagrimsson, who lived in the tenth century. Two of Egil's best-known poems are 'Höfuðlausn' ('Head Ransom'), which he is said to have composed in York, England, in order to save his life, which was under threat from his arch-enemy King Eirik Bloodaxe, and 'Sonatorrek' ('Lament for Sons'), which he is said to have composed after the death of two of his sons. The Danish pastor and philosopher N.F.S.

Grundtvig was probably the first to come up with the idea that Snorri had written *Egils saga,* in the introduction to his Danish translation of *Heimskringla* that was published between 1818 and 1822, but it was not until the twentieth century that scholars began to support this view in earnest. Unlike the debate over the authorship of *Snorra Edda* and *Heimskringla,* the arguments here are not based on testimony from earlier or later manuscripts of *Egils saga* – for nowhere in them is Snorri listed as author – but rather on a stylistic and literary comparison of the *Egils saga* text with other works attributed to Snorri. Although the conclusions deal in probabilities rather than certainties, an increasing number of people now take it for granted that the saga, and even Egil's own poetry, was authored by Snorri. A few scholars have even advanced elaborate interpretations of the saga narrative based on Snorri's biography.[39] The notion of Snorri's authorship of the saga received a kind of official blessing in 2002 when the Icelandic Parliament, in partnership with the Icelandic publisher Edda, released an edition of *Egils saga,* along with *Snorra Edda* and *Heimskringla,* as the *Ritsafn* (Collected Works) of Snorri Sturluson.[40]

From time to time Snorri's name has also been linked with *Njáls saga*. But in that context, he is just one of many candidates proposed as the potential author, and he is by no means the most likely, given the belief that the saga was probably not composed until some three or four decades after Snorri's death. Among others named as possible authors of *Njáls saga* are Sæmund the Learned, Jon Loftsson, Brand Jonsson (abbot at the Thingeyri monastery) and Sturla Thordarson. Debates on this topic have been quite lively in Iceland for almost a century and have reached out well beyond the small circle of specialist scholars in the field. Farmers in the area where the saga takes place have made interesting contributions to the discussion, with arguments often referring to the nature and extent of the geographical knowledge communicated in the saga. The search for the author of *Njáls saga* clearly reflects our modern need to link individual literary works with identifiable authors. This preoccupation takes various forms. Recently, the renowned Icelandic novelist Einar Kárason published a historical novel, *Skáldið* (The Poet, 2012), in which he proposes that Sturla Thordarson composed *Njáls saga* along with some other well-known sagas.

It is a little ironic that 'Háttatal', which was (almost definitely) written by Snorri and preserves his longest skaldic poem – 102 stanzas in all – has mostly been neglected by scholars. It is, for example, often omitted from editions and translations of *Snorra Edda*. The form of 'Háttatal' closely resembles that of 'Skáldskaparmál' in that its poetry, although composed by Snorri himself, provides examples for the author's discussion of the characteristics of traditional poetic metre and figurative language. We can take as an example the sixth verse of 'Háttatal', where Snorri discusses allegory:

> What is allegory?
> As follows:
>
> Svidr lætr sóknar nadra
> slídrbraut iöfurr skrída.
> Ótt ferr rógs ór réttum
> ramsnákr fetilhamsi.
> Linnr kná sverda sennu
> sveita bekks at leita.
> Ormr thyrr vals at varmri
> víggiöll sefa stígu.
>
> The wise prince makes the adders of battle [swords] creep the scabbard-path [be drawn]. The mighty war-snake goes swiftly from the straight strap-slough [scabbard]. The sword-quarrel serpent can seek the stream of blood. The worm of the slain rushes along the mind's path to the warm war-river:

> This is allegory to call a sword a worm and use an appropriate determinant, and call the scabbard its path and the straps and fittings its slough. It is in accordance with a worm's nature that it glides out of its slough and then often glides to water.[41]

As this example demonstrates, the literary discussion of the prose is fairly technical and it abruptly interrupts the flow of the poetic praise about King Hakon and Earl Skuli. It is therefore difficult for listeners or readers to enjoy the poem as a whole. Furthermore, a specialized knowledge of the skaldic tradition is required in order to enjoy the poem as a work of art. Accordingly, it is not surprising that 'Háttatal' is not one of the texts that have kept Snorri on his pedestal as a revered literary figure, although it is exactly these technical aspects of his work that Nicolas' mother proposes to discuss with Mrs Moucheboume.

In his study *Snorri Sturluson and the Edda* (2008), Kevin J. Wanner suggests that Snorri composed 'Háttatal' during the 1220s, in the wake of his first trip to Norway, after having discovered that King Hakon, then still in his teens, had a somewhat limited enthusiasm for Icelandic skaldic poetry. Snorri's attempts to use the old poetic tradition to win the king's favour had proved futile. On the other hand, during his trip Snorri had befriended Earl Skuli, who ruled over a third of the country and was a generation older than King Hakon. Skuli showered the Icelandic chieftain with praise for his poetic compositions and with gifts, including the ship in which Snorri sailed home. According to Wanner, Snorri duly decided to send King Hakon the long praise poem about Skuli and the king, with literary explanations. Later, he decided to write 'Skáldskaparmál', which not only explains the complex figurative language of the skaldic poetry, but includes a collection of examples from older praise poems dedicated to Norwegian kings by Icelandic court poets. Wanner suggests that Snorri finally completed his work by producing 'Prologus' and 'Gylfaginning'. Here, the pagan literary heritage, on which skaldic tradition drew heavily, is communicated in a more accessible way than in the eddic poems. According to Wanner, the implicit reader of all these texts was neither Ægir nor King Gylfi (Gangleri) of Sweden but rather King Hakon of Norway.

Wanner's argument is quite persuasive. Though he admits that considerable uncertainty surrounds the identity of the author or authors of 'Prologus', 'Gylfaginning' and 'Skáldskaparmál', there is good reason to believe that a literary-cultural-political agenda lay behind the compilation of *Snorra Edda* as a whole; namely, the desire to uphold the importance of the Icelandic skaldic poetry tradition within the Norwegian court. But all of these efforts were in vain. King Hakon based his power on the official blessing of the Christian Church and for cultural inspiration he looked to Britain and France, where chivalric tales were both fashionable and well suited to the promotion of courtly life and monarchical power. As Wanner observes:

> The scope and novelty of Snorri's efforts do nothing to alter the fact, however, that they were almost entirely ineffectual. By the time Snorri acted, the historical processes, structural forces, and events that conspired to rob skaldic verse of its cultural value had reached a point of critical mass and momentum that was probably impossible to counteract.[42]

Wanner stresses that Snorri's failure to establish trust in his dealings with King Hakon had indeed been his undoing. When he was killed in 1241, it was done precisely at the behest of the young Norwegian ruler.

Whether or not we are convinced by Wanner's argument, it represents a much needed reminder that although it is difficult to be certain about the extent of Snorri's contribution to the creation of *Heimskringla* and *Snorra Edda*, these texts, like other medieval Icelandic works of literature and history, were 'compiled' for political and personal purposes. In this chapter, I have highlighted that Snorri and many of his contemporaries should be regarded as compilers or rewriters of older pre-texts, but that does not rule out the possibility that their works were driven by the same compelling need for self-expression that shape compositions which are more original.

The same applies to most of the later adaptations of the eddas and sagas we have yet to examine, which so often have a personal story to convey. At the same time, such adaptations are conditioned by various conventions and constraints of the genres or styles in question. Both of these elements will be explored in the following chapter, which is devoted to playwrights who were eager to allow provocative saga heroines to take the stage. Speaking of whom, did you know that the lineage of Hedda Gabler can be traced to medieval Iceland?

Fredrikke Nielsen as Hiordis in a production of Henrik Ibsen's *Hærmændene paa Helgeland* in Bergen, 1859.

THREE

Hallgerd: A Bow-string Breaks

Edmund Gosse, who has been called 'Ibsen's First Prophet to English Readers',[1] wrote many essays about the works of the Norwegian playwright in the 1870s, conveying his firm belief that Ibsen was 'the greatest living dramatist and lyrist of Scandinavia'.[2] In Gosse's 1874 critique of *Hærmændene paa Helgeland* (The Warriors/ Vikings at Helgeland, 1858), a historical drama by Ibsen, the critic insists that although the work is not one of Ibsen's masterpieces, it should be of great interest to anyone interested in his development as a playwright. In the play, Gosse writes, Ibsen revives 'the serious brevity and force of the antique saga-literature'.

> There is a great deal of killing and cursing in the *Warriors*. To read it after such later books as *Brand* and *Peer Gynt*, is like returning to Marlowe after Shakespeare. . . . Many of the strokes are aimed in the dark by a hand strong enough and ardent enough, but not yet fully trained in sword-play.[3]

Ibsen's decision to write a play that takes place in Norway during the Middle Ages went hand in hand with a growing national consciousness among Norwegians during the nineteenth century.[4] Concurrently, he followed in the steps of previous generations of Scandinavian writers – poets in particular – who had sought inspiration in medieval texts under the influence of Romanticism. He seems, however, to have done so almost in spite of himself. Early in

1857, Ibsen stated in a lecture that the Sagas of Icelanders were not ideal material for a modern drama, and yet, just a few weeks later, he began writing *Hærmændene*.[5] The completed work was published in 1858 and premiered the same year in the Christiania (later Oslo) Norwegian Theatre under the direction of its author.

This was Ibsen's eighth play and as in some of his earlier works the dramatic conflicts revolved around a classic love triangle. The heroine is stuck in a dull marriage but dreams of spending her life with another man whom she can both look up to and love.[6] The playwright was certainly developing a winning formula; *Hærmændene* was well received when the play was first performed and enjoyed considerable popularity in the following decades.[7] Even so, as Bjørn Hemmer points out, it seems that Ibsen himself continued to have mixed feelings about the project:

> In a letter to the Royal Theatre, Copenhagen (8 February 1858) Ibsen admitted that this drama lacked any actual foundation in history; the characters were invented, structured on *literary* models from the Icelandic sagas and the Volsungasaga. His intention, he declared, had been 'to give a picture of the life of the saga age in general'.[8]

In terms of its success – well over a hundred productions from all over the world are listed in a database maintained by the Norwegian National Library – *Hærmændene paa Helgeland* is almost unique within the corpus of dramas inspired by the eddas and sagas.[9]

The earliest works of this kind were produced by Scandinavian, British and German writers in the eighteenth century, and during the nineteenth and early twentieth centuries there was a significant growth in their numbers.[10] The most productive dramatist in this field during the early period was the Danish poet Adam G. Oehlenschläger, who, under the influence of German Romanticism, recycled material from *Snorra Edda*, *Heimskringla* and the Sagas of Icelanders in several of his verse dramas. These include *Baldur hin Gode* (Baldur the Good, 1807), *Olaf den Hellige* (St Olaf, 1836), *Landet fundet og forsvundet* (The Found and Vanished Land, 1846) and *Kiartan og Gudrun* (Kiartan and Gudrun, 1848). Among other established Nordic authors who tried their hand at this sort of adaptation were Bernhard Severin Ingemann with *Kampen for Valhal* (The Battle of Valhalla, 1821), Bjørnstjerne Bjørnson with *Halte-Hulda* (Limping Hulda, 1858), August Strindberg with *Den fredlöse* (The Outlaw, 1871), Holger Drachmann with *Hallfred Vandraadeskjald* (Hallfred, Troublesome Poet, 1900) and Jóhann Sigurjónsson with *Løgneren* (The Liar, 1917).

Apart from Ibsen's play, none of these pieces has really left its mark on the history of dramatic literature. Yet many of them are still of some interest as they reveal quite clearly how modern artists working with the eddas and sagas are inevitably constrained by their forms, genres and modes of engagement. This is particularly evident when a written narrative is adapted for stage or screen, as Linda Hutcheon explains:

> to tell a story, as in novels, short stories, and even historical accounts, is to describe, explain, summarize, expand; the narrator has a point of view and great power to leap through time and space and sometimes to venture inside the minds of characters. To show a story, as in movies, ballets, radio and stage plays, musical and operas, involves direct aural and usually visual performance experienced in real time.[11]

With these concerns in mind, we will now investigate Ibsen's play and then compare it with two less familiar dramatizations of *Njáls saga*: Gordon Bottomley's *The Riding to Lithend* (1909) and Thit Jensen's *Nial den Vise* (Njal the Wise, 1934). While Bottomley's play is a traditional adaptation of a nineteenth-century translation of the saga, *Nial den Vise* was originally inspired by Jensen's trip to Iceland in 1904 and her romantic involvement with several of the natives.

'Life is not worth a handful of hair'

Hærmændene paa Helgeland tells of the loves and fates of Sigurd and Gunnar, foster brothers born in Norway during the tenth century. The lead-up to the events on stage is that these young warriors sail to Iceland looking for adventure. There they meet the chieftain Ornulf, a settler who has fled the tyranny of King Harald Fairhair in Norway. Ornulf has seven sons, a daughter called Dagny, and is also raising another girl, Hiordis, who is the daughter of a man killed by Ornulf in a duel. Hiordis has sworn to marry the man who can kill a polar bear that is in her possession. Sigurd accomplishes this deed under cover of darkness and lets Gunnar take the credit. Then the foster brothers run away with the two women, to the dismay of Ornulf. Hiordis marries Gunnar and they move to Helgeland in northern Norway. Sigurd marries Dagny and the couple soon set off raiding, but the friendship between Sigurd and Gunnar cools.

The first act commences with Ornulf having arrived with his sons in Helgeland from Iceland to take the two women back from the foster brothers. At the same time, Sigurd arrives with Dagny and his men, unaware that Gunnar and Hiordis live in the area. The play recounts the dealings between these three groups over the following days. Ornulf and Sigurd are quick to resolve their disagreements, but tension grows between the two of them and Gunnar. It is slowly revealed that Hiordis and Sigurd have had feelings for each other from the outset, and that they will need to dispense with their spouses in order to unite. Hiordis spurs on the animosity between the foster brothers and for a while it looks as though Gunnar and Sigurd will duel. Ibsen also weaves into the plot Gunnar's unremarkable disputes with the Norwegian farmer Kare, who ends up attacking Gunnar's farm. Kare describes the origin of their quarrel as follows: 'Our cattle fed together upon an island, hard by the coast; Gunnar's men carried off my best oxen, and one of them flouted me for a thrall. Then bare [sic] I arms against him and slew him.'[12] Kare adds that he suspects

Scene from a Norwegian production of *Hærmændene paa Helgeland* in 1927.

Hiordis is responsible for this skirmish because she stood in the way of Kare and Gunnar making peace and instead encouraged her husband to seek revenge for the slave. Though this suspicion is not confirmed in the work it accords well with the depiction of Hiordis. Being raised in the home of her father's slayer has hardened the girl's heart and she constantly resents Gunnar for not displaying more gallantry.

In preparation for writing the play, Ibsen read the Sagas of Icelanders, which had been translated into Danish by N. M. Petersen and published between 1839 and 1844. The Norwegian playwright was particularly influenced by *Egils saga*, *Laxdæla saga* (The Saga of the People of Laxardal) and *Njáls saga*, but he was also drawn to episodes from the legendary *Völsunga saga* (The Saga of the Volsungs).[13] Many of the motifs that Ibsen borrows from these works are all too obvious. It is apparent, for example, that the descriptions of the disputes between Kare and Gunnar in the play are inspired by the disputes between Thorstein Egilsson and Steinar Onundarson that are described in the final chapters of *Egils saga*. Another clear connection between these two works can be found in the final act when Ornulf is mourning his sons after Kare and his men killed six of them and Gunnar the seventh. According to the stage directions, the scene begins with Ornulf sitting on a rock holding his face in his hands. His men are nearby tending to his sons' graves. It is then up to Dagny to console her father, who, clearly lacking the will to live, plans to starve himself to death. A similar situation is described in *Egils saga* when Egil Skallagrimsson mourns the drowning of his son Bodvar, sinks into depression and decides to starve himself. Egil's stepdaughter sits by him in bed, and seems intent on accompanying him to Hel, the realm of the dead, but then tricks him into chewing some dulse and drinking milk. She then says: 'Now I want us to stay alive, father, long enough for you to compose a poem in Bodvar's memory and I shall carve it onto a rune-stick. Then we can die if we want to.'[14] Ibsen simplifies this situation slightly, omits the part about the dulse and the milk, and has Dagny instead impress upon Ornulf that he is the only person capable of composing a fitting memorial for her brothers:

> DAGNY: But needs must thou; honourable men were thy sons, one and all; a song must be made of them, and that can none of our kin but thou . . . Thy neighbours in Iceland will deem it ill done when the grave-ale is drunk over Ornulf's children, and there is no song to sing with it. Thou hast ever time enough to follow thy sons.
> ORNULF: Well well, I will try it; and thou, Dagny, give heed, that afterwards thou may'st carve the song on staves.[15]

Following this, Ornulf recites a poem reminiscent of Egil's famous poetic eulogy 'Sonatorrek'. Both poems, for example, open on a verse describing how difficult it is for the poet to compose when his heart is heavy with sorrow.

In his 1909 study, the Norwegian scholar Ferdinand G. Lynner systematically charted most of the parallels between *Hærmændene* and its Icelandic sources. He places particular emphasis on material from *Völsunga saga,* since Sigurd the Dragon Slayer and Gunnar Gjukason's relationship with Brynhild Budladottir is clearly a model for Ibsen's description of Sigurd and Gunnar's relationship with Hiordis.[16] In some of these examples, just as evident is the influence of the love triangle depicted in *Laxdæla saga* between Gudrun Osvifursdottir and the foster brothers Kjartan Olafsson and Bolli Thorleiksson. This can be explained by the fact that *Laxdæla saga* itself is to some extent inspired by *Völsunga saga*. Ibsen seems to have been fully conscious of such connections. Hence, in the introduction to the German translation of the play in 1876, he points out that in the sagas, mythological material was 'often brought down to human dimensions' and indicates that he has been chiefly inspired by just that quality in them.[17]

There are also some features of Hiordis's character that can be traced to Hallgerd Hoskuldsdottir 'Long-legs' (Icel. *langbrók*), one of the principal female protagonists in *Njáls saga*. The most memorable episode in the saga is the exchange between Hallgerd and her husband, Gunnar of Hlidarendi, shortly before he is killed. The preamble to the slaying is lengthy and interwoven with Gunnar's attempts to buy provisions from his neighbour, Otkel, who rejects the proposal but nonetheless sells Gunnar a slave. We learn nothing of Hallgerd's feelings concerning this transaction, but when Gunnar next rides to parliament she sends the slave home to Otkel on a dubious errand: 'You're to steal food from them, enough butter and cheese for two horses to carry. Then set fire to the storage shed, so that they will all think it was carelessness, and no one will suspect theft.'[18] The slave reluctantly acquiesces to Hallgerd's threats and steals from the larder, which he then burns down. Gunnar is furious when he discovers what has happened, and slaps his wife in the face: 'Hallgerd said she would remember this slap and pay it back if she could.'[19] After this, Gunnar tries unsuccessfully to compensate his neighbour, and ends up killing him and some of his men. These events and further conflicts, in which Hallgerd plays no part, culminate in a group of armed men coming to Hlidarendi intent on killing Gunnar, who is there on his own with only Hallgerd and his mother Rannveig for company. Gunnar kills several of his enemies by shooting at them with his bow and arrow from a window on the upper floor of his home, but things take a turn for the worse when the attackers start dismantling the roof of the dwelling and one of them manages to cut the hero's bowstring. Gunnar then says to Hallgerd:

> 'Give me two locks of your hair, and you and my mother twist them into a bowstring for me.'
>
> 'Does anything depend on it?' she said.
>
> 'My life depends on it', he said, 'for they'll never be able to get me as long as I can use my bow.'
>
> 'Then I'll remind you', she said, 'of the slap on my face, and I don't care whether you hold out for a long or a short time.'[20]

Gunnar is killed soon afterwards.

Ibsen was clearly moved by this scene. He refers to it at the beginning of the third act when Gunnar finds Hiordis sitting inside with a bow and arrow on the table in front of her, and asks what she is doing:

> HIORDIS: (without looking up). I am weaving a bow-string; canst thou not see?
>
> GUNNAR: A bow-string – of thine own hair?
>
> HIORDIS: (smiling). Great deeds are born with every hour in these times; yesterday thou didst slay my foster-brother, and I have woven this since day-break.[21]

Here we see influences from both *Njáls saga* and *Laxdæla saga* coming together. Hiordis's latter comment echoes Gudrun Osvifursdottir's acerbic words in *Laxdæla saga* after her husband Bolli has killed his foster brother at her instigation: 'A poor match they make, our morning work – I have spun twelve ells of yarn while you have slain Kjartan.'[22] It also transpires that Hiordis wants Gunnar to cut Sigurd's days short, and preferably Dagny's at the same time, and in return she promises to love him. It looks as though Hiordis will succeed in convincing Gunnar to commit this atrocity when Dagny appears and announces that Kare is now heading for the farm in the company of a group of outlaws, and that Sigurd will have his hands full heading them off. Gunnar then grabs his weapon and sets off.

Later in the third act, when Hiordis and Sigurd are alone on stage, the conversation returns to the bow-strings she had been turning. When Sigurd comments that she makes good weapons for her husband, Hiordis replies: 'Not for Gunnar, but against thee.'[23] She adds that in her daydreams she has seen Sigurd come sailing to Helgeland to burn her and Gunnar on their farm:

> All Gunnar's men have fallen; only he and I are left; they set light to the roof from without: – 'A bow-shot', cries Gunnar, 'one bow-shot may save us' – then the bow-string breaks – 'Hiordis, cut a tress of thy hair and make a bow-string of it – our life is at stake.' But then I laugh – 'Let it burn, let it burn – to me, life is not worth a handful of hair!'[24]

Ibsen uses material from *Njáls saga* very freely here, just as he does in his reworking of *Egils saga*. Interestingly, this most dramatic scene in the whole saga is not dramatized on the stage, but takes the form of an account of what Hiordis imagines could possibly happen. These examples shed light on how Ibsen's methodology can best be likened to that of collage in the visual arts or remix in contemporary music.

In his review of *Hærmændene* in 1874, Edmund Gosse suggested that the work's primary significance was for those interested in Ibsen's development as a playwright. This opinion is echoed in most discussion of the work since then. Michael Meyer, one of Ibsen's biographers, comments for instance: '*The Vikings at Helgeland* is a remarkable literary pastiche, and contains, buried in the impossible form of this pastiche, the kernel of what, over thirty years later, in a very different setting, was to become one of his greatest plays.'[25] The work Meyer refers to here is *Hedda Gabler*, which Ibsen completed in 1890. Like

Hiordis, Hedda is married to a man whom she scorns, and dreams of a passionate life with one of her husband's former friends. Meyer identifies parallels of varying degrees of transparency between the characters and dialogue in *Hærmændene* and *Hedda Gabler*.[26] Accordingly, Hedda can be regarded as among the fourth generation of robust female protagonists in Nordic literature, and among her foremothers are: a) Hiordis, b) Hallgerd and Gudrun Osvifursdottir, and finally c) Gudrun Gjukadottir and Brynhild Budladottir.

'There is no comfort in my breast to-night'

The Riding to Lithend (1909), one of more than thirty plays Gordon Bottomley wrote in verse, represents a very different kind of dramatic adaptation from that by Ibsen. Published in Britain some forty years after *Hærmændene* first appeared, Bottomley's work seems to have sprung from his reading of George Webbe Dasent's translation of *Njáls saga* that was originally published in 1861 under the title *The Story of Burnt Njal* before finding its way into the popular Everyman's Library series around the turn of the century. In a dedication to the writer Edward Thomas, Bottomley recalls a summer evening in 1907 when he related the story of the fall of Gunnar of Hlidarendi for Thomas and revealed his own desire to revitalize the ancient narrative. It appears that the dedicatee was deeply touched, and encouraged his friend to tackle this material and thus he became a kind of godfather to the resulting creation.

Both Bottomley and Thomas were part of a group of British writers often known as the Georgians, after King George v. The group was given its name by Edward Marsh, who, between 1912 and 1922, published several anthologies of poetry by his contemporaries under the name *Georgian Poetry*. One of Bottomley's plays, *King Lear's Wife*, appeared in the 1915 edition of the series and this led to greater exposure for his other works.[27] Bottomley's primary influence here was not only William Shakespeare – *King Lear's Wife* is written in blank verse and is full of Shakespearean metaphors – but Dante Gabriel Rossetti, an English poet and painter of Italian descent who sought inspiration from the art and narratives of previous centuries. Bottomley was also familiar with the works of Rossetti's colleague William Morris, who with Eiríkur Magnússon had translated a number of Icelandic sagas into English, and composed works inspired by several of them.[28] The best known of these is the epic poem 'The Lovers of Gudrun' (1869), which is inspired by *Laxdæla saga*. Morris also visited Hlidarendi during his two pilgrimages to Iceland in 1871 and 1873 and wrote an unusual poem about that experience, 'Gunnar's Howe above the House at Lithend'. There the poet describes Iceland as a mausoleum of the past and Gunnar's mound as a grave within that grave – he envisages the mound reopening and the hero speaking about his own death. Thus the words of the unknown author of *Njáls saga* have 'bridged all the days that have been' in the mind of the traveller.[29]

Bottomley's own adaptation of this saga seems to have grown from similar roots. In his dedication to Thomas he tells of his longing 'To body Hallgerd's ruinous / Great hair and wrangling mouth for us', and in particular to 'hear her voice deny again / That hair to Gunnar in his pain'.[30] Consistent with this, *The Riding to Lithend* is staged inside the farmhouse at Hlidarendi on the evening Gunnar is killed, and his conversation with Hallgerd about the bow-string represents the dramatic climax of the play. Bottomley's input involves creating new characters and dialogue within the lacunae of chapters 76 and 77 in the saga. Among the new characters are three house-women at Hlidarendi, as well as three beggar-women staying at the farm that night. Additionally, Bottomley amplifies the saga's descriptions of Hallgerd and Gunnar's mother Rannveig. For example, the harsh words Rannveig speaks to Hallgerd after the death of her son in *Njáls saga* – 'You are evil, and your shame will live long' – are better primed in *The Riding to Lithend* than in the saga narrative as a result of a quarrel between the two women that occurs earlier in Bottomley's work.[31] This animosity then continues to find expression, with a lively

'The Bill Sings to Rannveig', frontispiece by James Guthrie for the first edition of Gordon Bottomley's *The Riding to Lithend* (1909).

argument between Rannveig and Hallgerd taking place over the hero's bloodied corpse. Motherly love, or rather Rannveig's jealousy, also takes on a new dimension when Bottomley has her pointing out that Gunnar knew her 'bosom' before Hallgerd's.[32] We encounter the same tone and tenor at the end of the work when she tends to her son's corpse, shutting the eyes and mouth as though putting a child to sleep:

> RANNVEIG: Gunnar, my son, we are alone again . . .
> O, they have hurt you . . . but that is forgot.
> Boy, it is bedtime; though I am too changed,
> And cannot lift you up and lay you in,
> You shall go warm to bed – I'll put you there.
> There is no comfort in my breast to-night:
> But close your eyes beneath my fingers' touch,
> Slip your feet down, and let me smooth your hands;
> Then sleep and sleep.[33]

In the end, Rannveig picks up Gunnar's sword, kisses the weapon and 'shakes it on high' as the curtain falls.[34]

The Riding to Lithend neatly fulfils the requirements of the classical unities, according to which the tragedy should ideally consist of a single self-contained plot whose events occurred in one place and within the timeframe of a single day. These rules, based on Aristotle's *Peri poiêtikês* (Poetics, *c.* 335 BCE), were first proposed in any systematic fashion in the sixteenth century and have significantly influenced the work of many playwrights since then. However, such requirements were irreconcilable with the aesthetics of *Njáls saga*, which has a vast setting, extends over a sixty-year period and weaves together multiple storylines. For this reason, the saga needed to undergo a major process of simplification before it could succeed in the theatre. Broadly speaking, the choice to be made is between accurately portraying a few selected events or incompletely portraying many. Bottomley takes the first route, but the downside of his method is that few events are truly staged in *The Riding to Lithend*. A great deal of the dialogue of Hallgerd, Rannveig and the house-women at Hlidarendi in the first part of the play serves to introduce events and circumstances. Thus, incrementally, important information is communicated about Hallgerd's first two marriages, her initial meeting with Gunnar at Thingvellir and the slap on the face that she receives from her husband when she serves the stolen food at their home.[35] Such scenes inevitably lose their impact when presented as recollections of the characters.

At the same time, Bottomley's play is based on a series of pretexts. Most obviously, there is a connection between *The Riding to Lithend* and Dasent's 1861 translation of *Njáls saga*, with Bottomley apparently eager to preserve the style of the saga in his own text. Consequently, he includes entire sentences from *The Story of Burnt Njal* whenever the opportunity presents itself. Gunnar and Hallgerd's dialogue about the bow-string in Bottomley's play is a good example of his fidelity to the saga; the deviations in wording can primarily be explained in terms of the limits of blank verse. At the beginning of this dialogue in *The Riding to Lithend*, however, Gunnar displays striking independence when he likens his bow-string to the single string of a harp that has become 'voiceless'.[36] This is an example of how Shakespearean echoes reverberate in Bottomley's text, recalling here Macduff's line in *Macbeth*: 'I have no words; / My voice is in my sword.'[37] Indeed Bottomley's fascination with Shakespeare lay at the heart of his career as a playwright. Not only did he write *King Lear's Wife* (1915) as a prelude to Shakespeare's *King Lear*, but he also wrote a two-part prelude to *Macbeth* that was published under the title *Gruach* (1921).[38] We can regard Bottomley's work with the Icelandic saga as preparation for his subsequent engagement with the works of Shakespeare.

I have already noted the three beggar-women that Bottomley has visit Hlidarendi on the evening Gunnar is slain. It may seem natural to trace these characters back to several chapters in *Njáls saga* in which we encounter travelling women who spread gossip among the farming people in the area. But, as Alexander MacGill has pointed out, the beggar-women in *The Riding to Lithend* also recall the three witches from *Macbeth*.[39] Early in the 'Scottish play' Macbeth and

Banquo come across the witches on a desolate heath during a storm. Banquo asks:

> What are these
> So wither'd and so wild in their attire,
> That look not like th' inhabitants o' t' earth,
> And yet are on't? Live you? or are you aught
> That man may question?[40]

The witches reply by addressing Macbeth as a future king of the Scots, a prediction that will come back to haunt him.

When the beggar-women in *The Riding to Lithend* first appear, grey-haired and dressed in rags, Gunnar's reaction echoes Banquo's words when he asks the women, aghast:

> What men send ye here?
> Who are ye? Whence come ye? What do ye seek?
> I think no mother ever suckled you:
> You must have dragged your roots up in waste places
> One foot at once, or heaved a shoulder up –[41]

The women reply in verse and reveal that their home is in the rocky tors and cairns on the mountains above; they sweep the stony heath with the hems of their skirts. It is as though they have just come from meeting Macbeth and Banquo.

Other echoes of the same play include the moment when Biartey, one of the beggar-women, sits by the spinning wheel in the living room at the farm, singing rhymes that evoke the witches' song on the night Macbeth first meets them. In both cases, we find an emphasis on the three figures and the inversion of opposites. 'Fair is foul, and foul is fair', is the incantation of Shakespeare's witches.[42] Likewise, as Biartey spins the thread thinner and thinner, she sings: 'The outer is inner, / the core slips out.'[43] Here and elsewhere Bottomley creatively reprocesses his reading of Shakespeare and, in doing so, brings the saga material closer to his English audience.

Unlike *Hærmændene paa Helgeland, The Riding to Lithend* never achieved theatrical popularity, although it has been republished several times. In the 1920s the painter Paul Nash wrote to the playwright asking why it was that the work had never been performed. Bottomley thought it likely that the challenging set was to blame, as it was assumed, among other things, that Gunnar's killers would rip the roof off the dwellings at Hlidarendi at each and every performance.[44] The play was eventually performed one night in 1925 by The Manhattan Little Theatre Club at Wallack's Theatre in New York, under the direction of Conrad V. Norman, and again three years later during a drama festival in Cambridge, under the direction of Terence Gray. But these are the only performances I have been able to identify. As for its critical reception, Allardyce Nicoll claims unflatteringly in his history of English drama from 1900 to 1930 that the 'primitively Icelandic *The Riding to Lithend*', along with other works by Bottomley, 'must be regarded as too grim, too lacking in variety, often too allusive, to make a strongly favourable appeal even to dedicated repertory playgoers'.[45]

'The desire to be my own person'

In the spring of 1904, the Icelandic historian Bogi Th. Melsteð, then living in Copenhagen, wrote to his friends and relatives in Reykjavík asking whether they could provide accommodation for a Danish 'girl' (she was already 28 years old and his fiancée). Her full name was Maria Kirstine Dorothea Jensen but she was generally nicknamed Thit. In a letter to the physician Guðmundur Magnússon, Bogi claims that she intends to be in Iceland for about a year, 'and wishes to travel a little during the summer':

> I believe she would be like any other polite student in one's home, most often sitting in her room reading or writing. But

> given she is an 'intelligent' and polite lady, it would be more interesting for her to be among 'intelligent' and good people.[46]

Growing up in North Jutland, where her father worked as a vet, Thit Jensen had resolved early to dedicate her life to writing. As a teenager, she devoured the works of various key writers and poets of the time, with a wide variety of books available to her at home.[47]

When she arrived in Iceland, Jensen had taken the first steps on the path to becoming a novelist with her *To Søstre* (Two Sisters, 1903), and *Familien Storm* (The Storm Family, 1904) and was preparing for the publication of her third novel, *Martyrium* (Martyrdom, 1905).[48] The main characters of all these works are strong-willed young women who are faced with the choice of preserving their own independence or marrying the men they love. These competing impulses also crop up in *Nial den Vise*, the historical play Jensen started writing soon after her visit to Thingvellir during the summer of 1904.[49] A full thirty years would pass before the finished work was published, after it won first prize in a literary competition sponsored by the Danish breweries Tuborg and Carlsberg.[50] Meanwhile, Jensen had become one of Denmark's most influential women writers, often mentioned in the same breath as Karen Blixen (alias Isak Dinesen) and known for her outspoken views on women's rights. However, to the best of my knowledge, *Nial den Vise* has never been performed, perhaps because of the complexity of the staging, which would involve live horses, a great number of actors and an elaborate set. What's more, the published version of the play received dispiriting reviews in the Danish press. The most damning of these came from Hans Brix, who concluded his *Dagens Nyheter* piece with the words: 'It's nigh on impossible to imagine anything sillier than *Nial den Vise*.'[51]

Jensen's drama is divided into two parts, each of which is divided into three acts. The first act takes place at Thingvellir, the next three are set a year later at Hlidarendi, the fifth takes us to Bergthorshvol, the home of Gunnar's friend Njal, before we return to Thingvellir for the final act. Jensen has most of the key characters from *Njáls saga* appear on stage to take part in the three main events of the story: the killing of Gunnar of Hlidarendi, the killing of Hoskuldur Thrainsson (Hallgerd's grandson and Njal's foster son) and the burning of Njal. Still she partially follows Bottomley's commitment to the classical unities. In the second half of *Nial den Vise,* for example, Gunnar and Hoskuld and Njal are all killed within the same day. Jensen's play deviates, in this respect, significantly from the saga narrative, in which these three events occur years apart.

Kari Solmundarson, retainer to the Earl of Orkney, who only takes part in the action during the latter half of *Njâls saga,* proves to be a central character of *Nial den Vise* due to his complex relationships with three different women: Hildigunn, Hallgerd and Njal's daughter Helga. In the play Hallgerd is allegedly born and raised among royalty in the Hebrides; hence she and Kari have known each other all their lives. Although married to Gunnar, she tries to gain Kari's favour from the very start of the play. He, on the other hand, is in love with Hildigunn, who is herself engaged to Hoskuld and marries him once he becomes a chieftain. Njal then offers and Kari accepts Helga's hand in marriage. The two of them share a loving marriage but Kari still struggles to resist Hallgerd and also cannot stop thinking about Hildigunn.

This love rectangle finds no place in medieval versions of *Njáls saga,* in which Hallgerd is already Gunnar's widow before Hoskuld marries Hildigunn, and Kari comes to Iceland and marries Helga. In the saga, Hallgerd and Kari meet only once and even then we find no mention of them speaking to each other. On the other hand, though Kari and Hildigunn marry at the end of *Njáls saga,* that marriage may be thought of as quite implausible given that Kari takes part in killing Hoskuld, Hildigunn's husband. Jensen, on the other hand, keeps Kari well clear of the attack against Hoskuld. Overall, the hawkish Kari of *Njáls saga* is wildly different from the bewildered Kari of the play, who loves three women simultaneously and cannot choose between them. At the end of the first part he asks himself: 'Can one man have three souls?' – a question that reveals the nature of Jensen's hero.[52] This scene and many others give us cause to regard *Nial den Vise* as a loose adaptation, in the tradition of Ibsen; various scenes from the medieval saga can be identified, but they often operate in completely new contexts.

The fundamental difference between the works of Bottomley and Jensen become very clear when their interpretations of Chapter 75 are compared. In *Njáls saga*, Gunnar and his brother Kolskegg have been sentenced to outlawry and are riding towards their ship when Gunnar's horse stumbles and throws him to the ground:

> He turned with his face up towards the Lithe and the homestead at Lithend, and said –
>
> 'Fair is the Lithe; so fair that it has never seemed to me so fair; the corn fields are white to harvest, and the home mead is mown; and now I will ride back home, and not fare abroad at all.'[53]

In *The Riding to Lithend* this scene has taken place before the play begins and is only mentioned in a conversation that the house-women at Hlidarendi have with the three visiting beggar-women. When the visitors are surprised that Gunnar did not head off into exile, the house-woman Oddny says that on the way to the ship, Gunnar's horse had thrown him. Gunnar, having fallen, looked up towards the beautiful fields 'And said . . . What said he, girls?', adds Oddny.[54] Astrid answers by reciting Gunnar's famous speech, modified slightly from Dasent's translation:

> ASTRID: 'Fair is the Lithe:
> So fair I never thought it was so fair.
> Its corn is white, its meadows green after mowing.
> I will ride home again and never leave it.'[55]

It is undeniably strange to have a house-woman speak for the hero at this crucial moment. In Bottomley's play the scene is saved by the fact that Oddny doubts whether Gunnar really spoke the words, on the grounds that men wouldn't have the beauty of nature in mind under such circumstances. She thinks it more likely that Gunnar simply realized he was doomed, whether he set sail or not, and so decided not to go anywhere.

In *Nial den Vise* the scene of Gunnar's return is rewritten even more radically than in Bottomley's drama. Jensen's Hallgerd is immensely ambitious and will only truly be satisfied by becoming queen of Iceland. All her actions are dictated by this overriding goal, including her flirtation with Kari. And for the same reason, she wants to get rid of her husband. In the opening act, which takes place at Thingvellir, Hallgerd urges Gunnar not to leave Iceland despite having been outlawed. She explains that she fears the lonely nights ahead without him. In her heart, however, she knows that his remaining at home will cost him his life. At this point, Gunnar looks out through a doorway and sees the Almannagja rift gleaming in the evening sun:

> GUNNAR (*sighs deeply and looks out*): Fair is the Lithe. (*Turns around.*) And fair is *you*. And sweeter than honey is life, if you love me.
>
> HALLGERD: I love you.
>
> GUNNAR (*embraces her*): Hallgerd, my fair wife, it was first today that you were mine.[56]

As well as having Gunnar praise an entirely different landscape than the one in the saga, Jensen indicates that in the mind of our hero the beauty of the land is closely related to Hallgerd's own beauty.

Although the intertextual links with *Macbeth* are less explicit in *Nial den Vise* than in Bottomley's play, it is still tempting to compare Jensen's work with Shakespeare's play. Hallgerd's yearning to become queen of Iceland, for example, echoes the ambition of Lady Macbeth, who longs for, in her words, 'sovereign sway and masterdom.'[57] Such concepts of kingdom as expressed in Jensen's play are rather unconvincing, as Hans Brix noted in his review of *Nial den Vise*. We may, however, detect the influence of Ibsen here. In the third act of *Hærmændene paa Helgeland* it emerges, for example, that Hiordis is interested in Sigurd partly because she sees in him a man fit to be the king of Norway. She encourages him to rise up against the reigning monarch, adding: 'Plainly now I see my task in life: to make thee famous over all the world.'[58]

Another influence on the design of *Nial den Vise* may have been the writer's own life. In the years 1904 and 1905 Jensen's own emotions were no less complicated than those of the characters in her play. In her diary from this period we find several entries dealing with her relationship with Bogi Melsteð. While Bogi is looking for a place for the Danish 'girl' to stay in Iceland, the two of them are

The Valkyrie Thit Jensen, a cartoon by Herluf Jensenius from a Danish newspaper.

slowly becoming more intimate. He is sixteen years her senior and in her eyes, if her diary entries are any guide, a great Icelandic saga hero. At the same time, however, Jensen faces an inner struggle: 'The desire to be my own person, alone and undivided, is superior to my desire for love.'[59] A few weeks later, she adds in her diary: '*Summa summarum*: I don't wish to marry Melsteð, and I dare not ask him to be my lover.'[60]

If we are to believe the letters from Guðmundur Magnússon to Bogi, Jensen had attracted several admirers during her first months in Reykjavík.[61] It seems that Bogi's main rival was Gísli Skúlason, a priest in his early thirties who had been teaching Greek at the high school in Reykjavík that winter before eventually being appointed to the parish at Eyrarbakki, a small town in southern Iceland. It is not clear when Jensen met Gísli but in May 1905, after returning to Iceland by ship after a short visit to Copenhagen, she writes in her diary that she has finally decided to forget Bogi and focus on Gísli.[62] Just a few weeks later she reminds herself that she needs 'as cleanly as possible' to extract herself from the relationship with Bogi, whom she now no longer regards as a representative of the great 'primordial forces of the past', but as complacent, for the most part, 'with a pathologically heavy soul'.[63] Jensen's diary entry from 21 July relates the writing of *Nial den Vise* directly to these complications in her private life: 'I once wrote that I wanted to transform pent-up erotic desires into fiction! This is what I've truly done in recent days, harnessed the heat in my blood for fervent scenes in my play.'[64]

Gísli remains on Jensen's mind during these weeks and at the end of summer she writes in her diary: 'I love Gísli Skúlason and he me, I love him such that I will gladly become his wife, and I love him such that my heart is finally calm; I don't think of other men.'[65] These sentences reverberate in the first act of *Nial den Vise* when Kari takes Hildigunn in his arms and says: 'I love you, I love you, I wish to marry you, I shall (*yells*) I shall! (*He bites her hair.*)'[66] Still, it is not a simple case of Jensen *being* Kari and Gísli *being* Hildigunn, since it turns out that Kari and Hildigunn marry in the play whereas Jensen and Gísli separated. It seems more natural to regard *Nial den Vise* as a drama documenting the writer's personal struggle with the three different feminine roles represented by Helga, Hildigunn and Hallgerd. Helga is the gentle, obedient wife while Hallgerd plans to conquer the world at any cost. Hildigunn is somewhere in between; she is a woman with strong passions but her sense of responsibility prevails. Jensen clearly cannot imagine herself in Helga's role. After declaring in her diary a readiness to become Gísli's wife, she nevertheless adds that she cannot imagine living in a small, isolated village in Iceland.[67] She decides to return home to Copenhagen. Just as in her relationship with Bogi, the choice is between becoming a quiescent wife or an agent in her own life; finding a compromise seems impossible.

'Does it quench my thirst when my husband drinks?'

Before concluding the discussion of these three dramatic adaptations, let us briefly compare our female protagonists, all of whom owe some debt to Hallgerd's characterization in *Njáls saga*. In Ibsen's *Hærmændene paa Helgeland*, Hiordis is by far the most interesting character, driven by political ambition, burning passion and a thirst for revenge. At the same time, however, she leads the way for the other independent female characters in Ibsen's most famous works – not just Hedda Gabler but also Nora from *Et dukkehjem* (A Doll's House, 1879). For example, the discussion in that play about Nora as an ornamental bird in her husband's cage seems to echo the exchange between Dagny and Hiordis at the beginning of the second act of *Hærmændene*:

> DAGNY: Nay, Hiordis, I cannot understand thee. Thou hast shown me all the house; I know not what thing thou lackest, and all thou hast is fair and goodly; – then why bemoan thy lot?
> HIORDIS: Cage an eagle and it will bite at the wires, be they of iron or of gold.[68]

Although Hiordis is cunning and cruel, there are mitigating circumstances that should be noted. In the first place, she is orphaned at a young age and grows up under the iron fist of the man who killed her father. Secondly, she is tricked into marrying Gunnar, a coup for which Sigurd is responsible – the man she loved with all her heart. Furthermore, as the plot progresses she develops into a rather tragic heroine. The work concludes somewhat unexpectedly with Hiordis drawing her bow-string and shooting Sigurd in the chest. She plans on taking her own life so that the two of them can be united in Hel, the realm of the dead:

> Ay, Sigurd, so must it be here on this earth is no happiness for me. The White God is coming northward; him will I not meet; the old gods are strong no longer; – they sleep, they sit half shadow-high; – with them will we strive! Out of this life, Sigurd; I will enthrone thee king in heaven, and I will sit at thy side.[69]

But as Sigurd falls, he explains that he had become Christian while raiding in Britain, so he would be destined to rest in a different place from her: 'The White God is mine; King Aethelstan taught me to know him; it is to him I go.'[70]

In Bottomley's *The Riding to Lithend*, Hallgerd enjoys even less of the author's sympathy than Hiordis. Hallgerd is unambiguously dangerous, a kind of devil woman. When she first appears on stage she freely admits that her mother-in-law Rannveig is correct in accusing her of killing her first two husbands, and is not the least ashamed: 'I do not mar my face, / Though men have sunk in me as in a quicksand. / Well, death is terrible. Was I not worth it?'[71] Certainly, the stage directions in this scene indicate that Hallgerd's confidence is lacking. The actress playing her is supposed to bite her nails, twist her locks and chew their ends.[72] With the death of Gunnar, on the other hand, her words better match her body language:

> HALLGERD: (*laughing as she leans forward and holds her breasts in her hands*)
> O, clear sweet laughter of my heart, flow out!
> It is so mighty and beautiful and blithe
> To watch a man dying – to hover and watch.[73]

Hallgerd reminds us here of Lady Macbeth, who implores the spirits to 'unsex' her and thicken her blood before she plans the murder of King Duncan: 'Come to my woman's breasts, / And take my milk for gall', she inculcates.[74]

Jensen goes even further in 'unsexing' the female protagonist in her *Nial den Vise*. Not only is Hallgerd responsible for Gunnar's death but she is also behind most of the other murders in the play. This isn't surprising if we pause to consider 'Sigrid', the somewhat Nietzschean tale that Jensen published in 1909 as part of a collection of short stories relating to her stay in Iceland. The eponymous (anti-)heroine is a young maiden from Reykjavík who derives particular pleasure from the suffering and death of others. The most memorable incident in the story is when Sigrid pushes her friend into the waters of the Flosagja rift at Thingvellir and watches her drown. Shortly afterwards, Sigrid recalls how her father used to liken her to Hallgerd. The Hlidarendi housewife had in fact been the only character from the Sagas of Icelanders with whom she could identify, because 'she could well understand Hallgerd's billowy pleasure in seeing her husband, Gunnar, the male archetype, killed slowly and excruciatingly.'[75] In the play, Jensen magnifies this personal flaw by assigning to Hallgerd the role of Mord Valgardsson, the chief villain of *Njáls saga*. He does not appear in the play but in his place Hallgerd (disguised as a man) goes to meet Gunnar's enemies when they arrive at Hlidarendi and advises them on how best to exterminate her husband. When all is over for Gunnar, Hallgerd says triumphantly: 'See, the queen of Iceland advances!'[76] She then urges Njal's sons to kill Hoskuld before persuading Flosi Thordarson and his men to burn down the farmhouses at Bergthorshvol.

Hallgerd's objective in Jensen's play is not primarily to watch men die, but rather to end Njal's reign as Lawspeaker and create general chaos in society. In the final act, which takes place at Thingvellir the day after the burning of Njal, Hallgerd very nearly succeeds in convincing those present that the country needs a strong, regal leader and that she would be ideal for the role. However, Kari has seen through her plotting by this point and manages to expose her in the nick of time. The Assembly then turns against her; Kari is elected Lawspeaker and makes the play's final speech about the glories of peace, with Hildigunn by his side.

And yet Hallgerd is not portrayed as a total demon in *Nial den Vise*. It is clear that her ambition is deeply rooted. In the first act of the play, Hallgerd discusses with Njal the difference between her destiny and that of Kari. In youth, they both aspired to emulate powerful Vikings, but because of her gender she had to retreat from this desire, while he could realize his dreams. 'Why didn't my father make me a son?' she asks sadly.[77] Njal points out that Gunnar has accomplished enough for both of them, to which she offers the memorable reply: 'Does it quench *my* thirst when my husband drinks?'[78] Women's rights are again the focal point later in the act when Hallgerd and Hildigunn meet at Gunnar's booth at Thingvellir. Hallgerd points out the contrast between the sons of Vikings, who are expected to cultivate their heroism, while the daughters are made to renounce that same family trait: 'The son *should* be wild, the daughter *should* be tame.'[79] In order to challenge this disparity, Hallgerd takes the weapons and armour that are hanging on a wall and dresses for battle. This event, symbolic of her behaviour throughout the play, upsets Hildigunn, who asks the Valkyrie to take off the armour quickly, 'before the men arrive.'[80]

Jensen herself was often likened to a Valkyrie. She never settled for the narrow lot that men designated for her and her sex. After an intense meeting with Bogi Melsteð on 22 April 1904, she wrote in her diary: 'Why can't, why *doesn't* the man, respect the woman's desire to work?

'Unsex me now.' Lillie Langtry as Lady Macbeth, 1899.

Why is a man in love a pest?'[81] As a writer and active participant in the women's rights movement in Denmark, Jensen dreamed of a new type of person who united 'feminine' and 'masculine' characteristics:

> The woman who is called that by name but is in fact not that, but rather an asexual being, half man and half woman, without impulse but churning with the capacity to work, determined to make a difference, without conceit, but distinct from the eternal femininity that does not befit her.[82]

With the exception of the comment about conceit, could this not serve as a plausible description of both Jensen and Bottomley's Hallgerd, as well as Ibsen's Hiordis and Hedda?

FOUR

Gunnar: In Saddles, Armchairs and Land Rovers

A windy summer's day in 1872: Samuel Edward Waller was sitting close to a decrepit sheepcote by the ridge of Fljotshlid, in the south of Iceland, looking up at Hlidarendi. This young aspiring artist had spent the previous day sketching the view over the Rangarvellir plains from above the farm. Now he wanted to depict the landscape in the reverse direction. But as Waller was absorbed in his task, there was an unexpected intrusion:

> I became conscious, firstly, of the noise of something rapidly approaching, and then of a series of the most terrific bellowings I ever heard in my life. I looked up, much alarmed, and saw one of the savage little brindled bulls coming up the hill at me as fast as possible, his eyes glaring savagely, and his tail in the air. I dropped my brushes and crept inside the hut, and the brute, close at my heels, attempted to follow. Fortunately, the doorway was much too narrow; so, after a good deal of pushing and blustering and tearing the turf with his horns, he left off trying to force an entrance, and contented himself with marching up and down outside.[1]

Waller had been prompted to visit Iceland that summer by reading Dasent's 1861 English translation of *Njáls saga*. He was particularly captivated by the first half of the saga and regarded the heroic but tragic last stand of Gunnar of Hlidarendi as its artistic highpoint.

In fact, reading the saga had such a powerful effect on Waller that he felt compelled to explore its setting, particularly the farm where Gunnar lived. His aim was to gain the deepest possible understanding of the final scene in the life of the noblest character in Icelandic history. And in that respect, Waller's dramatic episode with the bull served a practical purpose, for it enabled him to find out for himself what it was like to sit inside a fortress of turf and rock with a ferocious enemy at the door. The key difference between Waller's experience and that of Gunnar of Hlidarendi nine centuries earlier was that the bull eventually abandoned his attack, unable to strip away the roof.

Shortly after his stay in Iceland, Waller published a book to which he assigned the title *Six Weeks in the Saddle* (1874). Among fourteen drawings included in the book are two that Waller sketched in the vicinity of Hlidarendi. These illustrations were certainly valuable for his travel story, but they were also intended to make it easier for British readers of *Njáls saga* to comprehend the topography of the saga setting. In many ways Waller's overall attitude to Iceland

'Victory!', from Samuel E. Waller's *Six Weeks in the Saddle* (1874).

typifies that of many foreign travel writers and artists who have visited the country during the past century and a half. The familiarity of these travellers with the sagas has tended to colour their sense of Icelandic landscape and its inhabitants, and in some instances it has been the principal impetus behind their visits. Furthermore, as we have already noted with William Morris and Thit Jensen, a visit to Iceland has often been the stimulus for further literary activity.

But what were the origins of this tradition of writing and how has it developed in more recent decades? To address these questions we will first examine some of the earliest British travel books in which sagas feature prominently, exploring in particular their treatment of *Njáls saga*. We will also discuss briefly an example where the genre of travel literature overlaps with that of the modern novel. Our focus will then turn to one of the most dynamic modern travel accounts inspired by the sagas, *Nord for Vatnajøkel* (North of the Vatnajokull Glacier, 1994) by the Danish writer and art critic Poul Vad. The book recounts the author's short visit to the landscapes of *Hrafnkels saga Freysgoða* (The Saga of Hrafnkel Frey's Godi) in eastern Iceland, but what makes this trip exceptional is that Vad seems convinced that the saga in question is a fictional account rather than history. Consequently, he cannot help questioning the overall purpose and validity of taking a pilgrimage to individual 'saga-steads'.

'You must visit Hlidarendi'

The first British travel descriptions from Iceland were the product of expeditions which were particularly motivated by an interest in the country's geology and nature. Most of the parties arriving during the period from 1772 to 1834 headed for one or all of the 'lions' of Iceland: Mt Hekla, Geysir and Thingvellir in the south of the country. At this time, however, Iceland's ancient literature and culture were rarely mentioned.[2] The expedition organized by the geologist Sir George Steuart Mackenzie in the summer of 1810 was a noteworthy exception. Mackenzie's *Travels in the Island of Iceland* (1811) opens with a detailed introduction by one of his party, Henry Holland, a medical student, who surveys Icelandic literature and history from the ninth-century settlement until the end of the eighteenth century. While travelling, Holland had discussed these topics with various Icelanders and examined most of the relevant writings and translations that had been published in Latin and English. Mackenzie was so impressed by one of the sagas Holland summarized in the book, *Gunnlaugs saga Ormstungu* (The Saga of Gunnlaug Serpent-tongue), that he adapted it quite freely as a drama, *Helga, or the Rival Minstrels* (1812). However, as Andrew Wawn has noted, the staged version of the saga 'enjoyed the shortest run imaginable at the Theatre Royal Edinburgh. Geological controversy ensured that the play, already holed beneath its artistic water-line before the curtain rose, was greeted with derision by a hostile audience.'[3]

There is no indication that either Holland or Mackenzie was aware at the time of the Latin translation of *Njáls saga*, which had been published in Copenhagen in 1809. This absence of any mention of the saga in their writings is all the more interesting given that the party travelled through the primary setting of the saga and even spent the night at Hlidarendi. There, they enjoyed the hospitality of the local sheriff, Mackenzie bought a woman's national costume for his wife and Holland used the occasion to make a sketch of the farm with Eyjafjallajokull Glacier in the background. An impressive watercolour by a British artist, based on this sketch, is included in Mackenzie's book. There we also find a description of the Markarfljot river and the view towards the Vestmannaeyjar (Westman Islands) to the south. But no smoke rises from Njal's old farmstead at Bergthorshvol and no ancient heroes are seen riding through the plains. The most remarkable character encountered there by Mackenzie and his companions was the local pastor, who offered Holland a pinch of snuff in the middle of the service in a neighbouring church, fortified himself by drinking spirits while the hymns were being sung and cut the service short so that he could accompany the Britons back to Hlidarendi.[4]

The new saga-inflected perspective that we find in the writings of later tourists such as Waller was shaped both by the sudden growth of saga translations in Britain in the second half of the nineteenth century and by improved transportation. In the summer of 1856, steamships began scheduled sailings to and from Iceland, ensuring that travellers could rely on relatively inexpensive fares and predictable arrival and departure dates. Some were interested in fishing and shooting sports, others in climbing mountains and exploring nature, and some were primarily readers of Icelandic literature. In the years that followed, the publishing of travel books about Iceland in English came to enjoy a new lease of life after a lapse of more than two decades. Between 1860 and 1863 alone at least three such works were published in London: Charles S. Forbes' *Iceland: Its Volcanoes, Geysers and Glaciers* (1860), Frederick Metcalfe's *The Oxonian in Iceland: or, Notes of Travel in That Island in the Summer of 1860, with Glances at Icelandic Folk-lore and Sagas* (1861) and Sabine Baring-Gould's *Iceland: Its Scenes and Sagas* (1863).

Metcalfe is generally regarded as the first Briton systematically to link his Iceland travels with his knowledge of the sagas. He had studied Iceland's ancient literature at Oxford and regarded his journey in 1860 as a kind of pilgrimage. His book opens with a quotation from an advertisement in *The Times* for a summer voyage to Iceland on board the steamship *Arcturus*. This is followed by the narrator's dramatized conversation with other prospective travellers, describing how this represents a unique opportunity for them to actually visit the places they have been reading about in the sagas:

> You must visit Hlidarendë, where that peerless, noble hearted, Gunnar lived, and Bergthorshvoll, where wise old Niál was burnt, house and family and all, by those stern incendiaries. It made me shudder when you read the tale.[5]

Compared with most other tourists of the second half of the nineteenth century, Metcalfe ventured unusually far and wide in Iceland. He went first to see the famous sights – and sites! – at Thingvellir and Geysir, before taking the Kjolur route north over the highlands, heading east as far as Lake Myvatn and then back through the districts in the north and the west. His final destinations included Mt Hekla and the southern Icelandic lowlands. Alongside his account of these travels, Metcalfe relates Iceland folktales and relevant episodes from five sagas: *Grettis saga* (The Saga of Grettir the Strong), *Vatnsdæla saga* (The Saga of the People of Vatnsdal), *Laxdæla saga*, *Egils saga* and *Njáls saga*.

Chapter 24 of *The Oxonian in Iceland* is devoted to *Njáls saga*. At Thingskalar, the western boundary of the saga setting, Metcalfe is shown the ruins of the booths of Gunnar and Njal at the assembly held there. Continuing towards Hlidarendi, he recalls at Knafarholar how Starkad and his men ambushed Gunnar and his two brothers. Metcalfe then pauses on the banks of the Eystri-Ranga river where Gunnar and Starkad arranged a horse fight earlier in the saga. At Breidabolstadur the expedition is met by Revd Skúli Gíslason, who accompanies them across the ridge of Fljotshlid. It is probably thanks to having Skúli as their guide that Metcalfe not only mentions where individual *Njáls saga* characters lived, but provides pen-portraits of the Milton translator Jón Þorláksson, born at the farm of Teigur, and poet Bjarni Thorarensen, who was brought up at Hlidarendi. Metcalfe points out how Fljotshlid has deteriorated since its beauty compelled Gunnar to remain there and meet certain death, and he cites Bjarni's poem about the hillside with its 'feet hidden in the mountain's mud'.[6]

It is interesting to compare this account with the description of Mackenzie's expedition to the same area half a century earlier. *Njáls saga* had given the British traveller a new perspective on the surroundings. Metcalfe admires the view from the farm at Hlidarendi and individual episodes from the saga come to life in his mind. Even the most minute features of the landscape can be laden with meaning.

'Thingvellir', frontispiece to Frederick Metcalfe's *The Oxonian in Iceland* (1861).

Thus, alongside the track leading from the farm to the mound where Gunnar is said to have been buried, there is a little tussock, a grass-covered reminder of where the hero's dog lies buried. Later that same day Metcalfe leaves Hlidarendi for Bergthorshvol and one of his companions mentions that they are following the same route to the farm that had been used by Flosi Thordarson and his men, who burnt Njal and his family to death inside. The people presently living at Bergthorshvol point out to them a hollow and a tarn named after Flosi and Kari respectively, and also the site of Njal's farm where local people had recently dug up charred wood, ashes and metal remains. Metcalfe implies that he took some of these relics back to England with him, incontestable evidence that the burning of Njal actually took place.

It is apparent from the title of his book, *Iceland: Its Scenes and Sagas,* that Sabine Baring-Gould was 'one of the new post-Metcalfe generation of Icelandic travellers', as Andrew Wawn puts it.[7] A school teacher and later an Anglican priest, Baring-Gould followed more or less the same route in 1862 as Metcalfe had taken two years earlier; from Reykjavík, across the country to Lake Myvatn and back along the coast, albeit without exploring the southern lowlands. The

'Almanna-gjá', frontispiece to Sabine Baring-Gould's *Iceland: Its Scenes and Sagas* (1863).

objective of Baring-Gould's trip was twofold, as he explains in his preface: 'examining scenes famous in Saga, and filling a portfolio with water-colour sketches'.[8] The main body of his text consists of lively and at times humorous travel description, interspersed with translated sections or summaries of *Vatnsdæla saga, Egils saga, Flóamanna saga* (The Saga of the People of Floi) and *Bandamanna saga* (The Saga of the Oath-bound Men), along with four different sections of *Grettis saga,* which were later recycled in his juvenile novel *Grettir the Outlaw* (1891). Baring-Gould's book also contains sixteen illustrated pages, several in colour, and some twenty smaller sketches of Icelandic landscapes and saga scenes.

When these expeditions to Iceland, translations of Icelandic literature and published travel books are set in context, a complex web of pre-texts and adaptations can be discerned. Three factors underpinning this process stand out. First, it is interesting how sagas serve to dictate the itineraries of travellers such as Metcalfe and Baring-Gould, and how their accounts in turn influence the way in which latter British readers of saga translation approach and understand these texts. To some extent, each new literary journey seems to be founded on earlier ones. Thus Samuel Waller's examination of the scenes of *Njáls saga* in *Six Weeks in the Saddle* is curiously similar to Metcalfe's account, since both parties stop at many of the same places. The difference is that Metcalfe's journey has now become part of the tradition from which Waller is working. When Waller visits Bergthorshvol he seeks out Kari's tarn, for instance, and mentions that remnants from the burning of Njal have been found during excavations on the farmland and sold to travellers.[9] As the number of journeys and published accounts increases the literary baggage carried by the authors grows heavier, while opportunities to find and visit unexplored or unfamiliar locations steadily diminish. Towards the end of the nineteenth century the travel literature tradition has become so extensive that Mrs Disney Leith begins her *Three Visits to Iceland* (1897) with an apology for adding yet another account of visits to Geysir and the setting of *Njáls saga* to the existing corpus.[10] One of Leith's innovations was to include as an appendix her translation of Jónas Hallgrímsson's poem 'Gunnarshólmi' (Gunnar's Holm, 1838), which was then and probably still is the best-known literary reflection on the topography of *Njáls saga* by any Icelander.

Second, these travel books reveal how different characteristics of cultural tourism emerged slowly in Iceland. During his first day at Hlidarendi, Waller looks at the supposed ruins of Gunnar's farmhouse and gazes out across the wilderness towards the sea with a feeling (just like Bjarni Thorarensen and Metcalfe before him) that the land has deteriorated since Gunnar turned back. Afterwards he settles down towards the top of the slope to sketch the farm site looking out to the southeast. He has not been at work for long before an old man approaches, pulls out a well-worn copy of *Njáls saga* and starts reading the chapter about the death of Gunnar. The raconteur then points out Gunnar's cairn to Waller:

> 'It is Gunnar's grave', said the old man. 'Here they buried him . . . But though his body was laid here in its grave, his spirit

> rested not in the stony chamber, for on the starlit nights the war songs he had sung in life were heard again upon the hillside, and magic lights were seen to burn within the cairn.'[11]

'How strange it all seemed', Waller adds, in a turn of phrase which Gary Aho sees as symbolic of his romantic attitude.[12] By this time, the traveller's encounter with a bookish Icelander was already becoming a literary topos. But the account also invites speculation as to whether Waller had not in fact witnessed a little dramatic interlude staged by the locals for foreign visitors.

Third, it is interesting to see how travel descriptions become more personal as the nineteenth century progresses; they are just as much an expression of the psychological state of the travellers themselves as of the sights that greet their eyes. It is a sign of the times in which he lived that Waller, unlike many of his predecessors, chose to travel alone in Iceland; he appears to believe that his experience will be different and perhaps even truer than it would have been had he travelled around the country in the company of others. His description of the first part of his journey is in this respect symbolic, emphasizing the delight of the solitary traveller (despite the constant presence of his Icelandic guide):

> Though entirely alone (excepting for Bjarni's company), I never felt so thoroughly comfortable in my life. There was something gratifying in being the sole proprietor of such a cavalcade, and being bound on such an errand as painting an unknown country; and again, the 'happy-go-lucky' air which pervaded the whole scheme, the delightful uncertainty about beds, meals, fires, and all home comforts, had a great deal of attraction for a Bohemian like myself.[13]

Alongside such enthusiastic descriptions are entertaining accounts of Waller's ordeals with a leaky tube of paint (tainting his painting equipment, clothes and the journey itself a deep blue), his battles with predatory fleas and his experience of the unbearably stale air in the main room of the farm at Herdisarvik in southwest Iceland. The account of that particular incident ends when the farmer leaps out of bed in the middle of the night, removes a cork plug from the wall and lets in some fresh air for half a minute before replacing the plug, sighing that everyone will now probably catch his death of cold.

'Hoskuldstead stood above the Laxa River'

The armchair travellers who have toured Iceland since the nineteenth century with the aid of Metcalfe, Waller and many others certainly have had various additional lazy-boy means of visiting this northern 'tomb of time past', to borrow William Morris's phrase from his poem about Gunnar's cairn at Hlidarendi.[14] One option has been the popular genre of Viking novels. Works within this tradition range from Friedrich de la Motte-Fouqué's *Die Fahrten Thiodolfs des Isländers* (The Rides of Thiodolf the Icelander, 1815) to Neil Gaiman's *American Gods* (2001). Such narratives enjoyed their initial heyday in Victorian Britain with the publication of a number of novels set in the medieval 'North' and featuring Vikings as principal characters. These include, among many others, Edward Bulwer-Lytton's *Harold* (1848), Charles Kingsley's *Hereward the Wake* (1866), R. M. Ballantyne's *Erling the Bold* (1869), H. Rider Haggard's *The Saga of Eric Brighteyes* (1890), W. G. Collingwood's *Thorstein of the Mere* (1895) and J. F. Hodgetts's *Kormak the Viking* (1902). Emphasizing the range of such works, Andrew Wawn writes:

> We find paraphrases of saga and chronicle that celebrate the Scandinavian and Norman heritage in the British Isles, or the Norse discovery of America. Some old northern tales promote images of stout-hearted masculinity for the schoolboys of middle England as they trained to become pillars of

> society and empire. There are novels that give imaginative substance to the distinctively regional old northern heritage which British antiquarians had begun to celebrate. Some tales were intended as spiritual and moral fables, while others, a blend of didacticism and sensationalism, transferred easily to the London stage.[15]

Throughout the twentieth century, the tradition continued to flourish on both sides of the Atlantic, with several major and many more minor authors taking on the challenge of reprocessing the plots of individual sagas or myths for a modern readership. Two ambitious examples of this genre are *Gerpla* (The Happy Warriors, 1952), by Iceland's only Nobel laureate Halldór Laxness, and *Berättelsen om Såm* (The Story of Sam, 1977) by the acclaimed Swedish novelist Per Olof Sundman. While *Gerpla* is a provocative medieval saga pastiche, based on the texts of *Fóstbræðra saga* (The Saga of the Sworn Brothers) and *Ólafs saga helga* in *Heimskringla*, in Sundman's novel the plot of *Hrafnkels saga Freysgoða* is recontextualized within a contemporary setting.[16]

If we leave out literary relocations such as *Berättelsen om Såm*, it seems that one of the great challenges in both translating and adapting the sagas in modern times is that the implied reader of the pre-texts is a medieval Icelander, or at least someone who knows the basics of Icelandic early history and geography. Accordingly, many saga translations are buttressed with commentary on the settlement of Iceland, its regional organizations, public life and parliamentary procedures. A vivid example of this sort of presentation is George Webbe Dasent's 1861 translation *The Story of Burnt Njal*. It was originally published in two volumes of around nine hundred pages, only two-thirds of which were devoted to the translation while the rest contained Dasent's preface, introduction and appendices, all designed to prepare potential readers who knew next to nothing about Iceland and its medieval past. But how are such elements relevant for saga adaptations by novelists? Dorothy James Roberts's *Fire in the Ice* (1961), inspired by both *Laxdæla saga* and *Njáls saga*, may supply us with some answers.

In the early 1960s Roberts was already a well-known novelist whose works featured both historical and contemporary settings. The daughter of a West Virginia oil producer, her graduate work had involved the study of medieval European literature, notably the legend of Tristan and Isolde, which became the source of her best-known novel *The Enchanted Cup* (1953). Her other historical works include *Launcelot, My Brother* (1954) and *Kinsmen of the Grail* (1963), both of which were inspired by Arthurian Romances. Roberts was also a passionate enthusiast of saga literature. In her preface to *Fire in the Ice* she claims: 'The best Icelandic Sagas approach the finest of modern novels, and are more closely related to them than to the European literature of their time.'[17] But still, she felt the urge to produce a modern adaptation of these works. Emulating the dramatists discussed in the previous chapter, she became fascinated by the character of Hallgerd Long-legs, whose family is not only portrayed in *Njáls saga*, but in *Laxdæla saga*.

As far as the sagas' historical context is concerned, an example from the opening of *Fire in the Ice* may serve to illustrate Roberts's method of adaptation. The reader is introduced to Hallgerd at the age of ten, sitting in her mother's 'wool house' at the family farm. When the girl grows tired she is allowed to go outside:

> She followed the nurse outdoors and stopped to draw a breath.
>
> Hoskuldstead stood above the Laxa River on the hill slope which made the southern side of the valley. Her father's seat was a cluster of buildings, the gabled fire hall, the home dairy, the stables and barns, the stout, locked storehouse, the wool house and loft above it which was used as the women's quarters. The long, narrow houses faced south, and were either built against each other or communicated by short paths

> and passages. All were constructed of blocks of porous lava rock, and to keep out the wind, their side walls were covered with thick slabs of turf, now grown over with brown-green autumn grass.[18]

Apart from the first sentence, this text could be mistaken for part of a learned introduction to a saga translation, but Roberts simply unites plot and commentary. Generally, her historical data is fairly accurate and presented as an integral part of the narrative.

Another concern of non-Icelandic saga readers is the reality of Iceland's geography. In most modern saga editions and translations it is presented through maps, illustrations and photographs. As already suggested, many authors of Icelandic travel books have attempted to achieve the same connection between narrative and landscape. One suggestive example is *A Pilgrimage to the Saga-steads of Iceland* (1899) by the painter W. G. Collingwood and the writer Jón Stefánsson. This 'picture book', as the authors explain in their preface, was designed to supply 'the background of scenery' for some major Icelandic sagas. The idea was to help 'the modern reader, out of Iceland' to '*stage* these dramas, to *visualize* the action and events'.[19] Another example might be William Morris's *Icelandic Journals*, in which the author describes, for instance, a visit to Thingvellir in the summer of 1871. Morris writes:

> My heart beats, so please you, as we near the brow of the pass . . . for this is the heart of Iceland that we are going to see: nor was the reality of the sight unworthy; the pass showed long and winding from the brow, with jagged dark hills showing over the nearer banks of it as you went on, and betwixt them was an open space with a great unseen but imagined plain between you and the great lake that you saw glittering far away under huge peaked hills of bright blue with grey-green sky above them, Hengill the highest of them, from the hot

> spring on whose flank rose into the air a wavering column of snow-white steam.[20]

I have chosen this passage because a strikingly similar description occurs in *Fire in the Ice* when Hallgerd visits Thingvellir:

> Yet in time they began to see the plain of Thingmeads over the pitch of the near hills. And now they perceived how the parliament site was ringed by mountains. To the south, rising above lesser eminences, stood Hengill, crowned with an immaculate plume of steam. And far beyond Armansfell in the north brooded the snowy dome of Skialdbreid.
>
> Above Mossfell Heath the road dropped into a smooth, grass-grown plain. The view shortened, and the lava abruptly ended.[21]

Descriptions of this sort imply that *Fire in the Ice* is not just a covert lesson in early Icelandic history but also partly a travelogue written for people with limited knowledge of Iceland's geography.

Additionally, Roberts transforms the impersonal and understated narrative style of the two sagas in accordance with the accepted poetics of the modern American novel. Although *Fire in the Ice* is written in the third person, as are the sagas, the narrator is omniscient. The difference between the two styles is apparent in the dramatic scene, set in Thingvellir, describing how Hallgerd presents herself to her future husband, Gunnar of Hlidarendi. In *Njáls saga*, the story is as follows:

> It happened one day that Gunnar was walking from the Law Rock and passed below the booth of the people from Mosfell. He saw some women coming towards him, and they were well dressed. The one in the front was the best dressed. When they met, she greeted Gunnar at once. He took her greeting well and asked who she was. She gave her name as Hallgerd.[22]

A map of Iceland, frontispiece to Dorothy James Roberts's *Fire in the Ice* (1961).

The events are being reported here from the point of view of someone who is following Gunnar and is able to listen to his conversation with Hallgerd. In Roberts's novel, however, we follow Hallgerd as she tricks several young women in to walking with her towards Gunnar's quarters, while at the same time we enter the characters' minds:

> 'Come with us, Hallgerda', said one of them.
>
> 'Not I, I'm not interested in catching any man's eye.'
>
> 'But you're a married woman, you – you will –'
>
> 'Protect you? I suppose it wouldn't be suitable for you just to run out and stare. I'll go for your sakes.'
>
> They were delighted to be involved in a romantic plot, especially with a woman their mothers did not approve of. 'Don't giggle and give him flirtatious looks', she cautioned them. 'We must seem to be enjoying a little stroll in the air.'
>
> They were childishly awkward and obvious. She moved among them gravely, thinking, if girls between fourteen and seventeen realized their gifts, if they could learn to walk, avoid grimaces, be mindful that light reflects on smooth hair but makes wool of hair allowed to bounce about their heads, what luck would even beautiful older women have?
>
> They approached Gunnar. Hallgerda let her eyes show a flicker of surprise.
>
> 'What woman are you?' Gunnar said.[23]

This passage offers a sense of Roberts's narrative control. The sentence 'Hallgerda *let her* eyes show a flicker of surprise [my emphasis]', for instance, carries a meaning quite different from 'Hallgerda's eyes showed a flicker of surprise', which would have more closely mimicked traditional saga style.

Finally, Roberts's implied audience is culturally different from that of the medieval sagas. A telling example is Hallgerd's conversation with her brother, Olaf the Peacock, at the end of the novel. Gunnar has been killed and Hallgerd is a widow for the third time. Olaf asks her how she is doing:

> 'Me, I am getting old.' But she watched him, to see denial in his eyes.
>
> 'This fate overtakes us all in time.'

> 'Though I am hardly gray', she added.
> 'I do not see a single gray hair.'
> 'Why did you say I was getting old, then?'
> He laughed at her. 'I did not say it, you did.'
> 'But you agreed with me.'[24]

Conversations of this sort were probably the primary source of annoyance for the critic, writing for the *New York Herald Tribune* in 1961, who complained that Roberts's portrait of the heroine fused 'elements of past and present', and added that Hallgerd's 'thoughts and motivations' were neither those of a modern nor medieval woman.'[25] I am inclined to agree with these words, but a similar judgement can possibly be passed on most of the adaptations, both modern and medieval, considered in this book. The universal tendency of their creators has been to fuse elements of past and present.

'The fictitious Adalbol'

In the latter half of the twentieth century, a range of literary scholars – among them Edward Said, Gayatri Chakravorty Spivak and Homi K. Bhabha – drew attention to the way Westerners' descriptions of developing nations, for instance in travel books and fiction, often revealed more about the authors and their colonialist attitudes towards their subjects than about the realities they purported to be describing. Such works tend to make a sharp distinction between 'us' and 'Other': that which should be considered normal, obvious and ordained (us), and that which may be regarded as abnormal, strange and primitive (Other). Sumarliði Ísleifsson has outlined how foreign writings about Iceland, as well as pictures and maps, were for a long time also tainted by such attitudes; Icelanders tended to be portrayed 'as primitive and immoral, as the opposite of civilization.'[26] By the nineteenth century, however, Icelanders were increasingly portrayed as noble (and sometimes exceptionally bookish) children of nature, while Iceland's natural environment continued to be characterized as the complete opposite of the 'tamed' fields of continental Europe. Key terms and concepts in Waller's descriptions of the landscape, for example, are 'wild', 'impressive', 'weird' and 'ancient'.[27]

Many of these same characteristics were also to be found in Anglophone travel literature dealing with mainland Scandinavia, and even as all the Nordic societies became ever more modern and in most respects socially progressive during the twentieth century, the exotic and at times Arcadian image of the North survives to the present day. Old habits and views die hard, as Heidi Hansson notes: 'the rural character of much of the Nordic North invited nostalgic interpretations that were continually reproduced due to the intertextual nature of the travel genre.'[28] This is particularly true of Iceland, which, even in the eyes of Scandinavians, continues to be regarded as a place apart, somehow immune to the demystifying effect of modernity. Iceland is frequently portrayed as the enchanted 'Saga Island', a somewhat primitive paradise of people who are in closer contact with their natural elements and cultural heritage than any other Nordic nation.

This perception is at the forefront in Poul Vad's travel book *Nord for Vatnajøkel* from 1994. A travel book, I say, but we should use the term cautiously; the book was certainly inspired by the author's trip to Iceland in 1970 and tells of some of the people and places he encountered, including the occasion on which he drove 60 kilometres up the remote Hrafnkelsdalur Valley in a Land Rover jeep rented in the local town of Egilsstadir. On the other hand, Vad's primary aim seems to have been to educate his readers about *Hrafnkels saga Freysgoða*. Several chapters of *Nord for Vatnajøkel* are devoted to explaining the storyline, analysing the saga's principal characters and comparing the saga with various celebrated works of world literature, such as Niccolò Machiavelli's *Il Principe* (The Prince, 1532) and Miguel de Cervantes's *Don Quixote* (1605–15). One chapter traces the publication history of *Hrafnkels saga Freysgoða* in Denmark, another is a harsh criticism of Sundman's novel *Berättelsen om Såm* and a third chapter offers Vad's reflections on how the saga might be made into a film, perhaps in the style of an Italian Spaghetti Western or a Japanese Samurai production. At the same time, Vad grapples with the influence of the traditional Danish approach to Icelandic sagas and their settings.

One notable late nineteenth-century work exemplifies this approach in every respect: the 1,200-page *Bidrag til en historisk-topografisk beskrivelse af Island* (A Contribution to a Historical-topographical Study of Iceland, 1877–82), by P. E. Kristian Kålund, a Danish scholar who travelled all over Iceland between 1872 and 1874 in order to acquaint himself in detail with Icelandic historical sites. The resulting two-volume study soon came to be regarded as an important contemporary description of the country. Kålund's discussion of the Hrafnkelsdalur Valley as the setting for *Hrafnkels saga* is characteristic of his overall methodology. He notes that in the nineteenth century there were only two farms there, Vadbrekka and Adalbol, where the saga hero Hrafnkel is said to have lived, but four farms in the valley are mentioned in *Hrafnkels saga*, and other medieval sources indicate that there were close to twenty. This discussion is followed by a short summary of the content of the saga, complete with Kålund's speculation about where the fateful cliff might have been, over which Hrafnkel's enemies drove his horse. Kålund found that local conditions contradicted the saga's description of the area.[29] He noted that there could be at least two explanations for this: Adalbol farm could have been moved to a new location in the valley, or the author of the saga might not have been familiar enough with the area. In this respect, Kålund's work is typical of the comparisons between landscape and saga made by many nineteenth-century travellers of Iceland. Such comparisons gradually developed into a separate field of research among those twentieth-century scholars who sought to identify the authors of particular sagas.

Vad does not name Kålund in his book but mentions two other compatriots: Daniel Bruun, whose publications included *Fortidsminder og nutidshjem paa Island* (Archaeological Remains and Contemporary Households in Iceland, 1897) and the multi-volume *Turistruter paa Island* (Iceland: Routes over the Highlands, 1912–16), and Martin A. Hansen, author of *Rejse paa Island* (Journey through Iceland, 1954). While the subject-matter of Bruun's works is not that different from Kålund's work, Hansen describes his jeep trip around rural Iceland in the company of Danish artist Sven Havsteen-Mikkelsen in the spring and summer of 1952. *Rejse paa Island* is full of learned speculation about the sagas and their settings but also includes descriptions of whatever catches the contemporary eye and ear. Although Hansen and his companion do not explore the remote area in which *Hrafnkels saga* is set, their visit to Hlidarendi follows tradition faithfully; they are 'greeted warmly and accompanied to some ruins, said to be the remains of Gunnar's hall.'[30] And the author's imagination makes up for any disappointments resulting from reality not living up to his saga-derived expectations:

> It was extraordinary indeed how unsightly everything was at Hlidarendi, that the poverty of many centuries could steadily strip the place of all dignity. The vitality and leverage of the saga consequently became greater perhaps than it ever could have become otherwise. In an instant, the fiction became so overwhelming and importunate, that everything that once was, at this derelict place, could surely rise up from the ground at any moment, yes, one moment the madness and wonder of this great work could be sensed there, with death as its core motif . . .[31]

Poul Vad speaks warmly of *Rejse paa Island* and admits that he himself followed in the footsteps of Hansen, he is taking a literary pilgrimage along the same historic paths. Yet an unusual consciousness about the limitations of such tourism is evident in Vad's writing. He takes the example of one of his friends, a book-loving painter who travelled to Florence with the sole purpose of visiting the house in which Fyodor Dostoyevsky wrote *Idiot* (The Idiot, 1869). Vad then describes the psychological and even religious powers at play here:

> By linking a point in space with spiritual value, we give it meaning, charge it with a power that in turn works on us – the magical power of the sacred place. The pilgrimage is a spiritual exercise and not far from being a kind of necromancy practised by cultivated tourists.[32]

In an article discussing three Danish travel books, including the works by Hansen and Vad, Henk van der Liet suggests that in the quotation cited above, Vad is describing his own experience as a traveller.[33] It seems to me, however, that here, and indeed widely in his text, we can discern the kind of self-consciousness often termed romantic irony, referring to writers that express profound doubts about the premises of their own writing. Vad's final sarcastic words about the artist who visited Dostoyevsky's house in Florence offer a good case in point: 'Exhausted by this experience, he spent the rest of the day at a cafe over a small glass of wine. Thus a week went by.'[34]

Vad's unusual position as a travel writer is informed to some extent by his sceptical view of the Icelandic sagas as historical sources. He was influenced here by early twentieth-century scholars associated with the so-called 'Icelandic School' of saga studies. Unlike Hansen, who discusses the saga characters 'as though they were old friends and family members and above all as though these were really historical figures and not characters created by writers', Vad approaches them as the fictional creations of a thirteenth-century author.[35] He refers to Sigurður Nordal's influential 1940 *Hrafnkels saga Freysgoða* study, in which it is suggested that the saga 'bears all the marks of a distinguished novel'.[36] Vad says that this is why he would have chosen to go on a 'pilgrimage to the grave of the writer or to the farmstead, rectory or monastery where the writer of *Hrafnkels saga* had lived and worked', rather than to visit the putative setting of the saga. He adds that he knows full well 'that the place would not be able to add to my perception and understanding of a text that built its reality on words'.[37] So it is that he sets off somewhat half-heartedly from Egilsstadir in the direction of Adalbol in the Hrafnkelsdalur Valley. The locals from whom he seeks directions seem to know little about whether the route is passable or, even if it is, how long the journey will take. More than once the Dane comes close to abandoning his quest and repeatedly suggests that the journey will not end well.

This is, of course, a deft rhetorical device designed to encourage the reader to keep turning the pages, and indeed it is curiosity about how the tour will end that sustains the interest of most readers as they make their way through the many digressions of this unusual travel book, heavily laden with literary theory and philosophical reflections. But there is more to it than that; while the destinations that pilgrims such as Metcalfe, Waller and Hansen visited were situated in the past – the settings of particular sagas – Vad seems mainly driven by curiosity about the present, in particular about Páll Gíslason, a farmer at Adalbol. A local priest by the name of Arnór tells the Dane that Páll was,

> even on an Icelandic scale, no ordinary farmer, for he was renowned as a great and passionate book collector . . . This sent my imagination soaring to such heights that anything else Arnór said was lost on me – a book collector in the wasteland, so close and yet so difficult to reach him.[38]

In *Nord for Vatnajøkel* Páll becomes a modern-day substitute for the unknown saga writer, and his library the equivalent of the farm, rectory or monastery where the saga was written. Vad rejects the classic relationship between landscape and saga that typifies earlier travel writing and instead takes it upon himself to promote the nineteenth-century cliché about the book-loving Icelandic farmer.

Vad's description of his visit to Páll's farmstead covers two chapters that form the climax of his book. In the first of these, 'Architecture and Domestic Warmth in Hrafnkelsdalur', the description of the house at Adalbol is almost surreal, and in stark contrast to Hansen's description of the derelict house at Hlidarendi. The building at Adalbol is a stately, three-storey, avant-garde concrete box that shows no sign of agriculture being practised around it, nor is there any evidence of a professional architect having been involved in its design: 'there was no way to espy proportions between walls and windows; walls and windows were just there, as though disconnected from the laws of anything as trivial as "proportion".'[39] Nevertheless, in the eyes of the guest the house fits very well into the bleak and bare landscape. The atmosphere inside the farmhouse produces a similar effect; as if the lack of furniture were not enough, Páll's wife and son remind the guest more of a silent, modernist work of art than of flesh and blood individuals: 'Neither of them moved so much as a finger the whole time I sat opposite them; perhaps they didn't so much as blink either; one might think that they were under some kind of spell and no longer present in time.'[40]

At the end of this chapter, after unsuccessful attempts to get the farmer to discuss the saga or the library with him, Vad begins to feel uneasy and regrets having come to the house with his inane questions. But as he prepares to leave, Páll suddenly awakens from his trance. Not only does he offer to show the guest around his library, but invites him to stay for dinner. The next chapter, 'The Farmer's Library', begins with Vad and Páll leaving the library, and is followed by a description, first, of their modest meal, then of the two men saying goodbye to each other and, finally, of Vad's trip back to civilization in his rented Land Rover. At that point, it seems as though readers will never have the chance to explore the library, but later in the chapter – and in fact in the three chapters that follow – Vad slowly provides a fragmentary account of what took place there, by unfolding his discussions with various Icelanders over the next few

Páll Gíslason in his library in Adalbol, 1978.

days about his remarkable visit to Adalbol. The Dane discloses that his interlocutors warmed to him more when they learned that he had met Páll Gíslason, and it becomes clear that there are many colourful stories about the farmer that concern not just his cultural interests but also his physical prowess. It is widely believed, for example, that in his younger years Páll once fell into a raging glacial river and only managed to save himself and reach the riverbank through a miraculous display of strength and determination. The description is somewhat reminiscent of a chapter from Halldór Laxness's epic novel *Sjálfstætt fólk* (Independent People, 1934–5), in which the main character, the farmer Bjartur, involuntarily crosses a glacial river on the back of a reindeer bull and is finally compelled to reach the far side on his own. At this point Páll not only becomes a modern incarnation of the old saga writers, but a symbol of the classic Icelandic saga hero, deterred neither by injury nor fear of death. So it is that (despite his best intentions) Vad is stuck in the same literary-cultural ruts as most of his predecessors.

The core of Vad's narrative is still that at Adalbol, of all places, can be found a remarkable library of old and newer books of every shape, size and theme, some of them very valuable:

> The mass of books itself had a strong effect on me; but I didn't forget either, for a single moment while I stood in that confined room with the softly spoken, and yet enormous farmer and passionate book collector, that I was in the middle of the wasteland; that I had first flown over sea and land to this island in the Atlantic, that I had subsequently come by coach half way around the island and finally by Land Rover to arrive at this desolate, bleak district, to reach this wonder of high culture preserved behind locked doors, to the amazing treasure there that was as inaccessible to thieves and predators as it was to ignorant eyes in his own house.[41]

In fact, the description of the library and its owner becomes an allegory for the miracle represented by the creation and preservation of the medieval sagas in Iceland, and the great influence they have exercised on reality over time. When it comes down to it, Vad's pilgrimage is not a journey into the Icelandic landscape but rather into the all-encompassing and evocative world of literature.

In the last chapter featuring the library at Adalbol, Vad recalls Páll drawing his attention to a book by Daniel Bruun. Vad admits he was inadvertently filled with pride when he saw a work by his compatriot in that remote place, but at the same time he reminds his readers that Bruun belonged to that earlier group of writers who believed that saga descriptions were historically reliable. Vad goes on to speculate about the changes that have taken place in Hrafnkelsdalur valley, not just since the time of settlement but also during the century or so since Bruun visited Adalbol and conversed with the farmer. His name was Elías, and he had been forced temporarily to abandon farming in the valley after the volcanic eruption in the area in 1875.

This fact provides Vad with the opportunity to contemplate the changing nature of both natural and man-made structures, at least when compared with literary artefacts:

> Even stone palaces crumble; and new volcanic activity could make the Hrafnkelsdalur Valley uninhabitable once again. Should that happen, people would doubtless return sooner or later. But so it seems that *Hrafnkels saga Freysgoða* and the fictitious Adalbol, seen from a human perspective – the only one we know – are the most enduring of all in Hrafnkelsdalur Valley.[42]

This and many similar comments in Vad's work may encourage us to describe his book as a postmodern travel story, a narrative that truly demonstrates how texts shape reality or, at least, our sense of it.

Amalie Materna as the Wagnerian heroine Brünnhilde, from a production of *Der Ring des Nibelungen*, 1898.

FIVE

Odin: From Wagner to Viking Metal

The actor Jack Black once summed up the repertoire of Led Zeppelin as 'songs about love, about Vikings, about Vikings making love'.[1] He was speaking in 2012 at the annual Kennedy Center Honors ceremony celebrating the influence of artists and entertainers on American culture. Black opened his tribute to the band by claiming they were 'the greatest rock 'n' roll band of all time, better than the Beatles, better than the Stones, even better than Tenacious D' (a comedy rock duo that Black himself formed with Kyle Gass in the 1990s). He suggested that those who didn't agree with his verdict were probably hampered by their never having done the Zeppelin marathon: 'the Zep-athon is where you sit your ass down and listen to all nine Zep albums in a row, the thing that every true fan must do at least once in their lifetime. [It's] the pilgrimage to heavy metal mecca.'[2]

I must admit that I belong to that tedious group of music lovers who think the Beatles were the greatest rock 'n' roll band of all time. More to the point, I disagree with Black's potted version of Led Zeppelin's subject-matter. The band – consisting of singer Robert Plant, guitarist Jimmy Page, bassist and keyboardist John Paul Jones and drummer John Bonham – certainly sang numerous songs about love, but very few about Vikings, and none of those (as far as I can tell) are concerned with lovemaking. Still, I believe that the quartet not only deserves an eminent place in the Rock and Roll Hall of Fame, but should be recognized for its decisive role in making Icelandic medieval literature topical in the context of modern music history. In this chapter, I seek to present Led Zeppelin, in particular Plant and Page's legendary 'Immigrant Song', as a link between two widely separated ends of the musical afterlife of the eddas, represented most notably in the past by Richard Wagner's opera cycle, *Der Ring des Nibelungen* (The Ring of the Nibelung, 1869–76), and in the present by that popular subgenre of heavy metal music known as Viking metal.

'In Walhall want I him not'

The imperative refrain of 'Immigrant Song' is a suicidal war cry in which Plant addresses Valhalla, as if it were a person, and claims that he and the band are coming to it. He is referring to the popular idea that Vikings were especially eager and valiant warriors because they believed that death in battle would secure them eternal life in the noble company of the gods. This notion is communicated in several medieval Icelandic texts, including *Snorra Edda*, where one of Odin's aliases is Valfadir (father of the slain), 'since all those who fall in battle are his adopted sons. He assigns them places in Val-hall and Vingolf, and they are then known as Einheriar.'[3] The women who serve Odin – the Valkyries – are said to be sent by him 'to every battle. They allot death to men and govern victory.'[4] Furthermore, *Snorra Edda* describes the afterlife of the Einherjar in Asgard as an endless rerun of their violent existence on Earth:

> Each day after they have got dressed they put on war-gear and go out into the courtyard and fight each other and they fall each upon the other. This is their sport. And when dinner-time approaches they ride back to Val-hall and sit down to drink.[5]

For the post-medieval dissemination of these ideas, Thomas Bartholin's *Antiquitatum danicarum de causis contemptae Danis adhuc gentilibus mortis* (Danish Antiquities Concerning the Causes of the Danes' Contempt of Death, 1689) became an essential source. As Margaret Clunies Ross has noted: 'One of Bartholin's most influential ideas about Nordic religion . . . was that the pagan Scandinavians were so brave in battle and scorned death because they believed in reincarnation and the transmigration of souls.'[6] Numerous works on Nordic mythology and Viking culture, along with translations and adaptations of material from the eddas and sagas, continued to inform generations of eighteenth- and nineteenth-century Europeans about the violent yet glorious afterlife of the Einherjar in Odin's Valhalla (the literal meaning of the word is 'the hall of the slain'). The idea was so ubiquitous that when King Ludwig I of Bavaria commissioned a memorial temple dedicated to the great figures from German history, which was to be constructed above the Danube River near Regensburg, he chose not to call it a Pantheon, like the Greek and French buildings on which it was modelled, but Walhalla. At the inauguration of the edifice in 1842, the king proclaimed: 'Might Walhalla be useful to the growing strength and to the increase of German feelings.'[7]

When it comes to early musical contributions to this tradition, Johann Ernst Hartmann was an important pioneer. He was a German-born violinist who moved to Denmark in the 1760s and became concertmaster of the Royal Danish Orchestra. In the late 1770s he composed music to *Balders Død* (The Death of Baldur, 1775), a play in verse written by the Danish poet Johannes Ewald. Loosely based on the myth about the death of Baldur, as related in *Snorra Edda* and *Gesta Danorum* (Deeds of the Danes), written by the twelfth-century Danish historian Saxo Grammaticus, Ewald and Hartmann's musical drama premiered in 1779. It later became a model for a series of theatrical works, primarily German, relating how Hod is tricked by Loki into killing his righteous brother Baldur. Ewald accentuates the tragic love of Nanna for her husband Baldur, but also the role of the three singing and dancing Valkyries, who echo the witches of Shakespeare's

Macbeth.[8] At the same time, these women, who were supposed to carry both shields and spears, pointed towards the future: 'Hartmann's Valkyrie music seems to anticipate that of Richard Wagner', writes Frederick Key Smith, referring to the dark minor-key elements characteristic of the opera's orchestral interludes.[9]

During the early nineteenth century, Hartmann's grandson and namesake, Johan P. E. Hartmann, became one the most prolific European composers involved in the recycling of medieval Scandinavian themes. In 1832 he was asked to write the background score for a public recital of 'Guldhornene' (The Golden Horns, 1802), a poem Adam Oehlenschläger had composed after two priceless medieval (musical or drinking) horns had been stolen from the Royal Chamber of Art in Copenhagen and melted down for their gold. A few years later, Hartmann wrote *Olaf den Hellige* (St Olaf), Op. 23 (1838) to accompany Oehlenschläger's 1836 verse tragedy inspired by *Heimskringla*. Hartmann's breakthrough, however, came first with his ten-minute overture to Oehlenschläger's earlier play, *Hakon Jarl hin Rige* (Earl Hakon the Great, 1807), also inspired by *Heimskringla*. This solemn, dramatic piece was first performed in 1844 at the Royal Danish Theatre, between the prologue and the first act of the play, and was warmly received. 'With the Hakon Jarl overture', Inger Sørensen states:

> Hartmann consolidated the Nordic sound he had begun in Guldhornene and continued in the music for Olaf den Hellige. The pairing of the gloomy minor motifs with the dark instrumentation with the many brasses was for the Danes of the Golden Age the epitome of the sound of the remote past.[10]

Hartmann also wrote music for several ballets created by the choreographer August Bournonville. These included *Valkyrien* (The Valkyrie, 1861) and *Thrymskviden* (The Lay of Thrym, 1868). The plot of the earlier ballet, which was inspired by Saxo Grammaticus' *Gesta Danorum*, focuses on Odin's dealings with King Harald Wartooth and his son Helge, who is killed in battle and falls in love with the Valkyrie who is supposed to deliver him to Valhalla. The second ballet was based on the eddic poem *Þrymskviða* which, as we noted in Chapter One, describes Thor's attempts to regain his stolen hammer from the giant Thrym. Hartmann then set out to compose a substantial choral work based on a selection of strophes from Frederik Winkel Horn's 1869 Danish retelling of *Völuspá*. During the composer's lifetime, *Vølvens Spaadom* (The Prophecy of the Seeress), Op. 71 (1870–72) 'became his most frequently performed work' and has remained a part of the Danish musical canon ever since.[11]

During this period, German intellectuals, musicians and artists began to regard the Middle High German poem *Das Nibelungenlied* (The Song of the Nibelungs) as 'a treasure of German cultural heritage', while at the same time realizing the extent to which it related to various medieval Icelandic sources, notably the eddas and *Völsunga saga*.[12] Respected composers such as Felix Mendelssohn considered composing operas based on this material. Friedrich Theodor Vischer went so far as to publish a libretto for such a work and the poetess Louise Otto-Peters tried to convince both Robert Schumann and Niels W. Gade to make music for the libretto that she was planning to write.[13] It was against this background that Richard Wagner, already an established opera composer, began to realize his ambitious plan of composing a series of 'dramas', as he chose to call them, based on characters and themes derived from Nordic mythology and from Icelandic and German poems and prose texts about the Nibelungen royal family.

Much has been written on the long and complex gestation of this monumental effort, which started with an exaggeratedly theatrical ten-page plot summary written by Wagner in the autumn of 1848. At the time, the composer's idea was to create just a single opera called *Siegfrieds Tod* (Death of Siegfried). According to this first draft it was to open with scenes explaining how the dwarf Alberich had a ring made from the noble Rhine gold 'that lent him rulership of all his race, the Nibelungen: so he became their master, forced them to work for him alone, and amassed the priceless *Nibelungen-Hoard*'.[14] The rest of the plot was supposed to centre around the attempts of different groups of characters – giants, gods and mortals – to seize either this treasure or the powerful but cursed ring. Lust, jealousy and revenge were also expected to play a part in the story, with the hero Siegfried being torn between his love for the Valkyrie Brünnhilde (Brynhild) and his desire for the mortal Gutrune (Gudrun). The most substantial part of the plot was devoted to the attempts of Hagen (Alberich's son and Gutrune's half-brother) to regain the ring from Siegfried. Hagen succeeds in killing Siegfried by hurling a spear at his back, but it is Brünnhilde who claims the reward, puts the ring on her own finger and mounts a burning funeral pyre with Siegfried's body:

> At like time the waters of the Rhine invade the entrance to the Hall: on their waves the three Water-maids bear away the Ring and Helmet. Hagen dashes after them, to snatch the treasure, as if demented, – the Daughters seize and drag him with them to the deep.[15]

Short as it was, this summary remained the blueprint for the composer's labours over the following thirty years.

Der Ring des Nibelungen developed into a cycle of four related works: *Das Rheingold* (The Rhinegold), *Die Walküre* (The Valkyrie), *Siegfried* and *Götterdämmerung* (Twilight of the Gods). The first two were premiered in 1869 and 1870 and the remaining two in 1876, when the whole Ring Cycle was staged for the first time. The total playing time of this monumental sequence amounts to some fifteen hours and it is usually divided into performances over four evenings. Its cast of characters includes the gods Wotan (Odin), Fricka (Frigg), Freia (Freyja), Donner (Thor), Froh (Freyr), Erda (Earth) and Loge (Loki), nine Valkyries, along with a handful of witches, Rhine maidens, giants, dwarfs and mortals. The mortals include Wotan's twin children Siegmund and Sieglinde, and their incestuous son Siegfried.

Walhall (Valhalla) itself is first mentioned in the final scene of *Das Rheingold* when Wotan, who has been busy finding a suitable way of paying the giants Fasolt and Fafner for building him an imposing castle, reaches out for Fricka's hand and says: 'Follow me wife! In Walhall.'[16] Fricka, who finds this name for their new home somewhat outlandish, asks her husband what it means, to which he replies rather mysteriously: 'What my spirit has found / to master my dread / when triumph is won, maketh the meaning clear.'[17] The implication of the name becomes somewhat clearer in the second act of *Die Walküre* when Wotan orders his Valkyrie daughter, Brünnhilde, to make sure that Siegmund will be successful in his impending combat with the warrior Hunding. But at the same time, Wotan is not interested in having Hunding join his force of Einherjar. Accordingly he declares: 'There let Hunding go, / where he belongs; / in Walhall want I him not.'[18] Later in the opera, Wotan enlightens Brünnhilde about her role as a Valkyrie and how it relates to his aim of making Walhall a secure fortress:

> I bade you to bring me:
> the slaves we had held
> by our laws in bondage,
> the mortals whom
> in their might we defied,
> whom, enthralled by darksome,
> treacherous bargains,
> we bound in obedience
> blindly to serve us –
> these ever to storm
> and strife should ye kindle,

their hearts rouse up
to ruthless war,
that valiant host of heroes
should gather on Walhall's height![19]

As Árni Björnsson has revealed, Wagner's ideas about 'Walhall' seem mainly to have been based on the testimonies of 'Gylfaginning' in *Snorra Edda* and on the eddic poem *Grímnismál* (Sayings of Grimnir). Both of these works were available to the composer in German versions, along with numerous other related works. In return, Wagner's operas made an immensely strong impact on popular Western European ideas about Nordic mythology for years to come. This influence was not limited to Europe, as can be seen by the choice of name for the American hamlet of Valhalla in Mount Pleasant in New York State. The local post office had been given this name in the nineteenth century – apparently because the postmaster's wife was a great fan of Wagner's operas – and in the early twentieth century the German immigrant Franz Xaver Reiter suggested that the name should be adopted by the small town.[20] A well-respected horn player, Reiter had taken part in numerous opera productions and was particularly well versed in Wagner's *Der Ring des Nibelungen*.[21]

The hundred-year period that leads from the debut of Wagner's *Das Rheingold* and *Die Walküre* to the release of Led Zeppelin's 'Immigrant Song' is criss-crossed by quite a few well-known European composers who wrote music for poems, librettos and plays based on the eddas or sagas, and by others who composed instrumental music inspired by this literature. In 1872 the Norwegian composer Edvard Grieg wrote incidental music to the *Heimskringla*-inspired play *Sigurd Jorsalfar* (Sigurd the Crusader, 1872) by his countryman Bjørnstjerne Bjørnson. Grieg composed the music as an orchestral suite, and later attempted to create a score for an opera about King Olaf Tryggvason. In 1898 the Swedish composer Carl Wilhelm Stenhammar composed music for *Tirfing*, an opera libretto by Anna Boberg based on the

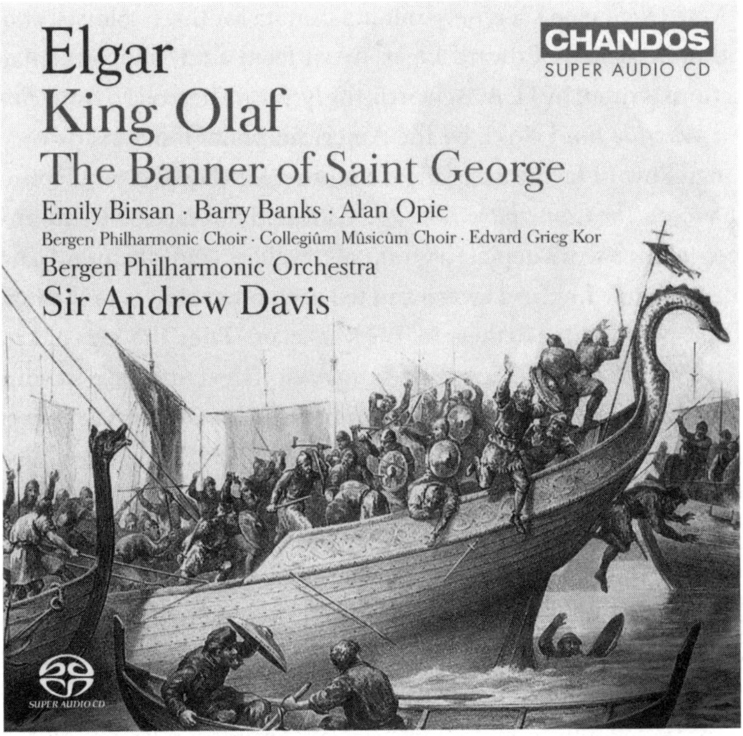

A cover of Elgar's *Scenes from the Saga of King Olaf*, released on a CD by Chandos in 2015.

legendary *Hervarar saga og Heiðreks* (Saga of Hervor and Heidrek). Ten years later, Carl Nielsen's *Saga-Drøm* (Gunnar's Dream, 1908) was first performed; this tone poem for orchestra was inspired by the chapter from *Njáls saga* in which Gunnar of Hlidarendi has a premonition of his younger brother's death in a dream. Later in the twentieth century, Icelandic composer Jón Leifs wrote a number of pieces, varying in scale, inspired by themes and motifs from the eddas and sagas. These include the symphony *Söguhetjur* (Saga Symphony, 1941–2), the 'choreographic drama' *Baldr* (Baldur, 1943–7) and the monumental oratorio *Edda I–III* (1939–64).

One of the compositions of this period that represent a clear landmark along the path which we are tracing is *Scenes from the Saga of King Olaf* (1896), a ninety-minute cantata for three soloists, choir and orchestra, by Edward Elgar. Apart from a few supplementary sections written by H. A. Acworth, the lyrics are borrowed from *Tales of a Wayside Inn* (1863), by the American poet Henry Wadsworth Longfellow (a favourite of Elgar's mother). Modelled on Geoffrey Chaucer's *The Canterbury Tales* and Giovanni Boccaccio's *Decameron*, Longfellow's work depicts a group of travellers who sit around a fireside in a New England tavern and tell each other stories in the form of epic poems. One of these is 'The Musician's Tale: The Saga of King Olaf', which relates King Olaf Tryggvason's eventful life in some twenty episodes, with particular emphasis on his attempts to convert Norway to Christianity. In the first episode, 'The Challenge of Thor', the Nordic thunder god challenges Olaf to battle, while in the final episode, which takes place after the king has been killed, his mother hears the voice of St John proclaiming: 'Love is eternal! / God is still God, and / His faith shall not fail us; / Christ is eternal!'[22] As Andrew Wawn notes, *Ólafs saga Tryggvasonar*, as related in *Heimskringla*,

> provided a little-known provincial composer with the raw material from which he produced an old northern cantata – the first ever in Britain, and the first of a series of major choral and symphonic works that made him one of Britain's best-loved composers.[23]

Nine of Longfellow's episodes became the backbone of Elgar's somewhat Wagnerian composition, including 'The Wrath of Odin', which describes how a mysterious one-eyed visitor sits at one of King Olaf's feasts and speaks 'of heroes and their deeds, / Of lands and cities he had seen, / And stormy gulfs that tossed between'. Furthermore, 'from his lips in music rolled / The Havamal of Odin old.'[24] Musically, however, 'The Challenge of Thor' is often regarded as the most striking part of the cantata. It opens with the bass soloist singing very deep lines supplied by Acworth: 'Summon now the God of Thunder, / Him who rives the heav'ns asunder / Sing the words of mighty Thor / Challenging the world to war.'[25] A powerful chorus of male and female voices then presents Longfellow's verses, while the orchestral writing lends the scene appropriate dramatic intensity:

I am the God Thor,
I am the War God,
I am the Thunderer!
Here in my Northland,
My fastness and fortress,
Reign I forever!

Here amid icebergs
Rule I the nations;
This is my hammer,
Miölner the mighty;
Giants and sorcerers
Cannot withstand it!

These are the gauntlets
Wherewith I wield it,
And hurl it afar off;
This is my girdle;
Whenever I brace it,
Strength is redoubled![26]

Elgar's treatment of Longfellow's poetry served further to strengthen the place of Nordic mythology in orchestral and choral music, and foreshadowed the adaptation of that mythology in late twentieth- and early twenty-first-century rock music.

'Rumbo al Valhalla'

Robert Plant and Jimmy Page's 'Immigrant Song' is both the earliest and the most influential of Led Zeppelin's Viking tracks. It was released in 1970, first as a single and then on the band's third studio album, *Led Zeppelin III*. The libretto begins with a legendary war cry from vocalist Plant, who then describes how he and his companions are rowing with their oars from a land which is characterized by midnight sun, snow, ice and hot springs. Their destination is the shores or new lands in the west, and their purpose is to fight in a battle with a horde.[27] References in the lyrics to Valhalla and Thor's hammer suggest this is a mantra chanted by a group of Vikings sailing their ship to battle. But in other respects, the lyrics are ambiguous, as is evident on Internet blog sites where Zeppelin fans debate both the origin and destination of these warriors. Some suggest that the Vikings must be leaving northern Norway and heading to the western coast of the British Isles, while others claim that the allusion to the geysers must point towards Iceland, and therefore associate the new lands they seek with Leif Eriksson's discovery of Vinland. But neither of these competing readings seems particularly well suited to explain the second half of the lyrics, in which the ferocious initial battle cry is juxtaposed with eccentric tropes of hope and harmony. Peace is supposed to replace the war between the invaders and the locals in the west. The addressees of the lyrics are encouraged to give in to their new overlords and reconstruct all their ruins.[28] The message seems to be that those who fall prey to Viking raids should have the good sense to lay down their arms and amiably submit to the aggressive immigrant force.

Page and Plant may have been familiar with the works of both Wagner and Elgar when they composed 'Immigrant Song', but another possible source for their reference to Valhalla is *The Mighty Thor* comic series that we discussed in Chapter One. Irrespective of how conscious the members of Led Zeppelin were of the earlier musical afterlife of the eddas, the lyrics referring to Valhalla probably stimulated more or less instinctively a set of images and ideas relating to Nordic mythology and Viking culture in the minds of the band's audience. By combining these ideas with a repeated staccato riff and the 'relentless chopping of the synchronized bass-guitar-drums rhythm', something new and exceptional was being created; in Andy Bennett's words, 'an aesthetic link between rock music and Pagan beliefs'.[29]

'Immigrant Song' and some later Led Zeppelin tunes – in particular 'No Quarter' from their album *House of the Holy* (1973) – are commonly seen as prototypes for the development of the genre of Viking metal. Musically and ideologically, the genre is generally associated with several other schools of metal rock, in particular death metal and black metal, as developed in the 1980s and '90s. Within all these genres, there is an emphasis on distorted guitar sounds and tremolo picking, aggressive drumming and prominent rhythm changes, along with death grunts and growled vocals. In their lyrics, costumes and performances, death and black metal bands eagerly flirt with mysticism, Satanism and atheist attitudes.[30] Within Viking metal this ideology is largely replaced by the principles of pagan tradition. Simon Trafford and Aleks Pluskowski link these three movements as follows:

> Extreme and obsessive loathing of Christianity had long been a norm – a cliché, even – of death and black metallers, but Bathory and, in the 1990s, many other bands and fans began to turn away from Satan and place their faith in the Vikings, and more specifically in Oðin, as the foremost champions of opposition to Christianity. Many claim affiliation to Ásatrú [modern belief in the pagan Nordic gods] . . . Whereas many proponents of Ásatrú are hippyish and peaceable New Agers, the slant put on the religion by most of the black metallers who claim devotion to the Aesir is militant and normally

> fiercely patriotic or racist: Christianity is regularly dismissed as a 'foreign, slave religion', whereas northern Europeans should actually be true to their old gods.[31]

Members of some of these bands went so far as to support and participate in church burnings – an endemic problem in Norway in the 1990s – but in other cases the adaptation of the pagan heritage has been a more frivolous affair, and even intertwined with a genuine interest in folk music and medieval literature.

The extent to which lyrics by numerous Viking metal bands represent formulaic echoes of Page and Plant's line announcing the Vikings' coming to Valhalla is quite remarkable. The lines to 'Gates of Valhalla' on the album *Into Glory Ride* (1983) by the American band Manowar are written from the perspective of a Viking about to die from his battle wounds, but he seems happy to acknowledge that the gods are waiting for him in Valhalla and implores Odin's hall to open its gates and embrace him.[32] The song 'Valhalla' from the album *Hammerheart* (1990) by the Swedish band Bathory is a parallel example; in the opening lines Thor, the god of thunder, is addressed and implored to swing his hammer, Mjolnir, but the lyrics end with a description of the dead warriors who are waiting

The cover of Mighty Thor's *Rumbo al Valhalla* (2011).

with golden shields for the speaker of the verse and his colleagues to join them in Valhalla.[33] A third example is found in the music of the Mexican band Mighty Thor: the refrain to the title song of their *Rumbo al Valhalla* (2011) goes: '*Y en manos de mi señor estoy / rumbo al Valhalla voy*' (I am in the hands of my master, / now I'm going to Valhalla at last).[34]

There are certainly several variations on the theme. A more elaborate perspective is found in the lyrics of 'Odin Owns Ye All' by the Norwegian band Einherjer on their 1998 album of the same name. A Viking sits by a fire facing four empty chairs and drinks to the memory of friends who have died in battle. He is certain that a Valkyrie has found them on the battlefield and is wishing them all the best on their journey to Odin's abode.[35] Similarly, the words to the song 'Hail to the Hammer' from the album *How Far to Asgaard* (2002), produced by the Faroese band Týr, describe the life of a Viking at home during winter, when the winds blow and darkness prevails. Men pass the time by telling stories of those who have already fallen in battle, while at the same time looking forward to setting off on raids the following summer. The text evokes Thor and the forces of nature that he represents:

> Hail to the hammer, Hail to the hammer
> To the god of thunder
> The god that's protecting us all
> All hail to the giant hunter
> And hail to the forces of nature all.[36]

Trafford and Pluskowski trace the development of Viking metal from bands such as Manowar and Bathory in the 1970s and '80s – where occasional references to the pagan past were largely embellishments – to Scandinavian bands of recent decades for whom the pagan beliefs of Viking times have become a central theme and shape not only the lyrics but album cover designs, stage performances and the bands' multifarious promotional material. They refer in that context to Moonsorrow from Finland, Thyrfing from Sweden and Enslaved from Norway, and also make particular reference to the cover of Einherjer's *Odin Owns Ye All*,

> which includes a representation of the one-eyed god and his two ravens, flanked by ornamentation reminiscent of the spiralling tendrils and animals found on Urnes stave church . . . You could be forgiven for assuming these were album covers from a Scandinavian folk band, but images of the band members themselves – sullen and aggressive, wearing black leather and chain mail – leave no doubt and exemplify the dual character of Viking Metal: the diabolical and masculine heritage of earlier Metal combined with a conscious link to a glorious pre-Christian ancestral past.[37]

This Janus-like appearance is the trademark of various Viking metal bands all around the globe, including Mighty Thor. The cover of *Rumbo al Valhalla* shows a Thor-like Viking with a winged helmet who fights his way through a blizzard towards a towering castle – perhaps Valhalla? On their posters, the band members are typically dressed in black T-shirts and black leather trousers, and are shown holding imposing swords.

The number and range of Viking metal bands is considerable.[38] Some of them, for instance the disreputable Varg Vikernes (alias Count Grishnackh) of the Norwegian one-man band Burzum, seem to have been inspired by the works of Tolkien – a tradition that can probably be traced back to the lyrics of Led Zeppelin's 'Ramble On' from 1969 and Black Sabbath's 'The Wizard' from 1970.[39] Others make explicit references to the operas of Wagner, as indicated by the album title *Rheingold* (2003), by the German band Grave Digger. In this context, it is also worth mentioning the Italian one-man metal band Solarsteinn, who recorded in 2013 'The Challenge of Thor', a

Promotional photo for the Mexican band Mighty Thor.

twenty-minute suite inspired by an episode from Longfellow's 'The Saga of King Olaf'.[40]

The most fanatical bands in the Viking metal tradition have been linked to neo-pagan groups and in some cases to National Socialist black metal.[41] Other bands have rejected neo-Nazism and racism and associate the pagan elements of their music with other political interests. The Faroese band Týr are a remarkable example. On their album *The Lay of Thrym* (2011), the lyrics of the title-song interpret Thrym's capture of Thor's hammer in a rather unusual way, namely as a dictator's attempt to suppress those who desire freedom: 'Hammertheft and all the world bereft / Of reason and of right overnight / Left between a tyrant's temper mean / And treason and betrayal, cold and stale'.[42] Yet in its conclusion, the song predicts that Thrym and other tyrants of the world will be toppled from power:

> You stand only for your own
> Any man may throw you off the throne
> Seat will not be set for thee
> At the league of free nations
> May this mark the end of your reign
> Let the lay of Thrym be heard
> Leave no tyrant out there undeterred
> Thunderstruck theocracy

Jimmy Page, from Led Zeppelin's concert in Reykjavík, 1970.

This theodicy heathen
In the end the giant was slain
Hammer home to any despot's dome
That tales of tyranny end with me.[43]

The song 'Take Your Tyrant' on the same album adopts a similar stance: 'Everybody take your tyrant / Make him pay for all his stay / Revolution take your tyrant / Bid him bleed for all his greed.'[44] In an interview, band singer Heri Joensen acknowledged that he was a supporter of Faroese independence from Denmark, but denied that 'Take Your Tyrant' and other songs with comparable lyrics by him on the album referred to the Faroese independence movement: 'That was mostly inspired by events in the Arab Spring. I was not really thinking about actual independence with us.'[45]

Some of the more original and inventive Viking metal bands have followed Wagner's (and Marvel's) example and created their own narratives to fit within the pagan mythological frame of reference. The album *Börn Loka* (Loki's Children, 2012), by the Icelandic band

Skálmöld, contains a series of linked lyrics about the hero Hilmar Baldursson, whom Odin calls upon to obliterate Loki's children in the opening song. The following tracks describe how Odin lends Hilmar his eight-footed horse Sleipnir and how Hilmar battles with Fenrir, the World Serpent, and Hel. Most of these lyrics refer cleverly to the narrative of the eddas. The lines of the song 'Gleipnir', for example, are based on the description in *Snorra Edda* of how Fenrir was tied up and, in revenge, bit off Tyr's hand.[46] Other bands have followed the example of Johan P. E. Hartmann and used lines from specific eddic poems, largely unaltered, either in translation or even in the original Icelandic. The words to the songs 'Out of Ginnungagap' and 'A New Earth' on Einherjer's *Odin Owns Ye All* (1998) are, for example, partially copied from W. H. Auden and Paul B. Taylor's 1969 English translation of *Völuspá*.

It is hard to say just how much influence Viking metal has had on public conceptions of pagan beliefs and Nordic mythology in the past decades. As Heather O'Donoghue points out, this kind of music 'has a cult following, rather than any appeal to popular culture. Popular appeal would probably be accounted artistic failure.'[47] On the other hand, it is interesting to note how widely Viking metal bands pop up and how unequivocally they connect with the mythological heritage, for instance in their choice of names. Ásmegin from Norway, Hel and Thrym from Sweden, Sleipnir from Britain, Helrunar from Germany, Baldrs Draumar from the Netherlands, Midgaard from Russia, Hildr Valkyrie from Greece and Horde Thor from Columbia are decisive examples. At the end of their article, Trafford and Pluskowski seek to explain the growing popularity of this musical genre and point to the influence of fantasy literature and films, among other things. But they also remind us of the classic role of rock music as a symbol of impatient youthful rebellion against all that is conventional and acknowledged: 'Escape into a stirring past, like rock 'n' roll decadence, may be an understandably attractive alternative to the horrors of respectable middle-class life in an affluent, enlightened European democracy.'[48]

Returning to Jack Black's claim that Led Zeppelin sang 'songs about love, about Vikings, about Vikings making love', I believe it would be more accurate to say that the band, just like so many Viking metal bands that followed their lead, sang songs about Vikings, about Vikings killing and about Vikings making their way to Odin's Valhalla. As for whether the land of the midnight sun described in 'Immigrant Song' was Norway or Iceland, I deliberately chose not to mention earlier that Robert Plant himself resolved that dispute by explaining that the lyrics were written during Led Zeppelin's summer tour to Reykjavík, Bath and Berlin in 1970: 'We did come from the land of the ice and snow', Plant stated:

> We were guests of the Icelandic Government on a cultural mission. We were invited to play a concert in Reykjavik and the day before we arrived all the civil servants went on strike and the gig was going to be cancelled. The university prepared a concert hall for us and it was phenomenal. The response from the kids was remarkable and we had a great time. 'Immigrant Song' was about that trip.[49]

This revelation, however, may force me to reconsider the earlier response to Jack Black. If the overlords of the 'Immigrant Song' are truly the four members of Led Zeppelin, the local kids coming to their concerts in Reykjavík, Bath and Berlin are possibly the subjects who should rebuild their ruins. Perhaps the song is, after all, about making love rather than war.

SIX

Leif: When Civilization Was Less Civilized

'From the pages of history, the missing chapter: *Erik the Viking*. A time when civilization was less civilized, dating was dangerous and peace looked a lot like war.'[1] These words are spoken in the voiceover for the trailer of *Erik the Viking* (1989) by the British writer and comedian Terry Jones. The film was partially inspired by Jones's children's book *The Saga of Erik the Viking* (1983), but it was no less shaped by the surreal humour that Jones and his collaborators had developed in the television series *Monty Python's Flying Circus* (1969–74). As the narrator says, 'A time when civilization was less civilized', we see a close-up shot of a group of drunk, bearded men in a feudal hall. One of them grits his teeth at the camera and throws an axe at a timber wall, landing it very close to the face of a frightened woman whose long, blonde plaits are nailed to the wood – it appears that she, or her hair, is the intended target. As we cut to a new scene, the actor John Cleese, also from the Monty Python group, appears in the role of an unkempt medieval man with fur across his shoulders, standing outside in the cold among a group of children. He holds a knife to the throat of one of the girls and says menacingly: 'Throw down your weapons – or we'll kill the children.'[2] He appears to be addressing a gawky group of men armed with swords and standing thigh-deep in a small pond. When they throw their weapons aside, Cleese adds: 'Well, now we'll just kill the children anyway.'[3] Finally, when the narrator declares that 'dating was dangerous', we see the film's eponymous hero, played by American actor Tim

'Odin's test' in Terry Jones's fantasy film *Erik the Viking* (1989).

Robbins, break through a door and make an awkward attempt to rape a defenceless woman.

These three scenes amount to no more than fifteen seconds, yet that's all it takes to present most of the key international cinematic clichés about Nordic Vikings. 'In the standard Viking film', writes Kevin J. Harty, 'the Viking is easily stereotyped as aggressive berserker – the savage, uncivilized other bent on marauding, pillaging, burning, raping, kidnapping, and killing.'[4] These words set the tone for *The Vikings on Film* (2011), a collection of articles edited by Harty, in which he and other scholars examine this particular film genre from a variety of perspectives. The history of the genre can be traced back to the beginning of the twentieth century when two silent films featuring Vikings were made: *The Viking's Bride* (1907) by the British director Lewin Fitzhamon, and *The Viking's Daughter: The Story of the Ancient Norsemen* (1908) by the American director James Stuart Blackton. Seven years later, a further two American films premiered: *The Oath of a Viking* (1914), directed by James Searle Dawley, and *The Viking Queen* (1914), directed by Walter Edwin. Apart from the last title, these were all romances. In *The Viking's Bride* and *The Oath of a Viking*, two Vikings fight over the same woman, while *The Viking's Daughter* is about an Anglo-Saxon prince enslaved by Vikings, but after he saves the life of the chieftain's daughter – who duly falls in love with him – the two of them are allowed to marry.

One or more of these early films may have influenced the production of *The Viking* (1928), directed by Roy William Neill. It was one of the last great American silent films, as well as the first feature-length Technicolor movie to feature a soundtrack. The script was loosely based on a popular novel by Ottilie A. Liljencrantz, which in turn was inspired by the Icelandic Vinland Sagas. The novel and the film deal with Leif Eriksson's journey to North America around the year 1000. Leif is depicted in both forms as a Christian emissary, and is in most ways the antithesis of the formulaic wild Viking described by Harty. In this chapter, we will trace the journey of Leif and his crew from the pages of Icelandic manuscripts to Liljencrantz's book, and then to the cinema. We will then focus on another influential movie, *The Vikings* (1958), directed by Richard Fleischer. Here, all the characteristics of the savage Vikings, which are condensed into the trailer of Terry Jones's *Erik the Viking*, find full expression.

'You shall carry good luck with you'

Ottilie A. Liljencrantz, who died in the prime of life in 1910, at the age of 34, had a short but productive career as a novelist. During a span of only a few years, she published four historical novels: *The Thrall of Leif the Lucky* (1902), *The Ward of King Canute* (1903), *The Vinland Champions* (1904) and *Randvar the Songsmith* (1906).[5] Apart from the second title, which focuses on the Danish conquest of Britain, all of these deal with the medieval discovery of America. On the promotional material sent out by the Chicago publisher of *The Thrall of Leif the Lucky*, Liljencrantz was apparently introduced as having 'Viking blood in her veins'.[6] Similarly, in a write-up published in the *Chicago Daily Tribune*, the novel was characterized as a work dealing with the author's 'hardy forefathers who sought to spread the Christian religion throughout Greenland'.[7] These comments, referring to the background of Liljencrantz's father as a Swedish immigrant to the United States, are illustrative of the way in which the nineteenth- and early twentieth-century discourse on medieval Icelandic literature on both sides of the Atlantic Ocean was preoccupied with questions of ethnic origins and race.[8]

In the write-up it was also stated that *The Thrall of Leif the Lucky* was 'based upon historical fact, but the author takes the privilege of the novelist in creating a number of exciting situations'.[9] The concept of 'historical fact' might be overstated in this context, but as Liljencrantz explained in the 'Note of Acknowledgement' in the first pages of the novel, she had studied much of what had been written about Leif Eriksson during her lifetime. In particular, she mentioned the works of Rasmus B. Anderson, an enterprising American scholar and translator of Scandinavian literature. His *America Not Discovered by Columbus* (1874) was instrumental in propagating information about the Vinland Sagas in North America. Liljencrantz's other sources included Paul du Chaillu's *The Viking Age* (1890), which contains English translations of most of the material from relevant Icelandic medieval sources.[10]

Our knowledge of Leif Eriksson's exploration is based mostly on two different texts: *Eiríks saga rauða* and *Ólafs saga Tryggvasonar*. *Eiríks saga* is preserved in two medieval manuscripts, *Hauksbók* and *Skálholtsbók*, which are thought to date from the fourteenth and fifteenth centuries respectively. As we noted in Chapter Two, there are several sagas devoted to King Olaf Tryggvason, varying in length, but the version preserved in the fourteenth-century *Flateyjarbók* manuscript is the only one that includes information about Leif Eriksson.[11] *Ólafs saga* and *Eiríks saga* share similar episodes and are probably based on the same oral or written sources. However, the way in which each saga describes Leif's discovery of North America varies so much that they are normally thought of as two independent narratives.

According to *Eiríks saga*, Leif sailed one summer to Norway from the Greenland farm of his parents, Erik and Thjodhild, and spent the winter in King Olaf Tryggvason's court. The king clearly held Leif in very high regard and 'Leif appeared to him to be a man of good breeding.'[12] Later in the saga we read:

> On one occasion the king spoke to Leif privately and asked, 'Do you intend to sail to Greenland this summer?'
>
> Leif answered, 'I would like to do so, if it is your wish.'
>
> The king answered, 'It would well be so; you shall go as my envoy and convert Greenland to Christianity.'
>
> Leif said the king should decide that, but added that he feared this message would meet with a harsh reception in Greenland. The king said he saw no man more suitable for the job than Leif – 'and you'll have the good fortune that's needed.'
>
> 'If that's so', Leif declared, 'then only because I enjoy yours as well.'
>
> Once he had made ready, Leif set sail. After being tossed about at sea for a long time he chanced upon land where he had not expected any to be found. Fields of self-sown wheat and vines were growing there; also there were trees known as maple, and they took specimens of all of them.
>
> Leif also chanced upon men clinging to a ship's wreck, whom he brought home and found shelter for over the winter. In so doing he showed his strong character and kindness. He converted the country to Christianity. Afterwards he became known as Leif the Lucky.
>
> Leif made land in Eiriksfjord and went home to the farm at Brattahlid. There he was received warmly. He soon began to advocate Christianity and true catholic faith throughout the country, revealing the messages of King Olaf Tryggvason to the people and telling them how excellent and glorious this faith was.

> Eirik was reluctant to give up his faith but Thjodhild was quick to convert and had a church build a fair distance from the house. It was called Thjodhild's church and there she prayed, along with those other people who converted to Christianity, of whom there were many. After her conversion, Thjodhild refused to sleep with Eirik, much to his displeasure.[13]

In this noteworthy description from *Eiríks saga,* there is a much greater emphasis on Leif's missionary work in Greenland than on his stay in North America, and his father's reluctance to convert to the new faith is also made clear.

In *Ólafs saga* in *Flateyjarbók* a similar story is related but in a different manner. First, it is briefly noted that some sixteen years after Erik the Red had settled in Greenland, his son Leif stayed one winter in Norway at the royal court and converted there to Christianity. Second, credit for the discovery of North America is given not to Leif but to one Bjarni Herjulfsson who, around the time Leif arrived in Norway, was caught up in a storm when sailing from Iceland to Greenland. Bjarni sighted land three times before reaching his intended destination in Greenland where his father lived. Third, at the end of a chapter describing the relationship of King Olaf with his wife, it is made clear that the king sent Leif, along with a priest and other clerics, to bring Christianity to Greenland. On the way Leif saved people who had been shipwrecked, and after he came to Brattahlid he was instrumental in having his father (without any reported protest) and everyone else living in Greenland christened.

Later, after learning of Bjarni Herjulfsson's journey, Leif bought Bjarni's ship and set off west from Greenland with 35 men to explore the coast of North America. In this context the saga introduces a man called Tyrkir, 'from a more southerly country', who joined Leif on the trip and who spoke both Norse and German.[14] Leif and his crew stepped ashore at all three of the places that Bjarni sighted, but in the reverse order. Leif named the first two of these Helluland and Markland. At the last location, where Tyrkir became the first to find vines and grapes, the group stayed for a whole winter. The local indigenous population is not mentioned here; Leif is simply said to have ordered his men fill the main ship with vines and the ship's boat with grapes.

> When spring came they made the ship ready and set sail. Leif named the land for its natural features and called it Vinland (Wineland). They headed out to sea and had favourable winds, until they came in sight of Greenland and the mountains under its glaciers.[15]

On his way home, Leif again saved people who had been shipwrecked and were marooned on a skerry; the group leader was a Norwegian called Thorir and his wife was Gudrid Thorbjarnardottir. 'After this', the saga notes, 'he was called Leif the Lucky.'[16]

From one perspective, Liljencrantz's *The Thrall of Leif the Lucky* may be regarded as a melodramatic romance, using the Vinland Sagas for historical background. The principal characters of her work are two young people from different backgrounds who fall in love. One is the Northumbrian nobleman Alwin, who has been captured in Britain during a Viking raid and is, in the first chapter of the novel, brought to a slave-market in the Norwegian city of Trondheim: 'the boy was of the handsomest Saxon type. Though barely seventeen, he was man-grown, and lithe and well-shaped; and he carried himself nobly.'[17] The other is the Norwegian girl Helga, who is introduced in the second chapter of the novel as her horse stumbles close to the hut where Alwin and other slaves are kept. At this point, Helga is wearing 'a helmet like a silver bowl, and a kirtle that stopped at the knee.'[18] Upon closer inspection Alwin discovers that she is exceptionally beautiful: 'Her face was as delicately pink-and-pearly as a sea-shell, and corn-flowers among the wheat were no bluer than the eyes that looked out from under her rippling golden tresses.'[19] Raised as a foster child at the farm of Erik the Red in Greenland, Helga has been staying for some time in Norway with her foster brother Leif, and her custodian Tyrkir, 'a puny little German, with a face as small and withered as a winter apple'.[20] Upon her suggestion, Tyrkir purchases Alwin for three marks of silver and before long the three of them are aboard Leif's ship along with a band of disorderly Vikings, heading back to Greenland. Leif's mission, laid out by King Olaf Tryggvason, is to christen the inhabitants of Erik the Red's settlement. After finishing this demanding task, Leif extends his travels further west along the coast of North America in the second half of the novel. Various obstacles delay Alwin and Helga's happy union in the course of these travels; one of them being Leif's crew member Egil Olafsson, who himself is in love with Helga and becomes dangerously jealous when he discovers that she has a soft spot for the Saxon slave.

From a different perspective, Liljencrantz's novel can be seen as an ambitious attempt to bring together the two different narrative traditions about Leif Eriksson's travels that can be found in the Icelandic medieval sources. In the first part of *The Thrall of Leif the Lucky*, Liljencrantz primarily looks for inspiration in *Eiríks saga*. The first seven chapters of the novel are devoted to Alwin and Helga's initial encounters in Norway. It is not until Chapter Eight that King Olaf entrusts Leif with the task of bringing Christianity to Greenland, and that episode is not staged directly. *The Thrall of Leif the Lucky* is written in the third person but the narration is mostly limited to the perspective of Alwin, who has not been introduced to Leif at this point. So it is that Liljencrantz has Leif's servant, a slave named Kark, tell Alwin and others about the meeting taking place between Leif and the king. Kark's description here is certainly based on *Eiríks saga*, but with some interesting additions:

> Kark went on: 'Leif said that he was willing to do whatever the King wished; yet it would not be easy. He spoke the name of

Helga and Alwin in the New World, illustration by Troy and Margaret Kinney in Ottilie A. Liljencrantz's *The Thrall of Leif the Lucky* (1902).

> Eric, and after that they lowered their voices so that I could not hear. Then at last Olaf leaned back in his high-seat and Leif stood up to go. Olaf stretched forth his hand and said, 'I know no man fitter for the work than you. You shall carry good luck with you.' Leif answered: 'That can only be if I carry yours with me.' Then he grasped the King's hand and they drank to each other, looking deep into each other's eyes.'[21]

In the following chapters, Leif sails to Greenland. On the way, he decides to entrust Alwin with the duties for which Kark had previously been responsible and this triggers an intense hatred between the two slaves. In the novel, Leif's ship does not run into a storm, as it does in *Eiríks saga*; instead Leif returns directly home to his parents in Brattahlid. There he attends a tense banquet at which Kark's father denigrates Alwin for his belief in Christ. Leif then stands up and declares that he himself was converted to Christianity two years earlier by King Olaf. Erik the Red's first reaction to this news is to cast his axe in the direction of his son but the weapon misses its target and ends up lodged in a timber beam behind Leif. The father and son and their respective followers come close to fighting but the audacious Leif takes control of the situation. Little by little, he manages to convert some of those around him to the new faith, while his father stubbornly sticks to his belief in the pagan gods.

At this point in the story, Liljencrantz begins to use *Ólafs saga Tryggvasonar* from *Flateyjarbók* as her primary source. A member of Bjarni Herjulfsson's crew, Grettir the Fat, arrives at Brattahlid and tells Leif and his men stories of Bjarni's ship drifting off course on the way to Greenland. Grettir's narrative here is taken almost word for word from the relevant passage in *Ólafs saga*, as it appears in Paul du Chaillu's *The Viking Age*. Following this visit Leif decides to explore the lands in the west that Bjarni had seen. He lands first in Helluland, then Markland and finally Vinland, where Tyrkir finds vines and grapes, just as he does in *Ólafs saga*. Additionally, two chapters in *The Thrall of Leif the Lucky* that recount Leif's exploration begin with quotations (in small font) from relevant episodes in *Ólafs saga* as printed in *The Viking Age*. Thus readers of the novel are reminded that Liljencrantz is drawing on her 'historical' sources. Nevertheless, those same readers have limited scope to discern exactly which part of the text is pure fiction and which is not.

An example of Liljencrantz's numerous embellishments occurs when during the winter in Vinland Leif discovers that Alwin (who at this point in the journey is disguised as a French nobleman) understands runic script. As a consequence, Leif has him writing down the official account of the expedition and promises to grant him anything he desires in return. This undertaking underpins Leif's decision ultimately to grant Alwin and Helga his blessing. There are still some doubts over whether Helga's parents in Norway are prepared to let her marry a slave, even if he is of noble blood. The novel ends, nonetheless, with Alwin and Helga sailing back home to Greenland with Leif. It seems quite probable that they will live there happily ever after.

'Leif built a watch tower of stone'

A quarter of a century passed from the publication of Ottilie A. Liljencrantz's debut novel until the premiere of Roy William Neill's *The Viking* (1928). Even though this ninety-minute silent movie is not held in high regard among contemporary film enthusiasts, it did mark an important milestone in cinematic history at the time. It was produced by Technicolor, a company founded in Boston by Herbert Kalmus, Daniel Frost Comstock and W. Burton Wescott in 1914. Over the next few years Technicolor developed two methods of colour filming with varying degrees of success, and by the end of the 1920s they had developed a third technique – the so-called 'Process 3' – which they claimed would make films last longer and be more colourful.[22] To introduce this new method to the American film industry, Kalmus hired Jack Cunningham to write the script for *The Viking*. Cunningham had previously written the script for the most popular silent Western of the period, *The Covered Wagon* (1923), and Kalmus felt that adopting a similar approach to tell 'a love story of the vikings with the epic quality of fighting mutiny and storms to conquer an ocean' would give his film a good chance of box-office success.[23] *The Viking* turned out to be a fine production in terms of Technicolor's state-of-the-art techniques, but as Kalmus would later confirm, there were two obstacles that prevented the film from achieving more widespread popularity: first, it was released at the same time as the first talking pictures, and second, Leif the Lucky

(Donald Crisp) was thoughtlessly given 'a long, curling mustache, whereas American audiences prefer their lovers smooth-shaven'.[24]

The storyline of *The Viking* is a significantly simplified version of *The Thrall of Leif the Lucky*. The main characters are indeed Leif's graceful Norwegian foster sister Helga (Pauline Starke) and the beardless Lord Alwin (LeRoy Mason), an Anglo-Saxon nobleman enslaved by Vikings. The couple, while sailing with Leif and his men to Greenland and then Vinland, fall in love and manage to overcome all the obstacles standing in the way of their happiness. One of the principal hindrances is that Leif himself considers marrying Helga (a deviation from the novel), but fortunately he abandons that ambition when Alwin saves his life and Helga reveals her warm affection for the slave. When Leif returns home to Greenland, the newlyweds stay behind, along with some members of Leif's crew, and establish a small European settlement in the New World (another deviation from the novel).

Arne Lunde has pointed out the extent to which *The Viking* 'borrows from other reigning film genres and conventions to construct a kind of "Vikings-in-America western" about land claiming and nation building'.[25] At the same time, the film certainly represents an important phase in Leif Eriksson's modern afterlife. In some respects, Leif's depiction on the silver screen is remarkably well aligned with the Icelandic medieval sources about him. He first appears in *The Viking* among guests at a feast or service held by King Olaf Tryggvason, 'first Christian ruler of Norway'.[26] Priests in white vestments read from the Bible and baptize a bearded Viking chieftain under the watchful eye of the monarch. Leif sits at a distance in the company of two other men, wears a knee-length tunic with a cape hanging from his shoulders, and has long hair and the curled moustache. He is introduced by name in the intertitles and said to be 'famed throughout the North for his strength, courage and justice'.[27] This echoes a description in *Ólafs saga*, where Leif is characterized as 'a large, strong man, of very striking appearance and wise, as well as being a man of moderation in all things'.[28]

In conversation with one of his companions in the film, Leif mentions that he is on his way to Greenland but only intends to call in there for provisions before continuing even further west to explore new lands. At a meeting with the king a little later, Leif shows Olaf a rough map of Norway, Britain, Iceland and Greenland, with the ocean to the west falling like a waterfall off the edge of the world. 'My father, Eric the Red, discovered Greenland . . . There must be other lands beyond', says Leif, referring to the map.[29] King Olaf reminds him: 'It has always been the belief that the edge of the world is not far west of Greenland . . . To sail out there and find new lands – that would be an adventure worthy of you Leif Ericsson!'[30] The king then removes his necklace with its huge crucifix and hangs it around Leif's neck, saying: 'Glory and success on your voyage.'[31] These words echo the words 'and you'll have the good fortune that's needed' that are spoken by King Olaf in *Eiríks saga*.[32] The primary deviation from the saga here (as well as from Liljencrantz's novel) is that instead of making Leif out to be a Christian missionary to Greenland, the film has the king give the explorer his Christian blessing.

As the story progresses the differences between the Vinland Sagas, *The Thrall of Leif the Lucky* and *The Viking* escalate. Scriptwriter Jack Cunningham profoundly simplifies, for instance, the scenes devoted to Leif's arrival and stay in Greenland. Particular emphasis is laid on Erik the Red's belief in the old pagan gods and his hatred of Christians. This is evident in a scene in which Erik kills one of his men with an axe after discovering that he wears a crucifix around his neck. On this occasion Greenland is described on the intertitles as 'that barren outpost of Norse civilization where hard stubborn paganism still held sway'.[33] The next scene is closely based on the chapter of *The Thrall of Leif the Lucky* in which Erik throws his axe at Leif, but the difference in the film is that a fight breaks out between Erik and Leif's men. The latter group manages to escape back to the ship with stolen provisions and sail west in search of new lands. As a result there is no time for Leif to preach Christianity during his visit,

The 'first white man' in the New World in Roy William Neill's *The Viking* (1928).

but at the end of the scene the audience is left with the impression that, despite everything, Erik is proud to have such a courageous son. This is one of many instances indicating that Leif is depicted in *The Viking* as a noble savage. Though he clearly knows how to wield a sword, he can also be merciful and compassionate at the right moment, characteristically grasping the crucifix that hangs around his neck on such occasions.

Another episode from the novel that Cunningham transforms is the ending. The final scene in *The Viking* takes place in North America and begins with the narrative intertitle: 'And the first white man set foot on the shores of the New World.'[34] The Vikings are seen coming ashore on a golden beach, where Leif erects a large wooden cross in the sand and falls reverently to his knees alongside his crew, many of whom hold flags. The next intertitle reads: 'As his Viking fathers had done in other lands, Leif built a watch tower of stone.'[35] Following this, we see the Vikings and a group of scantily clad Mohawks standing in front of a watch tower. Leif hangs the crucifix that King Olaf gave him early in the film around the neck of one of the natives, saying: 'Let this cross and the tower I have built be the signs of peace and friendship between us.'[36] Next we see Alwin embrace Helga, who speaks of the happiness they will find in this wilderness. The Norwegian girl, who appeared in the film's opening scenes wearing a winged helmet (resembling a Valkyrie of contemporary productions of Wagner's Ring Cycle), now wears a Charleston headband with Native American feathers. The last intertitle reads: 'What became of this little Viking colony, no one knows. But the watch tower they built stands today in Newport, Rhode Island.'[37] To reinforce this, we are then shown a car driving past the well-preserved ruins of the tower in modern Newport. At the same time the final chords of the 'Star-Spangled Banner' are heard.

As Arne Lunde skilfully points out, the end of *The Viking* weaves together various highly political messages. The scene in which Leif and his men come ashore with flags and a crucifix is a reference to typical nineteenth-century artistic representations of Christopher Columbus's discovery of the New World in 1492. The group falling to its knees may also be a reference to conventional paintings that show the arrival of the first English settlers in North America to the shores of Plymouth, Massachusetts in 1620. The watch tower is a reference to the lengthy dispute as to whether the ruins at Newport were relics of the Viking expeditions to Vinland or merely the remains of a seventeenth-century windmill. With reference to these symbols and the 'Star-Spangled Banner', Lunde declares that the film-maker 'appropriates the Norse Vinland sagas in order to construct a pre-Columbian, Anglo-Nordic narrative of mythologized American national origins'.[38]

As for the crucifix that Leif hangs around the neck of the Mohawk, and the feathers that Helga puts in her hair, these may be intended to indicate how the two groups of people can live in peace and harmony, with each adopting the other's customs. Needless to say, the scene in no way reflects the ways in which communication between white settlers and the native population of North America actually developed. As for the idea of Helga and Alwin establishing a settlement in North America, this probably derives from the chapters in *Eiríks saga* and *Ólafs saga* that tell of later voyages by Nordic explorers to Vinland. There was a significant expedition led by Thorfinn 'Karlsefni' ('makings of a man'), who is reported to have lived in Vinland along with his travelling companions for a couple of years. However, repeated skirmishes with the natives proved to be the main reason for Thorfinn and his company deciding to abandon Vinland. *Eiríks saga* records that they 'realised that, despite everything the land had to offer there, they would be under constant threat of attack from its prior inhabitants'.[39]

Lunde places *The Viking* in the context of North American racism and the influential American eugenics movement, partially driven by significant changes in immigration to the United States during this period.[40] For most of the nineteenth century, around 95 per cent of the immigrants had been arriving from northern Europe, but by the end of the century, almost 80 per cent were coming from southern and eastern Europe.[41] Many Americans of Nordic, Anglo-Saxon and German origin preferred the story of Leif Eriksson's 'Norse' discovery of America to the more traditional view that the continent had been discovered by Columbus, who was an Italian in the service of the king and queen of Spain.[42] This view was stressed in Rasmus B. Anderson's *America Not Discovered by Columbus*, and also formed the basis for his and other 'older' immigrants' struggle to institute an official 'Leif Eriksson Day' to be held each year. Columbus Day (12 October) had long been celebrated and was made an official state holiday in Colorado as early as 1906. Other states followed suit until Columbus Day was made a national holiday in 1937.

It is probable that *The Viking*, in addition to introducing new and exciting colour film-making technology, contributed to the dispute over who discovered America and which ethnic groups had the most symbolic claim to custody of the continent. It is difficult to gauge the effect of the movie in terms of these issues but in 1929,

Alexander Stirling Calder's statue of Leif Eriksson, unveiled in Reykjavík in 1932.

just a few months after it premiered, Anderson and his supporters finally managed to convince the authorities in Wisconsin to make 9 October an official Leif Eriksson day in the state. At around the same time the American Congress agreed to allow President Herbert Hoover 'to accept the invitation of the Kingdom of Iceland to participate in the celebration of the one thousandth anniversary of the Althing and in connection therewith to present to the people of Iceland a statue of Leif Ericson'.[43] The American sculptor

Alexander Stirling Calder was commissioned to create the work. In support of the motion, the official resolution referred to the fact that,

> the first white man to set foot on American soil was a native son of Iceland, Leif Ericson (the son of Eric the Red, a Norwegian who had settled in Iceland), an able and fearless sailor, who in 985 accompanied his father to Greenland, and thereafter went thence on a cruise to Norway, and on the return trip in the year 1000 discovered the American mainland, which feat constitutes the beginning of authentic American history.[44]

This echoes the final scene of *The Viking* in which the intertitles refer to Leif being 'the first white man' to set foot in the New World.[45]

All things considered, it is clear that Leif Eriksson's journey, from the oral accounts of his contemporaries in Greenland in the year 1000 to the silver screen in the United States of America in 1928, was both long and turbulent. The pre-texts of the film include the fourteenth- and fifteenth-century manuscripts of *Eiríks saga* and *Ólafs saga*, and Ottilie A. Liljencrantz's *The Thrall of Leif the Lucky*. In the novel, many characters and new events were added to the conflicting accounts of the Icelandic sources, but in developing the film script the storyline was again simplified and significantly altered. The greatest change is that while the Leif of the literary tradition brings Christianity to the Nordic settlers in Greenland, the cinematographic Leif acts as a missionary among the native inhabitants of North America.[46] The next stop on Leif's journey between media and continents might have been the majestic rise in downtown Reykjavík on which Calder's sculpture of Leif Eriksson was unveiled in 1932. The statue is set on a plinth reminiscent of the bow of a ship. There is no dragon prow to be seen but true to the image of the noble savage presented in *The Viking*, Leif wears a knee-length tunic, with a cape over his shoulders. In one hand he holds an axe and in the other a small crucifix, which he presses against his chest. The only thing missing is the curled moustache.

'The whole world trembled'

Another 25 years after the unveiling of the Leif Eriksson statue in Iceland, Richard Fleischer's *The Vikings* premiered in the USA. This was one of the many lavish historical motion pictures produced on the Hollywood assembly line in the 1950s and '60s. Other films of the same ilk include *Alexander the Great* (1956) with Richard Burton, *Ben-Hur* (1959) starring Charlton Heston and *Spartacus* (1960) with Kirk Douglas as the eponymous hero. Douglas played one of the leading roles in *The Vikings* and was also involved in producing the film through his own Bryna Productions. The same company would later produce *Spartacus* and the television series *Tales of the Vikings* (1959–60), which reused sets, costumes and props from Fleischer's film, including specially built and fully equipped Viking ships. These were replicas of the Gokstad and Oseberg ships that are preserved in the Viking Ship Museum at Bygdøy in Oslo. The vessels were such exact reproductions that the modern actors playing the oarsmen were too tall to fit into the available space, they had to sit on every second thwart.[47] In a newspaper interview, Icelander Stefán Karlsson, one of the many bearded extras in the film, revealed that each ship also had 'a motor with an accompanying mechanic and radio operator'.[48] And he added that there were other details of the set misrepresenting medieval reality:

> A great Viking town was erected, but it was built in such a way that a Norwegian archaeologist, who was supposed to be giving advice, stormed off when he saw the outcome. The same went for all the other Viking gear. The directors claimed to have had experts assist with all the gear, but the Norwegians said that only the hulls of the Viking ships were historically correct.[49]

The script of *The Vikings* was an adaptation of Edison Marshall's novel *The Viking* (1951), which in return was very loosely based on ancient sources about the Scandinavian legendary hero Ragnar 'Hairy Breeches' (Icel. *loðbrók*) and his many sons. The most influential of these sources is *Ragnars saga loðbrókar* (The Saga of Ragnar Hairy Breeches), which is thought to have been written in Iceland around the year 1230. It is preserved in two manuscripts: NKS 1824b 4to, from around the year 1400, and AM 147 4to, otherwise known as *Heynesbók*, probably written in the early sixteenth century. Other sources about Ragnar and his sons include *Ragnarssona þáttur* (The Tale of Ragnar's Sons), that seems to be based partly on *Ragnars saga*,

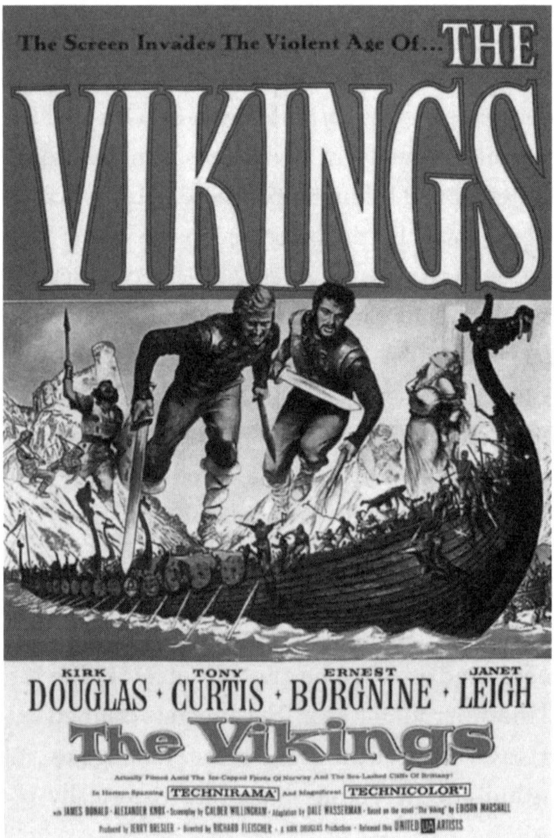

Poster for *The Vikings* (1958), directed by Richard Fleischer.

Saxo Grammaticus's *Gesta Danorum* and the skaldic poem *Krákumál* (The Lay of Kraka), possibly composed somewhere in the Scottish islands during the twelfth century. The poem takes the form of a monologue spoken by Ragnar Hairy Breeches on his deathbed.

Ragnars saga presents a detailed account of the operations of Ragnar and his descendants. While the sons rampage around southern Europe, and in fact almost reach Rome, Ragnar decides to attack the coast of England using just two ships. Unfortunately, King Aella of Northumbria has a spy in Ragnar's company and prepares for the attack by gathering a great army that kills all of Ragnar's men, except for Ragnar himself, who wears a long shirt, woven 'out of hoar-grey hair-strands', that functions as magic armour.[50] According to the saga the king doesn't intend to kill Ragnar, 'because he has left sons behind, who will never leave us alone if he falls'.[51] When the Viking chieftain refuses to identify himself, Aella tries to compel him to speak by throwing him into a snake pit. When that fails, the king has Ragnar stripped of all his clothes, including the long shirt, and so the snakes are now able to kill him. The second half of *Ragnars saga*, as well as *Ragnarssona þáttur*, describes the attempts of Ragnar's sons to avenge their father's death and destroy Aella's kingdom. In both narratives one of the sons, Ivar the Boneless, succeeds with great cunning.

First and foremost, it is the name and the death of Ragnar Hairy Breeches that links the medieval sources about him with Marshall's novel and Fleischer's film. The storyline of the novel is largely the fruit of Marshall's lively imagination, while the film script is a simplified and at times relatively loose interpretation of the novel. The names and roles of characters in these different works indicate clearly how independent they are from each other. In *Ragnars saga* the sons of Ragnar are called Eirik, Agnar, Ivar, Bjorn, Hvitserk, Sigurd and Rognvald; in Marshall's novel the main conflict is between Ragnar's son Hastings and the slave Ogier, while in Fleischer's film Ragnar's son is called Einar and the slave Erik. A considerable part of the action in the film takes place at the settlement of Ragnar (Ernest Borgnine) and Einar (Kirk Douglas), set in Norway. The other main setting of the film is the castle of King Aella (Frank Thring) in Northumbria, England, but the scenes there were filmed at Fort la Latte castle in Brittany, France. The storyline primarily follows Einar's contest with the slave Erik (Tony Curtis), who turns out to be his half-brother, as they compete for the love of Princess Morgana (Janet Leigh), who is promised to King Aella.

The Vikings is undeniably a violent movie. In the course of events, Einar loses an eye, for example, and Erik a hand. At the same time, the audience is presented with snapshots of 'typical' Viking ways, with their barbaric games, brutish table manners, excessive drinking and unrefined relationship with the gods. In the film, pagan religious customs amount to little more than shouting at the top of one's voice: 'Odin! Odin!' This is reinforced by the way Ragnar handles his drinking horn at a feast and the way Erik saves himself after Ragnar has had him tied down in a tidal pool to await certain drowning. Higher powers react by letting the wind blow in such a way as to keep the tide sufficiently low. The scriptwriters Dale Wasserman (adaptation) and Calder Willingham (screenplay) also make a great deal of the fact that the 'greatest wish of every Viking was to die sword in hand, and enter Valhalla where a hero's welcome awaited them from the god Odin', as spelled out (by Orson Welles) in the opening voice-over.[52] In one scene, when King Aella has ordered his men to throw Ragnar into a wolf pit, Erik passes his sword to the condemned man. Ragnar's fear vanishes immediately; he smiles triumphantly at his enemies and leaps towards the wolves with the name of Odin on his lips. There is a parallel episode at the end of the film, after Erik has fatally wounded his half-brother. When Einar reaches in vain for his sword, which he has dropped in the heat of battle, Erik picks up the weapon and nobly hands it to Einar, who smiles, raises the sword, looks towards the heavens, roars 'Odin!' and then dies. There seems to have been a slight misunderstanding here of the notion that 'all those who fall in battle are his adopted sons', as articulated with reference to Odin in *Snorra Edda*.[53]

At the same time, the first of these two scenes is clearly inspired by the medieval sources. In the version of *Ragnars saga* that is preserved in *Heynesbók*, Ragnar ends his life reciting *Krákumál*, rejoicing that Odin's Valkyries have come for him.

> On the high bench, boldly,
> beer I'll drink with the Gods;
> hope of life is lost now –
> laughing shall I die![54]

The moment in the film when Ragnar jumps into the pit laughing and calling out the name of Odin can be interpreted as a reference to these final words of *Krákumál*. Additionally, the scene is a simplified version of the corresponding chapter from Marshall's *The Viking*, except that in the novel there is neither a snake nor a wolf pit, but instead a deep pool of water swarming with sting rays, electric eels and octopuses. A closer comparison between these three works might well be interesting, but I am more inclined to examine how the director, scriptwriters and cinematographer of *The Vikings* were inspired by other pre-texts, in particular how they were picking up chauvinist threads from Roy William Neill's *The Viking*.

While there is considerable emphasis in the 1928 silent film on showing how Leif the Lucky was ennobled by his conversion to Christianity, there are also several key scenes that confirm the brutal nature of some of his contemporaries. The film starts with a few intertitles describing the Vikings as 'men of might, who laughed in the teeth of the tempest, and leaped into battle with a song. Plundering – ravaging – they raided the coast of Europe – until the whole world trembled at the very name – THE VIKING.'[55] Following this is a scene in which a group of full-bearded Vikings attack the castle of Alwin, Earl of Northumbria, in England. The homely atmosphere inside the castle is accentuated: a fire glows in the hearth, Alwin's mother sits embroidering, a young girl pets some kittens, another plays a lute, while a third recites the prayer 'From the sword and the chains of the Vikings, O Lord, deliver us.'[56] The invaders kill everyone in their path without mercy, and force the survivors, including Alwin, into slavery. The only thing missing here from the Viking film formula is sexual violence, but that absence can perhaps be explained by reference to the times in which the film was made. There is, however, a suggestive symbolism in showing how the Vikings break down solid castle doors with a large beam, immediately facing five terrified court maids.

The first few minutes of Fleischer's *The Vikings* are in several significant respects a remake of this scene. The film opens with an unusually long introduction by the narrator, explaining the bad reputation of Vikings in Europe during the eighth and ninth centuries. He talks not only about the Vikings' belief in the afterlife in Valhalla, but about their longing to conquer England: 'they exploited their skill as shipbuilders to spread a reign of terror, then unequalled in violence and brutality in all the records of history.'[57] As the narrator speaks, the audience views a simple cartoon inspired stylistically by the famous Bayeux Tapestry, which depicts the events leading to the Norse invasion of Britain in the eleventh century. While the cartoon shows a Viking ship come ashore near a Christian sanctuary, the narrator says: 'It was no accident that the English *Book of Prayers* contained this sentence: "Protect us, Oh Lord, from the wrath of the Northmen".'[58]

At the end of the introduction, the cartoon is replaced by a staged scene in which Ragnar bursts into the king and queen's tent in Northumbria, as they stand under a canopy on either side of a bed. The king draws his sword but Ragnar beats him to it, pushes the king onto the bed and runs him through with his sword. The queen screams and tries to escape but Ragnar grabs her in the doorway. Her screams are drowned by the noise of battle as the camera pans away to show Ragnar's men running amok. In the next scene, an English priest who is checking the dead and wounded finds the king lying dead and the queen crying by the bed. There is no doubt that Ragnar has raped her. It later transpires that she is pregnant – one of the main sources of drama in the film is that the slave Erik is the offspring of Ragnar's rape.

'Odin's test'

Men's sexual violation of women continues to be a prominent theme throughout *The Vikings*. Einar and Erik's dispute over Princess Morgana, who has been enslaved by the Vikings, is really about Einar's determined plan to have his way with her. Erik manages to spare her that fate at the eleventh hour and sails to England with her. On the way he takes Ragnar prisoner and considers handing him over to King Aella on the condition that Erik can be the one who marries Morgana. But the trip to England does not go quite as Erik planned, for after Ragnar is killed Aella also sentences Erik to death. It is only when Morgana consents to marry the king that he lets it suffice to chop off the slave's hand. For the rest of the film Erik looks to save Morgana from King Aella's bedchamber.

Another penetrating scene in Fleischer's film takes place during a feast at Ragnar and Einar's homestead in Norway. A woman with blonde hair is led into the room and placed in giant stocks, with her braided locks nailed to the wood, sticking out from her ears and jutting out above the crown of her head. Ragnar explains to an English nobleman who is present that this is no game but rather 'Odin's test', which Vikings subject their wives to when they are suspected of infidelity. If the husband manages to throw his axe so as to cut off the braids then the woman is deemed to be innocent, but if she is struck by the axe, this confirms that she is guilty and deserves to be punished. If, after three throws, the axe has not found its target then the husband is sentenced to be drowned. In this scene, the husband of the blonde-haired wife steps forward but when his throws have twice missed their mark, Einar (whom we have seen shortly before in an embrace with the woman in question) grabs the axe and throws it expertly, his skills apparently unhindered by his advanced state of inebriation. Having saved his mistress from the stocks, Einar lays another woman on a table, splashes mead from a drinking horn over her mouth and French kisses her.

In an ingenious analysis of this scene, Kathleen Coyne Kelly quotes an interview with Fleischer in which he says that he and his associates had 'invented this game' with the axes and braids.[59] Kelly takes Odin's test as an example of how, despite their assurances to the contrary, the makers of *The Vikings* were not much concerned about their film's historical accuracy. Their intention, Kelly suggests, was to exploit the putative historical setting in order 'to push the limits of violence that were hitherto accepted in Hollywood'.[60] While this seems a plausible analysis, I believe that Fleischer and his colleagues were also taking up where Roy William Neill's *The Viking* had left off. In the silent film we not only find a clear portrayal of Viking drunkenness but a comic encounter involving the Viking Sigurd and his wife with the blonde locks. Sigurd has purchased a young Greek slave girl for his wife, who tries to decide whether she should be grateful to her husband for the gift or filled with jealousy. She begins by affably slapping Sigurd on the chest, and after he responds in kind she pushes him with more force – and so the exchanges continue until she ends up pushing him over completely. The music during this episode would suit a classic silent Charlie Chaplin film. No axes are cast on this occasion, though that happens later in the film when Erik the Red discovers that his son Leif has pledged his allegiance to the Christian religion. The axes thrown in both films land dangerously close to their targets' heads.

Kelly points out that Einar losing his eye in Fleischer's film could well be a reference to the one-eyed Odin, and adds that Aella having Erik's hand chopped off might even be a reference to the scene in *Snorra Edda* in which Tyr loses his hand. She nevertheless notes that nothing more is made of this in the film and suggests that these passing motifs 'may well be the only real point of contact between *The Vikings* and medieval literature'.[61] Here, I am inclined to raise two objections. First, the description of how Tyr loses his hand in the jaws of Fenrir could well explain the otherwise strange decision of the film-makers to have Ragnar die in a wolf pit rather than in a pit of snakes or a pool of sea monsters. Secondly, there may well be some interesting parallels between the *Snorra Edda* chapter on the poetic mead and the film scene in which the Odin-like Einar and his Viking companions attack King Aella's castle in order to free Morgana.

In her article, Kelly reflects on the Vikings' use of a massive tree trunk on wheels to break through the raised drawbridge of the English castle. When we see this filmed from the castle moat below, Kelly observes, it 'appears to be the shaft of a huge penis (the tree trunk) and two equally huge testicles (the wheels)'.[62] A little later, attention is drawn to Princess Morgana in a chapel in a lofty tower within the castle walls. Einar uses a rope to climb the tower before swinging himself through a stained glass window (albeit one that seems made of paper), after which feat he declares his love for the princess. But when Morgana declares that she loves Erik, Einar drags

A tree trunk on wheels breaking through the raised drawbridge in Richard Fleischer's *The Vikings* (1958).

her up onto the roof of the tower where the showdown between the half-brothers takes place. Kelly takes both of these scenes as examples of how Fleischer and his cinematographer, Jack Cardiff, had fun in circumventing the rules laid down by the American film authorities that had been designed to prevent offensive elements of all kinds from appearing on the silver screen.

Others might wish to suggest that these scenes confirm the film-makers' preoccupation with Freud, but they could just as easily have been reading the chapter of *Snorra Edda* that we discussed in the Prologue. I refer here to the scene in 'Skáldskaparmál' in which Odin, disguised as Bolverk, breaks into Suttung's palace with the help of Baugi, Suttung's brother. Odin/Bolverk's aim is to win the poetic mead from Gunnlod, Suttung's daughter. This is the medieval text:

> Then Bolverk got out an auger called Rati and instructed Baugi to bore a hole in the mountain, if the auger would cut. He did so. Then Baugi said that the mountain was bored through, but Bolverk blew into the auger-hole and the bits flew back up at him. Then he realized that Baugi was trying to cheat him, and told him to bore through the mountain. Baugi bored again. And when Bolverk blew a second time, the bits flew inwards. Then Bolverk turned himself into the form of a snake and crawled into the auger-hole, and Baugi stabbed after him with the auger and missed him. Bolverk went to where Gunnlod was and lay with her for three nights and then she let him drink three draughts of the mead.[63]

The imagery is surely no less sexually suggestive than the scenes in the movie. In the same way, a number of other scenes from *The Vikings* that have been discussed here could be compared with particular chapters from the sagas, especially those of *Egils saga* that describe several feasts attended by Egil Skallagrimsson in Norway. Let it suffice here to recall the feast held by Armod the Bearded, in which

Egil behaves in a way that Kirk Douglas, in the role of the one-eyed Einar, would have been proud of:

> Egil started to feel that he would not be able to go on like this. He stood up and walked across the floor where Armod was sitting, seized him by the shoulders and thrust him up against a wall-post. Then Egil spewed a torrent of vomit that gushed all over Armod's face, filling his eyes and nostrils and mouth and pouring down his chest. Armod was close to choking, and when he managed to let out his breath, a jet of vomit gushed out with it.[64]

The next day, Egil thanks Armod for his hospitality by contriving to make the host resemble Odin: 'Egil cut off his beard close to his chin, and gouged out one of his eyes with his finger, leaving it hanging on his cheek.'[65]

It seems that Richard Fleischer's film is not only based on fragmented medieval sources about Ragnar Hairy Breeches and Edison Marshall's novel *The Viking*, but also represents a kind of tribute to Roy William Neill's film *The Viking*. Moreover, various echoes from other pre-texts, for example *Snorra Edda* and *Egils saga*, are detectable in *The Vikings*. We should, however, recollect once more that these two medieval Icelandic works were adaptations of even older pre-texts. In her article Kelly correctly points out that Fleischer's *The Vikings* paints an implausible picture of the historical reality of Norse Vikings, but the same can possibly be said about the eddas and sagas in general.

In the aforementioned press interview, Stefán Karlsson lamented that more care wasn't taken in truthfully representing the Scandinavian historical past in *The Vikings*: 'now we can expect that each Viking film will spur the creation of the next, because this is still a fertile field for movie makers.'[66] He was referring here to a planned British cinematic adaptation of the Viking novel *Röde Orm* (Red Serpent,

1941–5) by the Swedish writer Frans G. Bengtsson. The film premiered in 1964 as *The Long Ships*, with Richard Widmark and Sidney Poitier in the leading roles. At around the same time, several southern European films were released, including at least six Italian movies in which Vikings played a major role.[67] These were generally not based on the Icelandic eddas and sagas, but at least one of them, *Gli Invasori* (Erik the Conqueror, 1961) directed by Mario Bava, was clearly influenced by Fleischer's *The Vikings*. The only 1960s Viking film that was directly inspired by medieval sources was a Danish production, Gabriel Axel's *Den røde kappe* (The Red Mantle, 1967), based on Saxo Grammaticus's *Gesta Danorum*.

In the following decades the genre continued to proliferate. Most of the Viking films were produced by Scandinavian, British and American companies, but we also find a few produced in Turkey, Germany, Australia, Poland and Russia. Among the most recent European and American Viking films are *Pathfinder* (2007) directed by Marcus Nispel, *Outlander* (2008) directed by Howard McCain, *Valhalla Rising* (2009) directed by Nicolas Winding Refn and *Northmen: A Viking Saga* (2014) directed by Claudio Fäh. The popularity of the Irish-Canadian television series *Vikings* (2013–present), written and created by Michael Hirst and inspired by *Ragnars saga*, suggests that we may anticipate the appearance of many more works of a similar nature.

At the end of the 1980s Terry Jones completed his *Erik the Viking*, mentioned at the opening of this chapter. That film can certainly be placed in context by setting it alongside the other comedies produced by Jones and his Monty Python colleagues in the 1970s and '80s, not least *Monty Python and the Holy Grail* (1975) – in which the Knights of the Round Table undergo ironic reinvention – and *Monty Python's Life of Brian* (1979), inspired by the life of Jesus Christ. In some respects *Erik the Viking* can be seen as an adaptation of the eddas and sagas, but predominantly it represents a parody of the Viking film genre. At least two scenes from Fleischer's *The Vikings* (1958) that have already been discussed here are reworked by Jones. *Erik the Viking* begins on the same note as Fleischer's film, with a band of Vikings burning a small village and killing the inhabitants. Erik (Tim Robbins) breaks into a small hut where a woman named Helga (Samantha Bond) is standing by a bed. He forces her to lie down but when he has trouble taking his pants off, she calms herself down:

> HELGA: Have you done this sort of thing before?
> ERIK: Me? Of course! I've been looting and pillaging up and down the coast.
> HELGA: (*looking sceptical*) Looting and pillaging, eh?
> ERIK: (*on the defensive*) Yes.
> HELGA: What about the raping?
> ERIK: Shut up.
> HELGA: It's obvious you haven't raped anyone in your life.
> ERIK: Sh![68]

The scene exposes Erik's problem in fulfilling the macho demands that his fellow Vikings – in fact the whole Viking film tradition – place upon him.

Jones and his colleagues also have fun with the 'Odin's test' scene that Fleischer and his colleagues were so proud to have invented. In *Erik the Viking,* however, no drunken Viking succeeds in chopping the braids off the terrified woman who has been made a target. At the first attempt the axe hits a drinking cup held by a serving maid, and at the second attempt it lands between the shoulder-blades of a Viking who is there enjoying himself. Before the axe is thrown a third time, a priest approaches the woman and explains that this would be a good time for her to convert to Christianity. In typical Monty Python fashion, the woman doesn't appreciate this interruption and duly orders the priest to leave her alone. The expression on her face suggests haughty indignation at his failure to recognize that she has other and more pressing concerns.

Epilogue

Some three weeks apart, in the autumn of 2015, I received two almost identical emails from North America. Two college students – one living in Ontario and the other across the border in Illinois – were planning a pilgrimage to Iceland for the annual music festival Iceland Airwaves, and wanted to use the opportunity to work on school projects about the sagas. The American student wrote: 'I am writing a story on the history of Icelandic sagas and how it continues to thrive in modern Icelandic literature. I know that you have specializations in Icelandic culture, sagas and literature, so I feel like you would be a good resource.' Similarly, the Canadian student was doing a 'paper on the effect of Icelandic sagas on the education of Icelanders', and wrote: 'I wanted to talk with someone personally while I was there and I was wondering if you have any time during those days for a meeting.' These letters are by no means unusual. As a professor of Icelandic literature at the University of Iceland, I am contacted several times every month by someone abroad – students, scholars and journalists – who is interested in the eddas and sagas. Enquiries of this sort were one of the reasons for writing the book that you are now reading.

My correspondence with these two North American students confirmed to me (once again) that some of the contemporary adaptations we've been examining in previous chapters are instrumental in promoting the eddas and sagas internationally. When I asked the American student by what means she had developed an interest in the sagas, she replied:

> I would also say Tolkien's *The Lord of the Rings*. I grew up going to a high school with a focus in Creative Writing, so I have a lot of interest in literature. Until I began doing some research for this class I actually didn't know the sagas had originated in Iceland. I also didn't realize there were so many medieval sagas!

The response of the Canadian student demonstrated, on the other hand, that in this day and age people all around the world may well be more likely to connect the name of Iceland with experimental or post-rock musicians such as Björk (Björk Guðmundsdóttir, lead singer of The Sugarcubes before going solo) or Jónsi (Jón Þór Birgisson, lead singer of Sigur Rós) than with Hallgerd, Odin or Snorri.

> I first became interested in the sagas ever since I became aware of Icelandic culture through the music. I was actually in Iceland last year for Airwaves and during my visit I was able to travel for a bit and hear about the different saga stories. I ended up buying a large volume of Icelandic sagas when I returned to Canada.

These emails also suggested to me that I might end this study by saying something about the afterlife of the eddas and sagas in my native Iceland, and the natural assumption that their afterlife 'at home' might differ from the experience elsewhere.

'When had Gunnar of Hlidarendi ever done penance?'

In *Íslandsklukkan* (Iceland's Bell, 1943–6), a historical novel by Halldór Laxness, we meet one Arnas Arnæus. He is a character inspired by the life and personality of the Icelandic seventeenth-century manuscript collector Árni Magnússon, who was instrumental in saving from oblivion irreplaceable manuscripts of many of the works that we have been discussing so far. Arnæus makes his first appearance in the third chapter of the novel, looking for vellum leaves from valuable manuscripts in the home of a poor farmer called Jón Hreggviðsson. No sooner has the learned man entered the farmer's stone- and turf-built homestead than his host starts to praise the saga heroes. Unfortunately, declares Jón, the household has only a few books and nobody there really knows how to read except his mother. She has introduced him to

> all the necessary sagas, ballads, and old genealogies, and he claimed to be descended from Haraldur Hilditönn [Harald Wartooth], the Danish king, on his father's side. He said that he would never forget such excellent ancients as Gunnar of Hlidarendi, King Pontus, and Örvar-Oddur, who were twelve ells high and could have lived to be three hundred years old if they hadn't run into any trouble, and that if he had such a book he would send it immediately and for free to the king and his counts, to prove to them that there had indeed once been real men in Iceland. On the other hand, he reckoned, it was hardly due to impenitence that the Icelanders were now fallen into misery, because when had Gunnar of Hlidarendi ever done penance? Never.[1]

In these few lines, Halldór Laxness gives a good idea of the role that the sagas may have served in the lives of the common people in rural Iceland up until the late nineteenth century. First of all, they supplied the general public with suitable role models; second, they provided them with a noble ancestry; and third, they offered the Icelandic nation a Golden Age in the past to counter contemporary miseries. The premise for all these points seems to be a firm belief in the historicity of the sagas, in spite of the flickering verisimilitude that they display.

At the National Museum of Iceland we can find valuable sources that seem to confirm this analysis. These consist of surveys in which two groups of Icelanders – those born between 1850 and 1900, and those between 1900 and 1930 – answered questions about the impact of the sagas on their lives and ideas. The first survey was carried out by the Danish scholar Holger Kjær in the 1920s (HK survey) and the second by scholars at the National Museum of Iceland in 1994 (NM survey).

During the first five hundred years after the sagas were 'compiled' and written down, these texts primarily circulated within Iceland in the form of transcripts and were communicated by means of semi-public readings in individual farmsteads. Vésteinn Ólason suggests that in this period the sagas played a vital part in the life of the Icelandic public; the heroes served as role models, encouraging people to toughen up in their daily conflict with the harsh realities of Icelandic nature.[2] The HK survey implies that, to some degree at least, this was also the function of the sagas in the nineteenth and early twentieth century. A man born in 1889 remembered the sagas being read aloud at evening gatherings in his childhood home in the west of Iceland:

> The main readings were the ancient sagas about Icelandic heroes and strong-men, and the *rímur* [rhymed epic poems] were romances about valiant men and beautiful women . . . And I know that the stories about Gunnar and Egil and Grettir served to energise many Icelandic men. And I also know that the stories about Bergthora, Helga Jarlsdottir, and Audur, the wife of Gisli Sursson, have served as role models for many good women.[3]

During this period the sagas seem to have had a particular impact on the younger generation. A man born in 1892 stated that while toys were scarce in his youth, sometimes skilful adults would carve small human and animal figures out of wood: 'The children often gave these wooden figures various names, especially names drawn from the old literature, and with them, they acted out certain scenes from the sagas.'[4] It was also common for boys to take on the roles of certain saga heroes and imitate their fights and conflicts. A man born in 1898 described this tradition: 'Someone would be Gunnar of Hlidarendi, another Grettir, the third Skarphedin, and so on. Each would have his own "sword" which would be the shaft of a broken rake. You needed to break the "sword" of your enemy to win.'[5]

It was, however, not the case that Icelanders born in the second half of the nineteenth century viewed their pagan saga heroes uncritically. The saga characters were consistently used as exemplars in the discussion of fundamental ethical questions. A man born in 1861 claimed that debates of this sort often followed readings from individual sagas:

> Both the older and younger members of the audience paid close attention to what was being read, and at intervals people would discuss the subject; they would often have different opinions and when the sagas were being read people favoured different characters. Some even sought to excuse the evil deeds and flaws described in the sagas and tried to argue that these were inevitable, while others contradicted them; often there was heated debate. Such discussion would sharpen our sense of the personalities of individual characters; we could see how they wove their thread of destiny towards fame and valour, happiness and success, or towards disgrace and downfall, life or death. My heart was burning and my eyes were often filled with tears of happiness or sorrow.[6]

The HK survey also seems to confirm that nineteenth-century Icelanders tended to believe in the historicity of the sagas.[7]

In the late nineteenth and early twentieth century various societal changes brought an end to the tradition of the nightly saga readings in Icelandic farmsteads. A greater variety of literature, gradual industrialization and technical progress (notably, the arrival of radio) all had an effect in this respect. Some of those who took part in the HK survey mentioned these changes. One man born in 1852 wrote, for example:

> People hardly read the literature of our Golden Age any more. It is hard to find young people these days who are familiar with the family sagas for instance, but you can say that the public is to a large extent reading pulp-fiction and rubbish. The old literature has kept our language and culture alive but if we neglect it our nationality is at risk.[8]

The people taking part in the NM survey confirmed the diminishing importance of saga literature. A majority of correspondents claimed that the sagas had had little or no influence on their view of life and the rest saw themselves as somewhat exceptional cases. The latter were also well aware of the fact that some of their contemporaries found the sagas morally suspect. A man born in 1917 said that he had started to read the sagas at the age of ten. He then added:

> These were the thrillers of the time; the plots kept my interest awake. The feuds and the bloody fights were exciting. The hero, the champion, was elevated in the spotlight of fame. Most often, according to the saga, he was also more honourable than the villain. I never remember feeling bad for those who lost, or were cut into pieces or crippled from their injuries. And I'm afraid I never gave a thought to the surviving relatives, women, children or parents in their old age. I didn't doubt the historicity of the sagas; in my view their testimony was more or less accurate. I recognized that the difference between homicide in the saga-age and killing in our own times could be explained with reference to different religions and morals. Probably, I got that idea from people who were older and wiser than I was.[9]

Such comments suggest that the traditional heroic view towards the sagas was weakening in the early twentieth century. Similarly, a woman born in 1920 openly criticized the violent nature of the sagas' juvenile game playing and pointed out that the ferocity described in the sagas was irreconcilable with bringing up children in the Christian faith.[10] She did not denigrate the sagas directly, but another woman, born in 1913, certainly did, when she explained: 'I never read the old sagas; I found them ugly and boring.'[11]

It is also possible that Icelandic women in general had different attitudes towards the sagas than men did. One woman born in 1906 said that the ancient literature certainly influenced the worldview of her brothers, but not her own.[12] On the other hand, it is interesting to note how many Icelandic men born in the early decades of the twentieth century claimed to be untouched by the sagas, with some of them even suggesting that such works were dull and a bad influence on the young. A man born in 1905 noted: 'I did not particularly enjoy reading the sagas of Icelanders. I had a hard time figuring out all their complex genealogy and from early on I disliked all the killings described in them.'[13] Another man born in 1927 seemed to be fully aware of the possible negative side effects of saga reading but was nevertheless happy to acknowledge the sagas' influence on him:

> Heroes such as Gunnar of Hlidarendi and Kari Solmundarson became my role-models . . . I think the Sagas of Icelanders toughened me up for confronting the realities of life; they made me a better Icelander, but perhaps also more harsh-tempered.[14]

At the same time, it seems that modern Icelanders increasingly regarded the sagas as something of which they could be proud as a nation. A few of those who took part in the HK survey expressed sentiments of this kind; for example, a man born in 1857 wrote:

> The beauty of nature where majesty and elegance go hand in hand, tenderness and ruthlessness, scenes both lovely and sublime, all of these made an impression on us and empowered us, they kindled our love for our homes and our country. This is no wonder, as we would often hear the poems of the poets that we loved so dearly. Saga reading had the same effect and was combined with voices of nature. Right in front of us we could see the mountain of Thrihyrningur, the Fljotshlid Ridge and the Eyjafjallajokull Glacier, all reminding us of Gunnar and Njal, and at the same time of freedom and fame, but also its antithesis, the poverty and enslavement of the present.[15]

Such views find more frequent expression in the NM survey in 1994. A man born in 1914 answered the question, 'Have the sagas influenced your basic views of life?' as follows: 'Yes, most certainly. Primarily [they have] made me proud to be an Icelander, equal to anyone else.'[16] The most profound testimony came from a man born in 1924:

> Influenced my basic views of life? It's hard to say. I have always had the sense that I am an Icelander and nothing more, not even a European . . . rather than a member of the human race, but I am not sure that the sagas, more than anything else, had this influence . . . But their influence on society at large was twofold: they were the source of the language and they justified our striving for recognition as a nation.[17]

Additionally, the NM survey testifies that in the twentieth century the sagas gradually became a part of the curriculum within the developing Icelandic school system. A man born in 1916 had this illuminating tale to tell:

> My sister, Valgerður, was at the women's college, studying for exams. Our nephew, Eggert, was the farmer at Myrar;

> he was both intelligent and widely read. He stayed at our house in Bankastræti. He asks Valgerður what she is reading. She replies that she is reading *Njáls saga*, and that she is not enjoying it. He then offers to tell her the saga, which would make her life much easier. She accepts his kind offer and from then on she says that she knows *Njáls saga*. And in the exam she excelled with her knowledge of the saga.[18]

This development was not to everyone's liking. A man taking part in the HK survey wrote in 1929 that nightly readings of the sagas in the Icelandic farms had ensured that young people developed 'a firm knowledge of history and the human character, very different from the "summarised learning" that characterizes the elementary schools of the present'.[19]

'I am in the land of memories'

My personal interest in the afterlives of the eddas and the sagas can probably be traced to the fact that my childhood home in downtown Reykjavík was on the corner of two streets: Skólavörðustígur and Njálsgata (Njal's Street). The latter obviously takes its name from Njal Thorgeirsson, eponymous hero of *Njáls saga*, but it may also be relevant that at the eastern end of Skólavörðustígur stands Alexander Stirling Calder's statue of Leif Eriksson, which we encountered in Chapter Six. During my early years, I spent a lot of my time at two playgrounds in the neighbourhood; one on Grettisgata (Grettir's Street), named after the title hero of *Grettis saga*, and the other on Freyjugata (Freyja's Street). I had schoolmates living on Þórsgata (Thor's Street), Leifsgata (Leif's Street) and Snorrabraut (Snorri's Avenue), and a crush on a girl who lived on Óðinsgata (Odin's Street). I was, in short, surrounded by urban adaptations of the eddas and sagas.

Close to my home on Njálsgata was Ölgerð Egils Skallagrímssonar (The Brewery of Egil Skallagrimsson), a supplier of sodas and malt beverages. Other important manufacturing companies at the time included Freyja, Iceland's oldest sweets maker, and Frigg, one of the country's earliest soap-makers. While I was growing up in the 1970s, the Cod Wars between Iceland and Britain were raging, and the Offshore Patrol Vessels of the Icelandic Coast Guard fleet that I kept hearing about in the news were called Odin and Thor. One of our largest trawlers at the time was named Snorri Sturluson. I could go on like this for some time – did I mention that my grandfather's name is Gunnar, my father's Hakon and my brother's Snorri? The point is that some years before we ever read any eddic poems, sagas or works attributed to Snorri Sturluson, I and other kids in my neighbourhood had developed a strong subliminal sense of our native cultural heritage.

During my high school years in the early 1980s I was required to read *Völuspá*, *Þrymskviða*, *Snorra Edda*, *Njáls saga*, *Laxdæla saga* and *Egils saga*, but by that time I had already been exposed to a part of our medieval literary tradition in adaptations, both domestic and foreign. I knew by heart, for example, Jónas Hallgrímsson's *Njáls saga*-inspired poem 'Gunnarshólmi', as well as the lyrics of Led Zeppelin's 'Immigrant Song'. I had read an Icelandic translation of a Danish children's version of *Ragnars saga loðbrókar*, seen a German fantasy film based on *Völsunga saga* and several animated television episodes featuring Marvel's character the Mighty Thor. I owned both Haraldur Guðbergsson's illustrated version of *Þrymskviða* (1980) and Guðni Kolbeinsson's Icelandic translation of Peter Madsen's *Thors brudefærd*, titled *Hamarsheimt* (1980). I had been too young to be interested in Jón Ásgeirsson's pioneering Icelandic opera *Þrymksviða* (1974), but I was impressed by the musical *Grettir* (1980), by Egill Ólafsson, Ólafur Haukur Símonarson and Þórarinn Eldjárn, in which the rowdy hero of *Grettis saga* is transposed to the modern setting of Reykjavík.

The most influential Icelandic saga adaptations of this period were, however, several Viking films by Ágúst Guðmundsson and Hrafn

Gunnlaugsson. Ágúst Guðmundsson's *Útlaginn* (The Outlaw, 1981) is an adaptation of *Gísla saga Súrssonar* (The Saga of Gisli Sursson) and as of 2016 still the only film that draws directly on the Sagas of Icelanders.[20] Hrafn Gunnlaugsson made three films in quick succession – *Hrafninn flýgur* (When the Raven Flies, 1984), *Í skugga hrafnsins* (In the Shadow of the Raven, 1988) and *Hvíti víkingurinn* (The White Viking, 1991) – in which he recycled medieval literary motifs in creating independent narratives. These works have been compared with films by directors such as Japan's Akira Kurosawa and Italy's Sergio Leone.[21] More recent works in this tradition include celebrated choral performances of the post-medieval eddic poem *Hrafnagaldur Óðins* (Odin's Raven-Charm, 2002) to music by Hilmar Örn Hilmarsson, Steindór Andersen and Jónsi's Sigur Rós, as well as Embla Ýr Bárudóttir and Ingólfur Örn Björgvinsson's series of comic books based on *Njáls saga*, *Blóðregn* (Blood Rain, 2003), *Brennan* (The Burning, 2003), *Vetrarvíg* (Winter Killing, 2005) and *Hetjan* (The Hero, 2007).[22]

These are just a few examples from a very long list of adaptations, but the bottom line is that although the modern afterlife of Icelandic medieval literature may be more intense in Iceland than in any other part of our global village, it is essentially not that different. Some people are really into the tradition of the eddas and sagas, others are not. A few years ago, while visiting Japan, I met the local artist Makoto Yukimura, who has spent a decade creating the manga series *Vinland Saga* (2005–present). The story, which takes place in medieval Scandinavia, Britain, Iceland, Greenland and 'Vinland', is inspired by several medieval sources, featuring characters bearing the well-known names of Leif Eriksson and Thorfinn 'Karlsefni', but also others less familiar, such as Askeladd, who is a half-Danish and half-Welsh chieftain of Vikings. The worldview and ethics of these characters sometimes recall Icelandic saga heroes, though sometimes they seem to behave more like medieval Japanese samurai. Still, I discovered that as far as the immediate influence of the eddas and sagas was concerned, I – with my common name of Jón, which amounts to John Doe – probably had more in common with Yukimura than my own brother Snorri. Correspondingly, my three gifted children are definitely more conversant with Tolkien's *The Lord of the Rings* and individual episodes of the American sitcom *Friends* than with *Eiríks saga rauða, Snorra Edda* or *Völuspá*.

Every year seems to bring a number of new adaptations of the eddas and sagas to my nerd-like attention, along with adaptations of earlier adaptations. Recalling the role-playing games of my nineteenth-century ancestors, I find contemporary computer game design particularly curious. Kids of my children's generation, all around the world, have in recent years been introduced to the gods Odin and Thor, as well as Vikings by the names of Ragnar and Erik (or Eric), through video games such as *The Lost Vikings* (1992), *Rune: Halls of Valhalla* (2001), *Age of Mythology* (2002), *Viking: Battle for Asgard* (2008) or *The Banner Saga* (2014). Most of these games have been developed by either Japanese or American companies.

Closer to home, over the past twenty years a number of museums and exhibitions dedicated to particular Sagas of Icelanders, medieval archaeological finds or the cultural legacy of the Viking Age, have surfaced all around Iceland. The oldest of these museums is The Icelandic Saga Centre (also called the Njáls Saga Centre), which opened in 1997 in Hvollsvöllur, a small town in the vicinity of Hlidarendi and Bergthorshvol. The most substantial part of the exhibition there introduces tourists to the storyline of *Njáls saga*, but there is also a restaurant reminiscent of an ancient long house, as well as a brand new *Njáls saga* wall hanging, designed by artist and literary scholar Kristín Ragna Gunnarsdóttir, 'in a tapestry form using the Bayeux stitch (laid couching work)'.[23] Furthermore, the museum features a model of Thingvellir as it is thought to have looked in the Middle Ages when gatherings of the Althing were held there. Visitors can take trips to the nearby landscapes of *Njáls saga* and learn from information boards erected at key saga locations. A similar museum, The Settlement Centre, which opened in 2006 in Borgarnes, western Iceland, is mainly dedicated to the history of Iceland's settlement and the plot of *Egils saga*. In some respects these places institutionalize the old man who told Samuel E. Waller about the grave of Gunnar's dog at Hlidarendi in the 1870s and the farmer Páll Gíslason who welcomed Poul Vad into his private library at Adalbol a century later. Plays based on *Njáls saga* and *Egils saga* have been staged in Icelandic at both of these saga museums, including Benedikt Erlingsson's *Mr Skallagrimsson* (2006) and Hlín Agnarsdóttir's *Gestaboð Hallgerðar* (Hallgerd's Dinner Party, 2012). These performances indicate that the target audiences for these museums are just as much local as foreign tourists.

As further confirmation of how adaptations become pre-texts of further adaptations, I would like to conclude by drawing attention to *Íslandsförin* (Voyage to Iceland, 1996), a novel by the Icelandic novelist Guðmundur Andri Thorsson. It is written as a travelogue by an unnamed British aristocrat, born of an Icelandic mother. He visits Iceland with the scientist Cameron in the second half of the nineteenth century, perhaps the same year as Samuel Waller. The stated aims of his voyage are: (1) to see Geysir erupt, (2) to ascend Mt Hekla, (3) to meet rebels, (4) to sort out his own emotions, (5) to try to find out about his mother's family, (6) to find inspiration for writing an epic poem about Iceland, (7) to visit the setting of *Njáls saga* and (8) Thingvellir, (9) to experience in full the Nordic spirit of the Saga Island and (10) to have adventures.[24] As this list shows, *Íslandsförin* is an archetypal saga travelogue. The narrator's visit to the setting of *Njáls saga* sounds quite familiar, with the people at Bergthorshvol and Hlidarendi showing him the old farm sites, including Gunnar's cairn and his dog's grave. As in Waller's *Six Weeks in the Saddle*, the view from Hlidarendi is both majestic and melancholy:

> Markarfljot River has washed away the pink fields and mown meadows and now there is black sand gouged out by the merciless, ever-busy rivers. Such is the state it is in, the realm that Gunnar died for. Who would turn back to this country

> now if he had the chance of fame and fortune at foreign courts?[25]

At the same time Guðmundur Andri Thorsson's book differs from other travelogues in that it teems with remarks and allusions of particular relevance to an Icelandic reader in modern times. Confronted by the famous mountain of Ingolfsfjall, for example, the diarist entertains comic doubts as to whether the first settler of Iceland was named Ingolf, Beowulf or Bjartur (the last name refers to the principal character of Halldór Laxness's novel *Sjálfstætt fólk*).

Gradually one is haunted by the question of whether the relationship of us Icelanders with our history today has not come to resemble that of foreign travellers with the Saga Island at the end of the nineteenth century. Do we experience life in the afterlife of the eddas and sagas any differently from anyone else? We are visitors to a strange past and our attitude towards it is coloured by a mixture of admiration and disgust: 'I feel', writes the narrator of *Íslandsförin*, 'as if I am in the land of memories. Yet there seem to be no memories associated with me here.'[26]

TIMELINE

c. 870–930	Settlement of Iceland
c. 1000	Icelanders convert to Christianity
c. 1001	Leif Eriksson discovers North America
c. 1179	Snorri Sturluson born
c. 1220	*Snorra Edda* is compiled
c. 1230	*Heimskringla* is compiled
1241	Killing of Snorri Sturluson
1262	Iceland comes under Norwegian rule
c. 1280	*Njáls saga* is composed
1779	*Balders Død,* music drama by Ewald and J. E. Hartmann
1802	'Guldhornene', poem by Oehlenschläger
1807	*Baldur hin Gode,* play by Oehlenschläger
1811	*Travels in the Island of Iceland,* travel book by MacKenzie
1832	'Guldhornene', music of J.P.E. Hartmann
1858	*Hærmændene paa Helgeland,* play by Ibsen
1861	*The Oxonian in Iceland,* travel book by Metcalfe
1861	*Valkyrien,* ballet by Bournonville
1863	*Iceland: Its Scenes and Sagas,* travel book by Baring-Gould
1863	'The Saga of King Olaf', poem by Longfellow
1869–76	*Der Ring des Nibelungen,* operas by Wagner
1874	*Six Weeks in the Saddle,* travel book by Waller
1896	*Scenes from the Saga of King Olaf,* cantata by Elgar
1902	*The Thrall of Leif the Lucky,* novel by Liljencrantz
1908	*Saga Drøm,* music by Nielsen
1909	*The Riding to Lithend,* play by Bottomley
1928	*The Viking,* film directed by Neill
1934	*Nial den Vise,* play by Jensen
1937	*The Hobbit,* novel by Tolkien
1940	'Thor God of Thunder', comic by Lincoln
1941–2	*Söguhetjur,* symphony by Jón Leifs

1942	'The Villain from Valhalla!', comic by Kirby and Simon
1944	'The Shadow of Valhalla!', comic by Kirby and Simon
1952	*Gerpla*, novel by Halldór Laxness
1954	*Rejse paa Island*, travel book by Hansen
1957	'The Magic Hammer', comic by Kirby
1958	*The Vikings*, film directed by Fleischer
1959	'The Hammer of Thor', comic by Ditko
1961	*Fire in the Ice*, novel by Roberts
1962	'Thor the Mighty and the Stone Men from Saturn!', comic by Lee, Kirby and Lieber
1970	'Immigrant Song', song by Plant and Page
1976	'Saibōgu Zero-Zero-Nain: Edda-hen', comic by Ishinomori
1977	*Berättelsen om Såm*, novel by Sundman
1979	*Ulven er løs*, comic by Madsen and Rancke-Madsen
1980	*Thors brudefærd*, comic by Madsen
1989	*Erik the Viking*, film directed by Jones
1994	*Nord for Vatnajøkel*, travel book by Vad
1996	Íslandsförin, novel by Guðmundur Andri Thorsson
2011	*Rumbo al Valhalla*, album of Mighty Thor
2011	*The Lay of Thrym*, album of Týr
2011	*Thor*, film directed by Branagh
2015	*Avengers: Age of Ultron*, film directed by Whedon

REFERENCES

Prologue

1 Peter Bonerz, dir., 'The One Where They're Going To Party', *Friends*, season 4, episode 9, written by Andrew Reich and Ted Cohen (1997), 00:03:00.

2 Ibid., 00:03:34.

3 J.R.R. Tolkien, *The Hobbit, or, There and Back Again* [1937] (London, 1992), p. 3.

4 Snorri Sturluson, *Edda*, trans. and ed. Anthony Faulkes (London and Melbourne, 1987), p. 16.

5 Sturluson, *Edda*, pp. 16–17 (my italics).

6 Tom Shippey, *J.R.R. Tolkien: Author of the Century* (London, 2001), p. 180.

7 Fredric Jameson, 'Postmodernism and Consumer Society', in E. Ann Kaplan, ed., *Postmodernism and Its Discontents, Theories, Practices* (London and New York, 1990), p. 20.

8 Ibid.

9 Linda Hutcheon, with Siobhan O'Flynn, *A Theory of Adaptation*, 2nd edn (London and New York, 2013), p. 7.

10 Ibid.

11 Sturluson, *Edda*, pp. 61–2.

12 Ibid., p. 62.

13 Ibid., pp. 63–4.

14 Ibid., p. 62.

15 Ibid., p. 70.

16 Roberta Frank, 'Snorri and the Mead of Poetry', in *Speculum Norroenum: Norse Studies in Memory of Gabriel Turville-Petre*, ed. Ursula Dronke, Guðrún P. Helgadóttir, Gerd Wolfgang Webber and Hans Bekker-Nielsen (Odense, 1981), p. 159.

17 William Shakespeare, *Timon of Athens*, in *The Riverside Shakespeare*, ed. G. Blakemore Evans (Boston, MA, 1974), p. 1468.

18 Sturluson, *Edda*, p. 2.

1 Thor: From Superhero to 'Kitchin'-maid

1 Peter Madsen, *Thors brudefærd*, based on a story by Per Vadmand, Hans Rancke-Madsen, Peter Madsen and Henning Kure, colouring by Søren Håkansson, letters by Tore Bahnson, produced by Henning Kure (Bagsværd, 1980), p. 39. English translation Jón Karl Helgason (hereafter JKH).

2 See Peter Harris, dir., 'Sax and Violence', *The Muppet Show*, season 1, episode 20 (26 February 1977), written by Jack Burns, Jerry Juhl and Jim Henson.

3 Halldór Stefánsson, 'Foreign Myths and Sagas in Japan: The Academics and the Cartoonists', in *Beyond Boundaries: Understanding, Translation and Anthropological Discourse*, ed. Gísli Pálsson (Oxford and Providence, RI, 1993), p. 86.

4 Mark Evanier, *Kirby: King of Comics* (New York, 2008), pp. 111–63.

5 Snorri Sturluson, *Edda*, trans. and ed. Anthony Faulkes (London and Melbourne, 1987), p. 22.

6 Carolyne Larrington, trans., *The Poetic Edda* (Oxford and New York, 1996), p. 99.

7 Stan Lee, Jack Kirby and Larry Lieber, 'Thor the Mighty and the Stone Men from Saturn!', colouring by Stan Goldberg, inks by Joe Sinnott, letters by Artie Simek, *Journey Into Mystery*, 83 (August 1962), n. pag.

8 Larrington, *The Poetic Edda*, p. 101.

9 See Richard Kolkman, 'The Evolution of Thor & The Stone Men', in *The Collected Jack Kirby Collector*, ed. John Morrow (Raleigh, NC, 2004), vol. III, pp. 86–8.

10 Jack Kirby and Joe Simon, 'The Villain from Valhalla!', *Adventure Comics*, 75 (June 1942), n. pag.

11 Chris Sims, 'The Strange History of Jack Kirby's Three Thors', *Comics Alliance* (6 May 2011), http://comicsalliance.com, accessed 15 June 2014.

12 See Rich Morrissey, 'Commandos in Valhalla', in *The Collected Jack Kirby Collector*, vol. III, p. 86.

13 Jack Kirby and Joe Simon, 'The Shadow of Valhalla!', *Boy Commandos*, 7 (Summer 1944), n. pag.

14 Ibid.

15 Ibid.

16 Ibid.

17 Evanier, *Kirby: King of Comics*, p. 62; Kirby and Simon, 'The Shadow of Valhalla!', n. pag.

18 See Charles F. Hutchinson and Stefanie M. Herrmann, 'Weather Modification: More Than Bargained For?', in *The Future of Arid Lands – Revisited: A Review of 50 Years of Drylands Research* (Paris and Dordrecht, 2007), pp. 45–62.

19 Jack Kirby, 'The Magic Hammer', *Tales of the Unexpected*, 16 (August 1957), n. pag.

20 Ibid.
21 Ibid.
22 Sturluson, *Edda*, p. 60.
23 See Jón Karl Helgason, '"Þegi þú Þórr!": Gender, Class and Discourse in *Þrymskviða*', in *Cold Counsel: Women in Old Norse Literature*, ed. Karen Swenson and Sarah May Anderson (New York and London, 2002), pp. 160–62.
24 Tom Spurgeon, 'Obituary: Pierce Rice, 1916–2003', *The Comics Reporter* (30 June 2003), www.comicsreporter.com, accessed 6 July 2014.
25 Wright Lincoln, 'Thor, God of Thunder', *Weird Comics*, 1 (April 1940), n. pag.
26 See Karl E. H. Seigfried, 'Blond Thor: Stan Lee Wasn't Wrong', *The Norse Mythology Blog*, www.norsemyth.org, 30 September 2011. Seigfried discusses many of the early comics that I deal with in this chapter.
27 Wright Lincoln, 'Thor Goes to War', *Weird Comics*, 2 (May 1940), n. pag.
28 See Blake Bell, *Strange and Stranger: The World of Steve Ditko* (Seattle, WA, 2008).
29 Steve Ditko, 'The Hammer of Thor', *Out of This World*, 11 (January 1959), n. pag.
30 Ibid.
31 Kolkman, 'The Evolution of Thor & The Stone Men', vol. III, p. 88.
32 Martin Arnold, *Thor: Myth to Marvel* (London and New York, 2011), p. 158.
33 Stan Lee, Jack Kirby and Larry Lieber, 'Trapped by Loki, The God of Mischief', *Journey into Mystery*, 85 (October 1962), n. pag.
34 Sturluson, *Edda*, p. 50.
35 Arnold, *Thor: Myth to Marvel*, p. 158.
36 Heather O'Donoghue, *From Asgard to Valhalla: The Remarkable History of the Norse Myths* (London and New York, 2008), p. 197.
37 Stefánsson, 'Foreign Myths and Sagas in Japan', p. 89.
38 See Tina Hafner, *Peter Madsens Valhalla: Studien zur Rezeption altwestnordischer Mythen im modernen Comic* (Munich, 2008).
39 Sturluson, *Edda*, p. 38.
40 Peter Madsen and Hans Rancke-Madsen, *Ulven er løs*, colouring by Søren Håkansson, produced by Henning Kure (Bagsværd, 1979), p. 5. English translation JKH.
41 Sturluson, *Edda*, p. 29.
42 See Karl Weinhold, 'Die Sagen von Loki', *Zeitschrift für Deutsches Alterthum*, VII (1849), pp. 1–94.
43 Larrington, *The Poetic Edda*, p. 98.
44 Margaret Clunies Ross, *Prolonged Echoes: Old Norse Myths in Medieval Northern Society* (Odense, 1994), vol. I, p. 109.
45 Madsen, *Thors brudefærd*, p. 32.
46 I am grateful to Haukur Ingvarsson for pointing this out to me.
47 Larrington, *The Poetic Edda*, p. 97.

48 Ibid., p. 100.
49 Madsen, *Thors brudefærd*, p. 32.
50 See Clunies Ross, *Prolonged Echoes*, vol. I, pp. 108–11, and Helgason, '"Þegi þú Þórr!"', pp. 162–3.
51 Madsen, *Thors brudefærd*, p. 13.
52 Larrington, *The Poetic Edda*, p. 99. I substitute here 'big stones' for 'jewels' as a translation of 'breiða steina'.
53 Madsen, *Thors brudefærd*, p. 35.
54 Ibid., p. 43.
55 Ibid., p. 47.
56 Ibid., p. 37.
57 Ibid., pp. 22–3.
58 Ibid., pp. 34, 40.
59 Ibid., p. 39.
60 See Tsukusu (Jinn) Itó, 'Hokuō Shinwa no Sekai to Sono Image no Juyō' (The World of Northern European Mythology and Its Reception [Focusing on Japan]), *Eureka: Poetry and Criticism* (October 2007), pp. 187–98, and Akemi Itsuij and Tsukusu (Jinn) Itó, 'Sanshu Sareru Hokuō Shinwa: Ongaku, Kotoba, Image o Shōryō Suru' (Northern European Mythology Disseminated: Ranging over Music, Language, Images), ibid., pp. 58–75.
61 George Gene Gustines, 'Marvel Comics Reveals a Female Thor', *New York Times* (12 May 2015), http://artsbeat.blogs.nytimes.com, accessed 20 November 2015.

2 Snorri: The 'Real' Stories

1 Laurent Tirard, dir., *Le Petit Nicolas*, script by Laurent Tirard, Grégoire Vigneron and Alain Chabat (Paris, 2009), 1:00:44.
2 Ibid., 1:01:15.
3 See for example Slavica Ranković, 'Who Is Speaking in Traditional Texts? On the Distributed Author of the Sagas of Icelanders and Serbian Epic Poetry', *New Literary History*, XXXVIII/2 (2007), pp. 293–307, and Jón Karl Helgason, *The Rewriting of Njáls Saga: Translation, Politics and Icelandic Sagas*, Topics in Translation, 16 (Clevedon, Buffalo, NY, Toronto and Sydney, 1999).
4 Viðar Hreinsson, gen. ed., *Eirik the Red's Saga*, trans. Keneva Kunz, in *The Complete Sagas of Icelanders* (Reykjavík, 1997), vol. I, p. 6.
5 Snorri Sturluson, *Heimskringla: History of the Kings of Norway*, trans. and ed. Lee M. Hollander (Austin, TX, 1991), p. 251.
6 Ibid.
7 Erik J. Friis, gen. ed., *The Saga of Þorgils and Hafliði*, trans. Julia H. McGrew, in *Sturlunga Saga* (New York, 1974), vol. II, p. 43.
8 Ibid., p. 29.

9 Ibid., p. 44.
10 Ibid., pp. 43–4.
11 Erik J. Friis, gen. ed., *About Sturla Þórðarson*, trans. Julia H. McGrew, in *Sturlunga Saga*, vol. II, p. 495.
12 Ibid., p. 496.
13 Anthony Faulkes, 'Introduction', in Snorri Sturluson, *Edda: Prologue and Gylfaginning*, ed. Anthony Faulkes, 2nd edn (London, 2005), p. xiii.
14 Eiríkur Þormóðsson and Guðrun Ása Grímsdóttir, eds, *Oddaannálar og Oddverjaannáll* (Reykjavík, 2003), p. 146. English translation Jane Victoria Appleton (hereafter JVA).
15 Ólafur Halldórsson, ed., *Ólafs saga Tryggvasonar hin mesta* (Copenhagen, 1961), vol. II, p. 264. English translation JVA.
16 See Jakob Benediktsson, 'Hvar var Snorri nefndur höfundur Heimskringlu?', *Skírnir*, 129 (1955), pp. 118–27, and Ólafur Halldórsson, 'Sagnaritun Snorra Sturlusonar', in *Snorri: átta alda minning*, ed. Gunnar Karlsson and Helgi Þorláksson (Reykjavík, 1979), pp. 113–38.
17 See Jonna Louis-Jensen, 'Heimskringla – et værk af Snorri Sturluson?', *Nordica Bergensia*, 14 (1977), pp. 230–45; Jonna Louis-Jensen, 'Did Snorri Sturluson write "Heimskringla"?', in *Snorri Sturluson and the Roots of Nordic Literature*, ed. Vladimir Stariradev (Sofia, 2004), pp. 96–101.
18 Sverrir Tómasson, 'Veraldleg sagnaritun 1120–1400', in *Íslensk bókmenntasaga*, ed. Vésteinn Ólason (Reykjavík, 1992), vol. I, p. 368. English translation JVA.
19 See Patricia Pires Boulhosa, *Icelanders and the Kings of Norway: Medieval Sagas and Legal Texts*, The Northern World, XVII (Leiden and Boston, MA, 2005), pp. 6–21.
20 Sturla Thordarson, *The Saga of the Icelanders*, trans. Julia H. McGrew, in Friis, *Sturlunga Saga*, vol. I, p. 242. I substitute here 'compiling' for 'writing' as a translation of 'setja saman'.
21 Finnur Jónsson, ed., *Den norsk-islandske skjaldedigtning* (Copenhagen, 1967), vol. A-I, p. 584. English translation JVA.
22 Oddur Snorrason, *Ólafs saga Tryggvasonar*, in *Færeyinga saga; Ólafs saga Tryggvasonar*, ed. Ólafur Halldórsson, Íslenzk fornrit, 25 (Reykjavik, 2006), p. 232. English translation JVA.
23 Sturluson, *Heimskringla*, p. 4.
24 Ibid., p. 748.
25 See Bjarni Aðalbjarnarson, 'Formáli', in Snorri Sturluson, *Heimskringla*, ed. Bjarni Aðalbjarnarson, Íslenzk fornrit, 28 (Reykjavík, 1979), vol. III, pp. lxiii–vii.
26 Bjarni Einarsson, ed., *Ágrip af Nóregskonunga sögum: Fagrskinna – Nóregs konunga tal*, Íslenzk fornrit, 29 (Reykjavík, 1984), p. 145. English translation JVA.
27 Snorrason, *Ólafs saga Tryggvasonar*, p. 222.
28 Sturluson, *Heimskringla: History of the Kings of Norway*, p. 198.

29 Faulkes, 'Introduction', p. xiii.
30 Ibid., pp. xiii–xiv.
31 Tzvetan Todorov, 'Poetics and Criticism', in *The Poetics of Prose*, trans. Richard Howard (Ithaca, NY, 1977), pp. 29–41.
32 Snorri Sturluson, *Edda*, trans. and ed. Anthony Faulkes (London and Melbourne, 1987), p. 53.
33 Ibid., p. 3.
34 Ibid., p. 57.
35 Ibid.
36 Ibid., p. 59.
37 Ibid., p. 61.
38 Ibid., pp. 64–5.
39 See Torfi Tulinius, *The Enigma of Egill: The Saga, the Viking Poet, and Snorri Sturluson*, trans. Victoria Cribb, Islandica, 57 (Ithaca, NY, 2014).
40 Snorri Sturluson, *Ritsafn*, 3 vols, ed. Helgi Bernódusson, Jónas Kristjánsson, Örnólfur Thorsson (Reykjavík, 2002).
41 Sturluson, *Edda*, p. 170.
42 Kevin J. Wanner, *Snorri Sturluson and the Edda: The Conversion of Cultural Capital in Medieval Scandinavia* (Toronto, Buffalo, NY, and London, 2008), p. 160.

3 Hallgerd: A Bow-string Breaks

1 Olav Lausund, 'Edmund Gosse: Ibsen's First Prophet to English Readers', in *Anglo-Scandinavian Cross-currents*, ed. Inga-Stina Ewbank, Olav Lausund and Bjørn Tysdahl (Norwich, 1999), p. 139.
2 Edmund W. Gosse, 'The Warriors at Helgeland', *The Academy* (25 July 1874), p. 90.
3 Ibid., p. 91.
4 See Ingibjörg Jónsdóttir Kolka, '"Að ég gæti fundið það allt í einum manni." Baksviðs leikritsins Hærmændene på Helgeland eftir Henrik Ibsen, greining þess og viðtökur', unpublished MA thesis, University of Iceland, 2004.
5 Theodore Jorgenson, *Henrik Ibsen: Life and Drama* (Northfield, MN, 1963), p. 106.
6 See Gudleiv Bø, *Nationale subjekter: Ideer om nasjonalitet i Henrik Ibsens romantiske forfatterskap* (Oslo, 2000), p. 156.
7 Michael Meyer, *Henrik Ibsen: The Making of a Dramatist, 1828–1964* (London, 1967), p. 171.
8 Bjørn Hemmer, 'Ibsen and Historical Drama', in *The Cambridge Companion to Ibsen*, ed. James McFarlane (Cambridge, 1994), p. 16. Quotation from Henrik Ibsen, *Brev, 1845–1905*, ed. Øyvind Anker (Oslo, 1979), p. 83.

9 'Repertoardatabase: Hærmændene på Helgeland', *Nationalbiblioteket: Alt om Henrik Ibsen*, http://ibsen.nb.no/id/586.0, accessed 12 October 2015.

10 See Terry Gunnell, 'Early Representations of Old Nordic Religions in Drama', in *Pre-Christian Religions of the North*, ed. Margaret Clunies Ross (Turnhout, forthcoming), and Terry Gunnell and Sveinn Einarsson, 'Theatre and Performance (1830–2012)', ibid.

11 Linda Hutcheon, with Siobhan O'Flynn, *A Theory of Adaptation*, 2nd edn (London and New York, 2013), pp. 12–13.

12 Henrik Ibsen, *The Vikings of Helgeland*, trans. William Archer, in *Project Gutenberg Release #19205*, http://onlinebooks.library.upenn.edu, accessed 22 February 2016, act I.

13 Ferdinand G. Lynner, *Hærmennene paa Helgeland: Henriks Ibsens forhold til kilderne i den norrøne literatur* (Kristiania, 1909), p. 5.

14 Viðar Hreinsson, gen. ed., *Egil's Saga*, trans. Bernard Scudder, in *The Complete Sagas of Icelanders* (Reykjavík, 1997), vol. I, p. 151.

15 Ibsen, *The Vikings of Helgeland*, act IV.

16 Lynner, *Hærmennene paa Helgeland*, pp. 7–19.

17 Quotation from Jorgenson, *Henrik Ibsen*, p. 106.

18 Viðar Hreinsson, gen. ed., *Njal's Saga*, trans. Robert Cook, in *The Complete Sagas of Icelanders*, vol. III, p. 57.

19 Ibid.

20 Ibid., p. 89.

21 Ibsen, *The Vikings of Helgeland*, act III.

22 Viðar Hreinsson, gen. ed., *The Saga of the People of Laxardal*, trans. Keneva Kunz, in *The Complete Sagas of Icelanders*, vol. V, p. 79.

23 Ibsen, *The Vikings of Helgeland*, act III.

24 Ibid.

25 Meyer, *Henrik Ibsen*, p. 170.

26 Ibid., p. 172. See also Merrill Kaplan, 'Hedda and Hjørdis: Saga and Scandal in *Hedda Gabler* and *The Vikings at Helgeland*', *Ibsen Studies*, IV/1 (2004), pp. 18–29.

27 See Claude Colleer Abbott, 'Introduction', in Gordon Bottomley, *Poems and Plays* (London and Edinburgh, 1953), p. 16.

28 See ibid., and Gordon Bottomley and Paul Nash, *Poet and Painter: Being the Correspondence between Gordon Bottomley and Paul Nash, 1910–1946*, ed. Claude Colleer Abbott and Anthony Bertram (London and New York, 1955), p. xv.

29 William Morris, 'Gunnar's Howe above the House at Lithend', in *Poems by the Way & Love Is Enough* (New York and Bombay, 1898), p. 123.

30 Gordon Bottomley, *The Riding to Lithend*, in *Poems and Plays*, p. 94.

31 Hreinsson, *Njal's Saga*, p. 90.

32 Bottomley, *The Riding to Lithend*, p. 123.

33 Ibid., p. 127.

34 Ibid.
35 Ibid., pp. 101–6.
36 Ibid., p. 123.
37 William Shakespeare, *The Tragedy of Macbeth*, in *The Riverside Shakespeare*, ed. G. Blakemore Evans (Boston, MA, 1974), p. 1338.
38 See Abbott, 'Introduction', in Bottomley, *Poems and Plays*, p. 16.
39 See Alexander MacGill, 'Gordon Bottomley', *Eimreiðin*, XXXIII (1927), p. 71.
40 Shakespeare, *Macbeth*, p. 1314.
41 Bottomley, *The Riding to Lithend*, p. 108.
42 Shakespeare, *Macbeth*, p. 1312.
43 Bottomley, *The Riding to Lithend*, p. 113.
44 Bottomley and Nash, *Poet and Painter*, p. 185.
45 Allardyce Nicoll, *English Drama, 1900–1930: The Beginnings of the Modern Period* (Cambridge, 1973), vol. II, p. 302.
46 Guðmundur Magnússon to Bogi Th. Melsteð, 18 March 1904, in *Ut. 141* (Bogi Melsteð's collected letters), at The Royal Library, Copenhagen (Bogi's text is written on the back of Guðmundur's letter). English translation JVA.
47 See Cai M. Woel, *Thit Jensen* (Copenhagen, 1954), p. 14.
48 Books on Jensen's life include Woel's *Thit Jensen* and Jens Andersen, *Thit – den sidste valkyrie* (Copenhagen, 1996).
49 Thit Jensen, *Erindringerne: Hvorfra? Hvorhen?* (Copenhagen, 1950), p. 164.
50 See 'Tre Dramatikere belønnet med store Præmier', *Politiken* (24 August 1934), p. 3.
51 Hans Brix, 'Fru Thit Jensen præmierede Stykke', *Dagens Nyheter* (31 October 1934), p. 7. English translation JKH.
52 Thit Jensen, *Nial den Vise: Udstyrsskuespil fra Islands Storhedstid* (Copenhagen, 1934), p. 52. English translation JKH.
53 George Webbe Dasent, trans., *The Story of Burnt Njal; or, Life in Iceland at the End of the Tenth Century* (Edinburgh, 1861), vol. I, p. 236. Bottomley worked from Dasent's translation.
54 Bottomley, *The Riding to Lithend*, p. 111.
55 Ibid.
56 Jensen, *Nial den Vise*, p. 29.
57 Shakespeare, *Macbeth*, p. 1317.
58 Ibsen, *The Vikings of Helgeland*, act III.
59 Thit Jensen, *Jeg længes–: fra Thit Jensens dagbøger 1891–1927*, ed. Jens Andersen (Copenhagen, 1991), p. 128. English translation JKH.
60 Jensen, *Jeg længes*, p. 129.
61 Guðmundur Magnússon to Bogi Melsteð, 24 January 1905, in *Ut. 141*.
62 Jensen, *Jeg længes*, p. 137.
63 Ibid., p. 137.

64 Ibid., p. 138.
65 Ibid.
66 Jensen, *Nial den Vise*, p. 44.
67 Jensen, *Jeg længes*, p. 138.
68 Ibsen, *The Vikings of Helgeland*, act II.
69 Ibid., act IV.
70 Ibid.
71 Bottomley, *The Riding to Lithend*, p. 103.
72 Ibid., pp. 102–4.
73 Ibid., p. 125.
74 Shakespeare, *Macbeth*, p. 1316.
75 Thit Jensen, 'Sigrid', in *Sagn and Syner* (Copenhagen, 1909), p. 20. English translation JKH.
76 Jensen, *Nial den Vise*, p. 58.
77 Ibid., p. 11.
78 Ibid.
79 Ibid., p. 25.
80 Ibid., p. 26.
81 Jensen, *Jeg længes*, p. 129.
82 Quotation from Andersen, *Thit – den sidste valkyrie*, p. 112.

4 Gunnar: In Saddles, Armchairs and Land Rovers

1 Samuel Edward Waller, *Six Weeks in the Saddle: A Painter's Journal in Iceland* (London, 1874), p. 117.
2 See Gary Aho, '"Með Ísland á heilanum": Íslandsbækur breskra ferðalanga 1772 til 1897', trans. Jón Karl Helgason, *Skírnir*, CLXVII (Spring 1993), pp. 207–33.
3 Andrew Wawn, *The Vikings and the Victorians: Inventing the Old North in Nineteenth-century Britain* (Cambridge, 2000), p. 51. See also Andrew Wawn, '*Gunnlaugs saga Ormstungu* and the Theatre Royal Edinburgh 1812: Melodrama, Mineralogy and Sir George Mackenzie', *Scandinavica*, XXI (1981), pp. 139–51, and Andrew Wawn, '"The Courtly Old Carle": Sir Henry Holland and Nineteenth-century Iceland', in *Saga-book of the Viking Society for Northern Research*, XXI/1–2 (1982–3), pp. 54–79.
4 See George Steuart Mackenzie, *Travels in the Island of Iceland during the Summer of the Year MDCCCX* (Edinburgh, 1811), p. 257.
5 Frederick Metcalfe, *The Oxonian in Iceland: or, Notes of Travel in That Island in the Summer of 1860, with Glances at Icelandic Folk-lore and Sagas* (London, 1861), p. 3.
6 Bjarni Thorarensen, 'Vísur um Fljótshlíð', *Kvæði Bjarna Thórarensens amtmanns* (Copenhagen, 1847), p. 57. English translation JVA.
7 Wawn, *The Vikings and the Victorians*, p. 299.

8 Sabine Baring-Gould, *Iceland: Its Scenes and Sagas* (London, 1863), p. xiii.
9 Waller, *Six Weeks in the Saddle*, p. 76.
10 Disney Leith, *Three Visits to Iceland: Being notes taken at sea and on land: comprising a pilgrimage to Skalholt, and visits to Geysir and the Njala district* (London, 1897), n. pag.
11 Waller, *Six Weeks in the Saddle*, p. 115.
12 Aho, '"Með Ísland á heilanum"', pp. 255–6.
13 Waller, *Six Weeks in the Saddle*, p. 40.
14 William Morris, 'Gunnar's Howe above the House at Lithend', in *Poems by the Way & Love Is Enough* (New York and Bombay, 1898), p. 122.
15 Wawn, *The Vikings and the Victorians*, p. 313.
16 See Ástráður Eysteinsson, 'Er Halldór Laxness höfundur Fóstbræðrasögu?: Um höfundargildi, textatengsl og þýðingu í sambandi Laxness við fornsögurnar', *Skáldskaparmál*, I (1990), pp. 171–88, and Massimiliano Bampi, 'Revisiting the Past: P. O. Sundman's rewrite of *Hrafnkels saga Freysgoða*', in *The Garden of Crossing Paths: The Manipulation and Rewriting of Medieval Texts. Venice, October 28–30, 2004*, ed. Marina Buzzoni and Massimiliano Bampi (Venice, 2007), pp. 219–24.
17 Dorothy James Roberts, *Fire in the Ice* (Boston, MA, and Toronto, 1961), p. viii.
18 Ibid., p. 6.
19 W. G. Collingwood and Jón Stefánsson, *A Pilgrimage to the Saga-steads of Iceland* (Ulverston, 1899), p. v.
20 William Morris, *Icelandic Journals* (London, 1996), p. 130.
21 Roberts, *Fire in the Ice*, p. 238.
22 Viðar Hreinsson, gen. ed., *Njal's Saga*, trans. Robert Cook, in *The Complete Sagas of Icelanders* (Reykjavík, 1997), vol. III, p. 37.
23 Roberts, *Fire in the Ice*, p. 245.
24 Ibid., p. 317.
25 Quotation taken from *Book Review Digest, 1961* (New York, 1962), p. 1197.
26 Sumarliði Ísleifsson, *Ísland, framandi land* (Reykjavík, 1996), p. 210. English translation JVA.
27 Waller, *Six Weeks in the Saddle*, p. 39.
28 Heidi Hansson, 'Between Nostalgia and Modernity: Competing Discourses in Travel Writing about the Nordic North', in *Iceland and Images of the North*, ed. Sumarliði Ísleifsson and Daniel Chartier (Québec, 2011), p. 258.
29 P. E. Kristian Kålund, *Bidrag til en historisk-topografisk Beskrivelse af Island* (Copenhagen, 1882), vol. II, pp. 218–19.
30 Martin A. Hansen, *Rejse paa Island*, illus. Sven Havsteen-Mikkelsen (Copenhagen, 1954), p. 194. English translation JKH.
31 Ibid.
32 Poul Vad, *Nord for Vatnajøkel* (Copenhagen, 1994), p. 37. English translation JKH.

33 Henk van der Liet, 'Iceland: A Postcolonial Literary Landscape?', *Amsterdamer Beiträge zur älteren Germanistik*, LXVII (2011), p. 459.
34 Vad, *Nord for Vatnajøkel*, p. 36.
35 Ibid.
36 Sigurður Nordal, *Hrafnkels saga Freysgoda: A Study*, trans. R. George Thomas (Cardiff, 1958), p. 57.
37 Vad, *Nord for Vatnajøkel*, p. 39.
38 Ibid., p. 51.
39 Ibid., p. 87.
40 Ibid., pp. 91–2.
41 Ibid., pp. 97–8.
42 Ibid., p. 123.

5 Odin: From Wagner to Viking Metal

1 Dave Swanson, 'Jack Black Hails Led Zeppelin as "The Greatest Rock and Roll Band of All Time" at Kennedy Center Honors', *Classic Rock* (27 December 2012), http://ultimateclassicrock.com, accessed 7 August 2014.
2 Ibid.
3 Snorri Sturluson, *Edda*, trans. and ed. Anthony Faulkes (London and Melbourne, 1987), p. 21.
4 Sturluson, *Edda*, p. 31.
5 Ibid., p. 34.
6 Margaret Clunies Ross, 'The Measure of Old Norse Religion in Long-term Perspective', in *Old Norse Religion in Long-term Perspectives: Origins, Changes and Interactions, An International Conference in Lund, Sweden, June 3–7, 2004*, ed. Anders Andrén, Kristina Jennbert and Catharina Raudvere (Lund, 2006), p. 414.
7 Adalbert Müller, *Donaustauf and Walhalla* (Regensburg, 1846), p. 28.
8 See Terry Gunnell, 'Early Representations of Old Nordic Religions in Drama', in *Pre-Christian Religions of the North*, ed. Margaret Clunies Ross (Turnhout, forthcoming).
9 Frederick Key Smith, *Nordic Art Music: From the Middle Ages to the Third Millennium* (Westport, CT, and London, 2002), p. 17. Smith also refers here to John Horton, *Scandinavian Music: A Short History* (Westport, CT, 1975), p. 79.
10 Inger Sørensen, 'J.P.E. Hartmann', *Dacapo Records* (March 2007), www.dacapo-records.dk, accessed 14 October 2015.
11 Ibid.
12 Árni Björnsson, *Wagner and the Volsungs: Icelandic Sources of Der Ring des Nibelungen*, trans. Anna Yates and Anthony Faulkes (London, 2003), p. 79.
13 Ibid., p. 80.

14 Richard Wagner, 'The Nibelungen Myth', in *Pilgrimage to Beethoven and Other Essays*, trans. William Ashton Ellis (Lincoln, NE, and London, 1994), p. 299. Quotation from Björnsson, *Wagner and the Volsungs*, p. 118.
15 Wagner, 'The Nibelungen Myth', p. 311. Quotation from Björnsson, *Wagner and the Volsungs*, p. 125.
16 Richard Wagner, *The Rhinegold*, complete vocal score in a facilitated arrangement by Karl Klindworth, trans. Frederick Jameson (New York, 1904), p. 213.
17 Wagner, *The Rhinegold*, p. 214.
18 Richard Wagner, *The Valkyrie*, trans. Frederick Jameson (Mainz, London, Paris and Brussels, 1900), p. 26.
19 Ibid., p. 38.
20 David Mannes, *Music Is My Faith: An Autobiography* (New York, 1938), p. 159.
21 See Norman Schweikert, *The Horns of Valhalla: Saga of the Reiter Brothers* (Gurnee, IL, 2012).
22 Edward Elgar, *King Olaf* (London, 1896), pp. 167–71.
23 Andrew Wawn, *The Vikings and the Victorians: Inventing the Old North in Nineteenth-century Britain* (Cambridge, 2000), p. 111.
24 Elgar, *King Olaf*, pp. 78–9.
25 Ibid., pp. 5–6.
26 Ibid., pp. 7–10.
27 Jimmy Page and Robert Plant, 'Immigrant Song', on Led Zeppelin, *Led Zeppelin III* (New York, 1970).
28 Ibid.
29 Andy Bennett, 'Paganism and the Counter-culture', in *Pop Pagans: Paganism and Popular Music*, ed. Donna Weston and Andy Bennett (Durham and Bristol, 2013), p. 18.
30 See Michael Moynihan and Didrik Søderlind, *Lords of Chaos: The Bloody Rise of the Satanic Metal Underground* (Port Townsend, WA, 2007).
31 Simon Trafford and Aleks Pluskowski, 'Antichrist Superstars: The Vikings in Hard Rock and Heavy Metal', in *Mass Market Medieval: Essays on the Middle Ages in Popular Culture*, ed. David W. Marshall (Jefferson, NC, and London, 2007), p. 63.
32 Joey DeMaio, 'Gates of Valhalla', on Manowar, *Into Glory Ride* (New York, 1982).
33 Quorthon, 'Valhalla', on Bathory, *Hammerheart* (Berlin, 1990).
34 Mighty Thor, 'Rumbo al Valhalla', on Mighty Thor, *Rumbo al Valhalla* (San Bartolo Ameyalco, 2011).
35 Frode Glesnes and Gerhard Storesund, 'Odin Owns Ye All', on Einherjer, *Odin Owns Ye All* (Dortmund, 1998).
36 Heri Joensen and Pól Arni Holm, 'Hail to the Hammer', on Týr, *How Far to Asgaard* (Torshavn, 2002).
37 Trafford and Pluskowski, 'Antichrist Superstars', pp. 65–7.

38 See Florian Heesch, 'Metal for Nordic Men: Amon Amarth's Representation of Vikings', in *The Metal Void: First Gatherings*, ed. Nial W. R. Scott and Imke von Helden (Oxford, 2010); pp. 71–80; Imke von Helden, 'Barbarians and Literature: Viking Metal and Its Links to Old Norse Mythology', ibid., pp. 257–63.

39 Trafford and Pluskowski, 'Antichrist Superstars', p. 63. See also Joshua Chaplinsky, 'Lord of the Strings: The Influence of Tolkien on Heavy Metal Music', *Litreactor* (7 January 2013), https://litreactor.com, accessed 14 October 2015.

40 Solarsteinn, 'The Challenge Of Thor', released online (9 December 2014), https://solarsteinn.bandcamp.com, accessed 25 February 2016.

41 See Christian Dornbusch and Hans-Peter Killguss, *Unheilige Allianzen: Black Metal zwischen Satanismus, Heidentum und Neonazismus* (Münster, 2007); Heather O'Donoghue, *From Asgard to Valhalla: The Remarkable History of the Norse Myths* (London and New York, 2008), pp. 196–7.

42 Heri Joensen and Gunnar H. Thomsen, 'The Lay of Thrym', on Týr, *The Lay of Thrym* (Torshavn, 2011).

43 Ibid.

44 Heri Joensen, 'Take Your Tyrant', on Týr, *The Lay of Thrym*.

45 Karl E. H. Seigfried, 'Interview with Heri Joensen of Týr, Part One', *The Norse Mythology Blog* (24 October 2013), http://www.norsemyth.org, accessed 30 May 2014.

46 Snæbjörn Ragnarsson, 'Gleipnir', on Skálmöld, *Börn Loka* (Eisenerz, Styria, 2012).

47 O'Donoghue, *From Asgard to Valhalla*, p. 197.

48 Trafford and Pluskowski, 'Antichrist Superstars', p. 71.

49 Chris Welch, *Led Zeppelin: The Book* (London, 1994), p. 55.

6 Leif: When Civilization Was Less Civilized

1 *Erik the Viking Official Trailer* (London, 1989), available at www.youtube.com, accessed 13 September 2015.

2 Ibid.

3 Ibid.

4 Kevin J. Harty, 'Who's Savage Now?! – The Vikings in North America', in *The Vikings on Film: Essays on Depictions of the Nordic Middle Ages*, ed. Kevin J. Harty (Jefferson, NC, 2011), p. 107.

5 On these and other early American Vinland novels, see Geraldine Barnes, *Viking America: The First Millennium* (Cambridge, 2001), pp. 117–43.

6 Jeannette L. Gilder, 'Jeannette L. Gilder's Literary Reviews', *Chicago Daily Tribune* (15 March 1902). Reference borrowed from Jim Craig, 'She Made the Vikings Come Alive – Ottilie Adalina Liljencrantz', *Under Every Stone*

(16 January 2015), http://undereverystone.blogspot.co.uk, accessed 26 February 2016.

7 'Chicago Young Woman Becomes a Novelist', *Chicago Daily Tribune* (11 March 1902). Reference borrowed from Craig, 'She Made the Vikings Come Alive'.

8 See Jón Karl Helgason, *The Rewriting of Njáls Saga: Translation, Politics and Icelandic Sagas*, Topics in Translation, 16 (Clevedon, Buffalo, NY, Toronto and Sydney, 1999), pp. 47–82.

9 Gilder, 'Jeannette L. Gilder's Literary Reviews'.

10 Ottilie A. Liljencrantz, *The Thrall of Leif the Lucky: A Story of Viking Days* (Chicago, IL, 1902), p. 5.

11 I refer hereafter to these sections with the title *Ólafs saga*, but it should be noted that the chapters of *Flateyjarbók* concerning the settlements in Greenland and Vinland are frequently printed separately as *Grænlendinga saga* (The Saga of the Greenlanders).

12 Viðar Hreinsson, gen. ed., *Eirik the Red's Saga*, trans. Keneva Kunz, in *The Complete Sagas of Icelanders* (Reykjavík, 1997), vol. I, p. 8.

13 Hreinsson, *Eirik the Red's Saga*, p. 8.

14 Viðar Hreinsson, gen. ed., *The Saga of the Greenlanders*, trans. Keneva Kunz, in *The Complete Sagas of Icelanders*, vol. I, p. 21.

15 Ibid., p. 23.

16 Ibid., p. 24.

17 Liljencrantz, *The Thrall of Leif the Lucky*, p. 13.

18 Ibid., p. 19.

19 Ibid., p. 21.

20 Ibid., pp. 20–21.

21 Ibid., p. 87.

22 See Richard W. Haines, *Technicolor Movies: The History of Dye Transfer Printing* (Jefferson, NC, 2003).

23 H. T. Kalmus. 'Technicolor Adventures in Cinemaland', in *A Technological History of Motion Pictures and Television: An Anthology from the Pages of the Journal of the Society of Motion Picture and Television Engineers*, ed. Raymond Fielding (Oakland, CA, 1967), pp. 54–5.

24 Ibid., p. 55.

25 Arne Lunde, *Nordic Exposures: Scandinavian Identities in Classical Hollywood Cinema* (Seattle, WA, 2010), p. 26.

26 Roy William Neill, dir., *The Viking* (Boston, MA, New York, Los Angeles, CA, 1928), 00:18:38.

27 Ibid., 00:19:42.

28 Hreinsson, *The Saga of the Greenlanders*, p. 23.

29 Neill, *The Viking*, 00:21:32.

30 Ibid., 00:21:49–00:22:05.

31 Ibid., 00:22:35.
32 Hreinsson, *Eirik the Red's Saga*, p. 8.
33 Neill, *The Viking*, 00:40:14.
34 Ibid., 01:27:02.
35 Ibid., 01:28:00.
36 Ibid., 01:28:15.
37 Ibid., 01:29:06.
38 Lunde, *Nordic Exposures*, p. 16.
39 Hreinsson, *Eirik the Red's Saga*, p. 16.
40 Lunde, *Nordic Exposures*, pp. 17–21.
41 See George M. Stephenson, *A History of American Immigration, 1820–1924* (Boston, MA, 1926), p. 9.
42 See Inga Dóra Björnsdóttir, 'Leifr Eiríksson versus Christopher Columbus: The Use of Leifr Eiríksson in American Political and Cultural Discourse', in *Approaches to Vínland*, ed. Andrew Wawn and Þórunn Sigurðardóttir (Reykjavík, 2001), pp. 200–226.
43 'Alþingishátíðin og þjóðin íslenzka viðurkend í Congress Bandaríkjanna', *Heimskringla* (24 April 1929), p. 1.
44 Ibid.
45 Neill, *The Viking*, 01:27:02.
46 See Harty, 'Who's Savage Now?!', pp. 110–11.
47 See Kathleen Coyne Kelly, 'The Trope of the Scopic in *The Vikings* (1958)', in *The Vikings on Film*, p. 12.
48 H. H., 'Rætt við Stefán Karlsson: Með víkingum í verkfalli', *Frjáls þjóð* (20 July 1957), p. 2.
49 Ibid.
50 Ben Waggoner, trans. and ed., *Saga of Ragnar Lodbrok and his Sons*, in *The Sagas of Ragnar Lodbrok* (New Haven, CT, 2009), p. 29.
51 Ibid., p. 30.
52 Richard Fleischer, dir., *The Vikings* (Los Angeles, CA, 1958), 00:01:00.
53 Snorri Sturluson, *Edda*, trans. and ed. Anthony Faulkes (London and Melbourne, 1987), p. 21.
54 Ben Waggoner, trans. and ed., *Krákumál*, in *The Sagas of Ragnar Lodbrok*, p. 83.
55 Neill, *The Viking*, 00:01:50.
56 Ibid., 00:03:43. On possible Latin sources for this prayer see Magnus Magnusson, *Vikings!* (London, Sydney, Toronto, 1980), p. 61.
57 Fleischer, *The Vikings*, 00:01:10.
58 Ibid., 00:01:50.
59 Kelly, 'The Trope of the Scopic in *The Vikings* (1958)', p. 15. The interview is a part of a DVD version of the film: 'Photo gallery with audio commentary by Director Richard Fleischer'.

60 Kelly, 'The Trope of the Scopic in *The Vikings* (1958)', p. 16.

61 Ibid., p. 22.

62 Ibid., p. 17.

63 Sturluson, *Edda*, p. 63.

64 Viðar Hreinsson, gen. ed., *Egil's Saga*, trans. Bernard Scudder, in *The Complete Sagas of Icelanders*, vol. I, pp. 140–41.

65 Ibid., p. 142.

66 H. H., 'Rætt við Stefán Karlsson', p. 2.

67 See Kevin J. Hardy, 'The Vikings on Film: Filmography', in *The Vikings on Film*, pp. 193–213.

68 Terry Jones, dir., *Erik the Viking* (Stockholm and London, 1989), 00:01:50.

Epilogue

1 Halldór Laxness, *Iceland's Bell*, trans. Philip Roughton (New York and Toronto, 2003), p. 20.

2 Vésteinn Ólason, 'Bóksögur', in *Munnmenntir og bókmenning: Íslensk þjóðmenning*, ed. Frosti F. Jóhannsson (Reykjavík, 1989), vol. IV, p. 209.

3 HK 45, p. 407. One of the answers to questions posed to Icelanders between 1927 and 1930 by the Danish teacher Holger Kjær, preserved in the Department of Ethnology at the National Museum of Iceland. Material from this collection is referred to by the initials HK, together with the number assigned to each correspondent, and a page number referring to the collection as a whole. English translations from this source JVA.

4 HK 35, pp. 319–20.

5 HK 24, p. 199.

6 HK 1, pp. 5–6.

7 See for instance HK 12, p. 107.

8 HK 12, p. 109.

9 NM 12262. One of the answers to questionnaire #86 about daily life in rural and urban areas in the twentieth century, distributed by the Department of Ethnology to its correspondents in 1994, preserved at the National Museum of Iceland. Those who responded to the questionnaire will be referred to by the initials NM, together with the number assigned to each correspondent in the Department of Ethnology archive at the museum. English translations from this source JVA.

10 NM 11298.

11 NM 11251.

12 NM 11359.

13 NM 11323.

14 NM 11930.

15 HK 13, p. 121.
16 NM 11250.
17 NM 11872.
18 NM 11406.
19 HK 28, p. 251.
20 See Bergljót Soffía Kristjánsdóttir, '"Hann er kominn." – "Hann er farinn." Um *Útlagann* og *Gísla sögu Súrssonar*', *Ritið*, I (2001), pp. 23–40.
21 See Bjørn Sørensen, 'Hrafn Gunnlaugsson – The Viking Who Came in from the Cold?', in *Transnational Cinema in Global North: Nordic Cinema in Transition*, ed. Andrew Nestingen and Trevor G. Elkington (Detroit, MI, 2005), pp. 341–56.
22 See Fulvio Ferrari, 'From Saga to Comics: Njáls Saga and the Graphic Novels of Embla Ýr Bárudóttir and Ingólfur Örn Björgvinsson', in *Lost in Translation?*, ed. Denis Renevey and Christiania Whitehead (Turnhout, 2009), pp. 351–64.
23 'The Njal's Saga Tapestry', *Njálurefill*, http://njalurefill.is, accessed 27 February 2016.
24 Guðmundur Andri Thorsson, *Íslandsförin* (Reykjavik, 1996), pp. 25–6. English translation JVA.
25 Ibid., p. 148.
26 Ibid., p. 157.

SELECT BIBLIOGRAPHY

Primary sources in translation

Friis, Erik J., gen. ed., *Sturlunga Saga*, 2 vols (New York, 1974)
Hreinsson, Viðar, gen. ed., *The Complete Sagas of Icelanders*, 5 vols (Reykjavík, 1997)
Larrington, Carolyne, trans., *The Poetic Edda* (Oxford and New York, 1996)
Sturluson, Snorri, *Edda*, trans. and ed. Anthony Faulkes (London and Melbourne, 1987)
—, *Heimskringla: History of the Kings of Norway*, trans. and ed. Lee M. Hollander (Austin, TX, 1991)
Waggoner, Ben, trans. and ed., *The Sagas of Ragnar Lodbrok* (New Haven, CT, 2009)

Scholarly works on the afterlife of the eddas and sagas

Arnold, Martin, *Thor: Myth to Marvel* (London and New York, 2011)
Barnes, Geraldine, *Viking America: The First Millennium* (Cambridge, 2001)
Benson, Adolph Burnett, *The Old Norse Element in Swedish Romanticism* (New York, 1914)
Böldl, Klaus, *Der Mythos der Edda: Nordische Mythologie zwischen europäischer Aufklärung und nationaler Romantik* (Tübingen, 2000)
Clunies Ross, Margaret, *The Norse Muse in Britain, 1750–1820* (Trieste, 1998)
Engster, Hermann, *Germanisten und Germanen: Germanenideologie und Theoriebildung in der deutschen Germanistik und Nordistik von den Anfängen bis 1945 in exemplarischer Darstellung*, Texte und Untersuchungen zur Germanistik und Skandinavistik, 16 (Frankfurt a.M., 1986)
Ewbank, Inga-Stina, Olav Lausund and Bjørn Tysdahl, eds, *Anglo-Scandinavian Cross-Currents* (Norwich, 1999)
Hafner, Tina, *Peter Madsens Valhalla: Studien zur Rezeption altwestnordischer Mythen im modernen Comic* (München, 2008)
Helgason, Jón Karl, *Hetjan og höfundurinn: Brot úr íslenskri menningarsögu* (Reykjavík, 1998)

—, *The Rewriting of Njáls Saga: Translation, Politics and Icelandic Sagas*, Topics in Translation, 16 (Clevedon, Buffalo, NY, Toronto and Sydney, 1999)

—, *Höfundar Njálu: Þræðir úr vestrænni bókmenntasögu* (Reykjavík, 2001)

Jørgensen, Keld Gall, *Betydningens grænser. Oversættelsesvidenskab og saga* (Copenhagen, 1995)

Kunz, Keneva, *Retellers of Tales: An Evaluation of English Translations of Laxdæla Saga* (Reykjavík, 1994)

Larsen, Annette, ed., *Det norrøne og det nationale: studier i brugen af Islands gamle litteratur i nationale sammenhænge i Norge, Sverige, Island, Storbritannien, Tyskland og Danmark* (Reykjavík, 2008)

Malm, Mats, *Minervas äpple. Om diktsyn, tolkning och bildspråk inom nordisk göticism* (Stockholm, 1996)

Mjöberg, Jöran, *Drömmen om sagatiden*, 2 vols (Stockholm, 1967–8)

O'Donoghue, Heather, *From Asgard to Valhalla: The Remarkable History of the Norse Myths* (London and New York, 2007)

Quinn, Judy, and Maria Adele Cipolla, eds, *The Hyperborean Muse: Studies in the Transmission and Reception of Old Norse Literature*, Acta Scandinavica (Turnhout, 2016)

Schulz, Katja, and Florian Heesch, eds, *'Sang an Aegir': Nordische Mythen um 1900* (Heidelberg, 2009)

Schulz, Katja, ed., *Eddische Götter und Helden: Milieus und Medien ihrer Rezeption* (Heidelberg, 2011)

See, Klaus von, *Deutsche Germanen-Ideologie: Vom Humanismus bis zur Gegenwart* (Frankfurt a.M., 1970)

—, *Barbar Germane Arier: Die Suche nach der Identität der Deutschen* (Heidelberg, 1994)

—, *Ideologie und Philologie: Aufsätze zur Kultur- und Wissenschaftsgeschichte* (Heidelberg, 2006)

Tómasson, Sverrir, ed., *Guðamjöður og arnarleir: Safn ritgerða um eddulist* (Reykjavík, 1996)

Wawn, Andrew, ed., *Northern Antiquity: The Post-medieval Reception of Edda and Saga* (Enfield Lock, 1994)

—, *The Vikings and the Victorians: Inventing the Old North in Nineteenth-century Britain* (Cambridge, 2000)

Zernack, Julia, *Geschichten aus Thule: Íslendingasögur in Übersetzungen deutscher Germanisten*, Berliner Beiträge zur Skandinavistik, 3 (Berlin, 1994)

Adaptations analysed

Baring-Gould, Sabine, *Iceland: Its Scenes and Sagas* (London, 1863)

Bottomley, Gordon, *The Riding to Lithend* (Flansham, Sussex, 1909)

DeMaio, Joey, 'Gates of Valhalla', on Manowar, *Into Glory Ride* (New York, 1982)
Ditko, Steve, 'The Hammer of Thor', *Out of This World*, 11 (January 1959)
Einherjer, *Odin Owns Ye All* (Dortmund, 1998)
Elgar, Edward, *Scenes from the Saga of King Olaf* (London, 1896)
Fleischer, Richard, dir., *The Vikings* (Los Angeles, CA, 1958)
Ibsen, Henrik, *Hærmændene paa Helgeland* (Christiania, 1858)
Ishinomori, Shōtarō, 'Saibōgu Zero-Zero-Nain: Edda-hen', *Shūkan Shōjo Komikku*, 31–3 (1976)
Jensen, Thit, *Nial den Vise: Udstyrsskuespil fra Islands storhedstid* (Copenhagen, 1934)
Jones, Terry, dir., *Erik the Viking* (Stockholm and London, 1989)
Kirby, Jack, 'The Magic Hammer', *Tales of the Unexpected*, 16 (August 1957)
—, and Joe Simon, 'The Villain from Valhalla!', *Adventure Comics*, 75 (June 1942)
Lee, Stan, Jack Kirby and Larry Lieber, 'Thor the Mighty and the Stone Men from Saturn!', colouring by Stan Goldberg, inks by Joe Sinnott, letters by Artie Simek, *Journey into Mystery*, 83 (August 1962)
—, 'Trapped by Loki, The God of Mischief', *Journey into Mystery*, 85 (October 1962)
Liljencrantz, Ottilie A., *The Thrall of Leif the Lucky: A Story of Viking Days* (Chicago, IL, 1902)
Lincoln, Wright, 'Thor God of Thunder', *Weird Comics*, 1 (April 1940)
—, 'Thor Goes to War', *Weird Comics*, 2 (May 1940)
Madsen, Peter, *Thors brudefærd*, based on a story by Per Vadmand, Hans Rancke-Madsen, Peter Madsen and Henning Kure, colouring by Søren Håkansson, letters by Tore Bahnson, produced by Henning Kure (Bagsværd, 1980)
—, and Hans Rancke-Madsen, *Ulven er løs*, colouring by Søren Håkansson, produced by Henning Kure (Bagsværd, 1979)
Metcalfe, Frederick, *The Oxonian in Iceland: or, Notes of Travel in that Island in the Summer of 1860, With Glances at Icelandic Folk-lore and Sagas* (London, 1861)
Mighty Thor, *Rumbo al Valhalla* (San Bartolo Ameyalco, 2011)
Neill, Roy William, dir., *The Viking* (Boston, New York, Los Angeles, 1928)
Page, Jimmy, and Robert Plant, 'Immigrant Song', on Led Zeppelin, *Led Zeppelin III* (New York, 1970)
Quorthon, 'Valhalla', on Bathory, *Hammerheart* (Berlin, 1990)
Roberts, Dorothy James, *Fire in the Ice* (Boston, MA, and Toronto, 1961)
Skálmöld, *Börn Loka* (Eisenerz, Styria, 2012)
Týr, *How Far to Asgaard* (Torshavn, 2002)
Vad, Poul, *Nord for Vatnajøkel* (Copenhagen, 1994)
Wagner, Richard, *Der Ring des Nibelungen* (Mainz, 1877)
Waller, Samuel Edward, *Six Weeks in the Saddle: A Painter's Journal in Iceland* (London, 1874)

ACKNOWLEDGEMENTS

The idea of writing this book was presented to me by my friend Sigurður Gylfi Magnússon, who, having already published a book with Reaktion Books, indicated to me that the same publisher was also interested in publishing a study on the afterlife of the eddas and sagas. A considerable part of the book was originally written in Icelandic and has been translated by Jane Victoria Appleton, save for the first section of Chapter Four, which was translated by the late Bernard Scudder. Jane has also served as the primary editor of the work, considerably refining its structure and style.

Parts of the text are based on chapters from my two Icelandic books on the afterlife of *Njáls saga*: *Hetjan og höfundurinn* (1998) and *Höfundar Njálu* (2001), both published by Heimskringla under Ólöf Eldjárn's editorship. The first part of Chapter Four is an adaptation of my 'Reading Saga Landscapes: The Case of Samuel E. Waller', published by Háskólaútgáfan in *The Cultural Reconstruction of Places* (2006), edited by Ástráður Eysteinsson. The first part of the Epilogue is an abridged version of my 'Continuity? The Icelandic Sagas in Post-medieval Times', published in Blackwell's *A Companion to Old Norse-Icelandic Literature and Culture* (2004), edited by Rory McTurk. Chapter One and the second part of Chapter Five were originally written as part of my chapter 'Nordic Gods and Popular Culture', prepared under Margaret Clunies Ross's editorship for the forthcoming three-volume series *Pre-Christian Religions of the North*, to be published by Brepols. I am grateful for permission to use all of this material here. I am also grateful for a generous grant from The University of Iceland Research Fund, and to my inspiring students in the 'Adaptation of Icelandic Medieval Literature' course that I taught at the University of Iceland in the spring of 2014. I also want to thank musicians and labels for permission to quote from the songs 'Rumbo al Valhalla' from Mighty Thor's album *Rumbo al Valhalla* (2011), 'Hail to the Hammer' from Týr's album *How Far to Asgaard* (2002), and 'The Lay of Thrym' and 'Take your Tyrant' from Týr's album *The Lay of Thrym* (2011).

A number of friends and colleagues have read over the text in its various stages and helped me in numerous other ways. I would like to express warm gratitude to them all, in particular those who took an active part in the development of this work:

Jane Victoria Appleton, Martin Arnold, Ármann Jakobsson, Fríða B. Jónsdóttir, Guðrún Baldvinsdóttir, Simon Halink, Helgi Hákon Jónsson, Haukur Ingvarsson, Helgi Grímsson, Katrín Helena Jónsdóttir, Olga Holownia, Snœbjörn Arngrímsson, Tsukusu Jinn Ito, Magnús Örn Sigurðsson, Daisy L. Neijmann, Orri Tómasson, Sigurður Gylfi Magnússon, Sigrún Davíðsdóttir, Sveinn Yngvi Egilsson, Terry Gunnell, Torfi Tulinius and Andrew Wawn. I would also like to thank Amy Salter, Becca Wright and other members of the staff at Reaktion Books for all their help and encouragement, in particular publisher Michael Leaman, whose idea it was to attempt a book on this dauntingly wide-ranging topic.

PHOTO ACKNOWLEDGEMENTS

The author and publishers wish to express their thanks to the following sources for illustrative material and/or permission to reproduce it. Some locations of works are given below rather than in the captions for brevity.

Courtesy of Ulrik Andersen: p. 97; courtesy of Gunnar V. Andrésson (photographer): p. 150; courtesy of The Arnamagnaean Institute, Copenhagen, photo Suzanne Reitz: p. 57; courtesy of The Árni Magnússon Institute for Icelandic Studies, Reykjavík, photo Jóhanna Ólafsdóttir: p. 53; photo Solange Bied-Charreton: p. 49; courtesy of Kristján Einar Einarsson (photographer): p. 129; © Everett Collection/REX/Shutterstock: pp. 104, 132, 172; courtesy of Ishinomori Production, Japan: p. 33; courtesy of Katrín Helena Jónsdóttir (photographer): p. 169; © Keystone USA-ZUMA/REX/Shutterstock: p. 30; © Steve Meddle/ITV/ REX/Shutterstock: p. 20; courtesy Mighty Thor, logo and design Fernando Ricciardulli, Chromatic Chaos: pp. 146 (illustrator Arturo Anaya), 149 (photo Federico Robledo); courtesy of MyNDIR (My Norse Digital Image Repository), University of Victoria, photo P. A. Baer: p. 65; courtesy of The Norwegian National Library: p. 81; courtesy of Peter Madsen Studio: pp. 16, 35, 38; from Dorothy James Roberts, *Fire in the Ice* (Boston, MA, and Toronto: Little, Brown and Company, 1961): p. 120; and courtesy of Snorrastofa at Reykholt, photo Guðlaugur Óskarsson: p. 46.

INDEX

Page numbers for illustrations are in *italics*